Big Business and Brazil's Economic Reforms

In the 1990s, Brazil launched a comprehensive economic liberalization programme. It lifted its trade barriers, adopted new market-oriented regulations, opened up its capital market and abandoned earlier efforts to internalize production and to build vertically integrated systems across several sectors of the economy. In spite of the visible gap that separated the top global giants from the large local enterprises, Brazilian companies seemed to be willing to join in an economic liberalization process that was bound to expose them to unprecedented levels of competition, bring about a high degree of uncertainty and, in many cases, ultimately put their own businesses at risk.

Big Business and Brazil's Economic Reforms examines the most emblematic aspect of the Brazilian economic reforms, the support from parts of the local entrepreneurial class for the opening up of the economy. It investigates the reasons Brazil carried out these economic reforms in the 1990s, the transition process and the impact of the opening up of the economy on some of its most important sectors, such as the aerospace, auto and auto parts, food processing, oil and petrochemicals, ethanol, steel, telecoms and telecom equipment industries.

This book offers an in-depth analysis of Brazil's distinctive development paths, from the Latin American economic thinking of the early stages of its industrialization to the neo-liberal stance of the present day. It sheds new light on one of the main challenges facing all the large developing economies in their move to become more integrated into the world economy, the fostering of large enterprises. *Big Business and Brazil's Economic Reforms* is a great resource for students and researchers interested in global business, development economics and Latin American economic history.

Luiz Fernando Kormann holds a PhD from the Judge Business School, University of Cambridge, UK.

Routledge Studies in International Business and the World Economy

For a full list of titles in this series, please visit www.routledge.com

Big Business and Brazil's Economic Reforms

Luiz F. Kormann

Routledge
Taylor & Francis Group

NEW YORK AND LONDON

First published 2015
by Routledge
711 Third Avenue, New York, NY 10017

and by Routledge
2 Park Square, Milton Park, Abingdon, Oxon OX14 4RN

Routledge is an imprint of the Taylor & Francis Group, an informa business

Library of Congress Cataloging-in-Publication Data
Kormann, Luiz.
    Big business and Brazil's economic reforms / Luiz Kormann.
        pages cm. — (Routledge studies in international business and the
world economy)
    1. Big business—Brazil.   2. Brazil—Economic policy—21st century.
3. Brazil—Politics and government—2003–   I. Title.
    HD2356.B7K67 2015
    338.981—dc23
    2014045742

ISBN: 978-1-138-81388-5 (hbk)
ISBN: 978-1-315-74782-8 (ebk)

Typeset in Sabon
by Apex CoVantage, LLC

For my parents
Mário and Iracy Kormann

Contents

Tables

Figures

Preface

In June 2012, Brazilians took to the streets. The movement had a timid start, with small demonstrations against the rise of bus fares in the city of São Paulo. It reached other capital cities and gained momentum after a street rally in São Paulo was violently suppressed by the police. Within a couple of days, protest marches had spread all over Brazil, and what was initially an uprising against fare rises turned into a nationwide movement encompassing a wide variety of new demands.

The most impressive feature of this movement that mobilised millions of people was that it didn't count on the sponsorship of any political party. On the contrary, all the attempts by political parties to involve themselves in the movement were faced with strong opposition. It was easy to find people on the streets holding banners claiming that they didn't feel represented by any politician. Brazil was going through a serious crisis of political representation.

There were banners against corruption and others calling for better education and health systems and for more efficient use of public money. There was room as well for more specific but equally important demands related to civil rights. These protesters in Brazil were not asking for a regime change or attempting to overthrow the president. Actually, President Rousseff went through this wave of protests relatively unscathed, although her popularity substantially dropped. This fall was not sufficient to obstruct her re-election in the following year.

The international media were taken by surprise. According to all accounts, Brazil had been the protagonist of a success story. Over the last ten years, nearly 40 million people had acquired middle-class status, unemployment had reached a record low and the economy had been only mildly affected by the world economic crisis of 2008. Brazil was the only large developing economy in those years to temper growth with much-needed reductions in social inequality. Credit was cheaper and more easily available. There was a boom in consumption. The housing market was heated, brand new cars were flocking to the streets and all sorts of expensive IT novelties were becoming part of the daily life of millions of Brazilians. Perhaps the most lasting gain was related to a substantial increase in schooling years. Many families envisaged for the first time the prospect of sending their children to college.

In the world arena, two decades of economic and political stability had allowed Brazil to take great strides forward. This was definitely not the stance expected of a world leader, but it was certainly a more assertive one. Brazil has been the flagship of the Mercosur, an outspoken affiliate of the G20 and the Latin American member of BRICS (Brazil, Russia, India, China and South Africa). Whenever it was needed, Brazil has lent its voice to the modernisation of multilateral organisations like the International Monetary Fund (IMF), the World Bank and the World Trade Organization (WTO). This is a position that was virtually unthinkable two decades ago.

Even so, in the midst of this positive scenario, there was still room for strong popular discontent. This originated perhaps from a collective fear that growth would become unsustainable and recent achievements would soon be lost. For those millions of Brazilians that had joined the 'new middle class', there were still vivid memories of economic instability and hardship. They still remembered a recent past that must by all means be avoided. Moreover, despite real improvements, Brazil's living standards still have a long way to go before they catch up with those of any developed economy.

This sudden shift towards a more pessimistic stance can be traced back to a variety of causes. But one of these is certainly related to the mid- and long-term perspective of the future of the Brazilian economy. This is an outcome that may reflect the way that Brazil has been integrated into the world economy. It is the growing understanding that Brazil is inadvertently becoming a technology adaptor as opposed to a technology innovator. It is becoming a net exporter of primary goods as opposed to manufactured products at the upper end of the value chain. This has led to an unpleasant perception that, in an age of great industrial progress, Brazil is still vulnerable to the swings of commodity prices. It is no less emblematic that the Federation of Industries of the State of São Paulo (FIESP), Brazil's powerful association of industries, has recently called for the 'reindustrialisation' of the Brazilian economy. The weight of manufacturing in the Brazilian economy has gone back to the same levels as in 1955, the period that marked the beginning of its industrialisation.

Big Business and Brazil's Economic Reforms turns its sights on big business in Brazil in an attempt to understand its implications for the Brazilian economy. It takes a look at the capacity of Brazilian companies to produce, invest and compete locally and abroad. These are the building blocks of any dynamic economy. It may give us some clues as to why millions of Brazilians went out onto the streets despite the prospects of sunny days, because they realised there were instead patches of grey clouds in the sky.

Big Business and Brazil's Economic Reforms is the follow-up of my doctoral studies at the University of Cambridge, UK. Writing this book has been a challenging experience, and I couldn't end this project without expressing my profound gratitude to Prof. Peter Nolan for all his help and intellectual guidance. I always felt inspired by the numerous discussions we had in his office at Jesus College, Cambridge. This was a completely new research area for me, and without his support, this work would not have been done.

I am highly indebted to the funding institutions that provided me the required financial support for my studies at the University of Cambridge, namely the British Council's Chevening Scholarship Programme, the Cambridge Overseas Trust's Citigroup Cambridge Scholarship and the Lundgren Research Award. I would also like to thank all managers, chief executives and representatives of cross-industry bodies who kindly agreed to give part of their time to answer my questions and for providing me with their valuable testimonies and insightful information during my research in Brazil.

My deepest gratitude to Mrs Julie Coimbra, librarian of the University of Cambridge Centre of Latin American Studies, for her friendship and relentless sense of solidarity. I would like to express my gratitude to all my dear friends from Jesus College and the Judge Business School. Thanks to them, my time in Cambridge was a truly enjoyable experience.

Finally, I would like to express my special gratitude to my parents, Mário and Iracy, for all their love and encouragement, for their unreserved emotional and financial support. This book is dedicated to them.

Introduction

A wave of optimism hit the Brazilian economy in the first decade of the twenty-first century. This rise in confidence was shared equally by the business community and the Brazilian government. Signs of prosperity could be seen everywhere. Brazil's latent fear of soaring inflation seemed dimmer than ever, its basic interest rate was on a course of steady decline and unemployment showed, for the first time in many years, evidence of finally receding. For nine consecutive years since 2003, average income had also shown a steady rise.[1] On the account of Brazilian external relations, the scenario was just as positive. Integration into the world economy was followed by record levels of trade surplus and by a growing amount of foreign investments.[2] In early 2008, Brazil finally shifted from its long-lasting condition of a major international debtor to become, for the first time in history, a net creditor. The move helped to dissipate the risk of default that had pervaded the Brazilian economy and that lay beneath the dramatic crises of the previous three decades. In April 2008, Brazil even had its credit rating raised to 'investment grade' by Standard & Poor's. In the following month, this same rate upgrading was given by Fitch.

On the business front, numbers were equally promising. In 2013, the top 500 companies in Brazil hit a new record by breaking for the first time the ceiling of one trillion US dollars in total sales (Revista Exame Melhores e Maiores 2014). Brazil's mergers and acquisitions market remained heated even in the midst of the world economic crisis of 2008. In 2011, it reached a new peak of 817 transactions (KPMG 2012).[3] Usually seen as recipients of foreign investments, Brazilian companies made large investments abroad. In the last decade, the stock of Brazilian direct investments grew more than five-fold, jumping from US$49.7bn in 2001 to US$266.3bn in 2012.[4] In 2007 alone, Brazilian direct investments reached the striking amount of US$27.2bn (Sobeet 2007).[5]

Economic stability, which by the early twenty-first century had already lasted for more than a decade, opened up a completely new business environment for Brazilian companies. Further to improvements in Brazil's capital market, a whole new credit market also began to take shape. Although interest rates in Brazil moved back to double digits in November 2013, their bumpy decline since 2003 along with short periods when they were single digit have been sufficient to give a strong boost to the domestic market. The two most notable examples are perhaps the automotive and housing sectors, which together account for nearly 30% of Brazil's industrial GDP. In tandem with inflation control and economic growth, the introduction in 2003 of a comprehensive programme of income transference also played a momentous role in reducing poverty. Thanks to these three factors, it is estimated that between 2002 and 2012, more than 40 million Brazilians had their living standards raised to middle-class status and joined the consumer market[6]. In 2010 alone, it was estimated that 40% of fridges and 39% personal computers sold in Brazil went to this growing new middle class (Valor Econômico 2011). In the years following the 2008 economic crisis, while most countries witnessed the widening of their social gap, Brazil managed to combine economic growth with better income distribution. Between 2001 and 2013, Brazil's Gini coefficient for income per capita dropped from 0.563 to 0.495.[7] This was the biggest fall in income inequality since the beginning of its time series in the early 1960s.

These were all encouraging developments that helped to feed, even further, the confidence of local entrepreneurs. In the midst of such a positive environment, some analysts even dared to cast predictions of long-term economic growth. This was the case of the investment bank Goldman Sachs, which, following estimates of productivity and economic growth, projected Brazil along with other large developing economies such as Russia, India and China to become the top six economies in the next fifty years (Goldman Sachs 2003). The acronym BRIC (Brazil, Russia, India and China) was promptly assimilated by the world business media and was quickly replicated into investment strategies, trade analyses and stock options by many international financial institutions. It was not unusual for this select group of countries to be associated with the dynamism and growing influence of the emerging markets in the world economy.

Despite the atmosphere of optimism that has engulfed Brazil in recent years, a more in-depth analysis of the economy may reveal a different reality. Brazil's latest record of economic expansion, although a real improvement when compared to the bumpy growth of previous years, has still been markedly lower than that of many other developing economies. Brazil may have shown signs of growth, but other economies have done much better. Between 2001 and 2013, Brazil's annual GDP growth of 3.2% was lower than the world (3.6%), developing world (6%) and South American (3.9%) averages. Brazil's economic expansion was also lower than countries like South Korea (3.8%), Chile (4.3%) and Argentina (4.6%), as well as the other BRIC economies. In the same period, China grew by 9.9%, India by 7% and Russia by 4.4% a year.[8]

The major economic crisis into which the world was plunged in the second half of 2008 was relatively less severe in Brazil. The local banking system remained resilient to the global liquidity shock (*Financial Times* 2009), and in December 2009, the São Paulo stock exchange had practically recovered to its pre-crisis level. Net public debt per GDP, which skyrocketed in the worst-affected countries over the post-crisis years, actually dropped in Brazil to the manageable rate of 33.6%.[9] Fiscal incentives put forward by the government to stimulate the economy were successful at keeping a few selected sectors like automotive and white goods afloat, and the unemployment rate started to fall again after a brief rise in the first half of 2009. In December 2013, the unemployment rate of 4.3% was the lowest under the new methodology implemented by the Brazilian Institute of Geography and Statistics back in 2001.[10]

Brazil may have recently reached economic stability, but its cost has also been notably high. Brazil's basic interest rate is still one of the highest in the world and is a frequent target of fierce criticism from the local business community. Considered as too austere on the monetary front, Brazil's macroeconomic policy was constantly blamed for not allowing the country to take full advantage of the period of world economic expansion that marked the turn of the millennium and lasted until the global economic crisis of 2008. For many analysts, Brazil's monetary policy, in addition to being too fierce at hindering demand, stimulated the inflow of volatile capital, which added pressure to the overvaluation of the local currency and sponsored an indiscriminate spree of imports. In many cases, these were imports that took the place of locally produced consumer goods. The stringency of Brazil's adjustment programme in the mid-90s is still a matter of intense debate. Most notably, Brazil's market-oriented reforms and its strict observance of the macroeconomic agenda contributed to hinder the implementation of more specific microeconomic policies. This poses a crucial question to Brazil's long-term economic development—specifically, the one that deals with the fostering of large companies to operate abroad. Unlike other catching-up approaches carried out by Japan and South Korea in the past or by China in the present, the development of strategic sectors to compete in the global market was not part of Brazil's economic policies in the 1990s.

The market-oriented reforms carried out by Brazil in the 1990s and the country's move towards a greater integration into the world economy coincided with a period of great changes in global business. This was a particularly complex period of transition for the world economy, which, as will be discussed later in this book, was marked by an unprecedented rise in the international flow of capital; by record numbers of cross-border mergers and acquisitions; by a higher concentration of businesses among a few global players; and by a complete reshuffle of global supply chains that were reshaped to accommodate tighter links between system integrators and select groups of first- and second-tier suppliers (Nolan 2001). It is right in the middle of this worldwide restructuring process, which was very much created by the logic of competition, and in most cases uneven competition, that the large Brazilian companies have been forced to find their way into global business. In the face of this new business environment of growing concentration among a few global players, one of the first questions that comes to mind has to be inevitably related to the real chances of Brazilian companies to compete with their foreign counterparts. This is a matter of prime relevance, as it will indicate in the end what role Brazil is going to play in the world economy.

A quick analysis of the opening up of the Brazilian economy in the 1990s may suggest, however, that this was not the best time for local companies to engage in head-to-head competition with their large global counterparts. In the first half of the 1990s, market conditions in Brazil were particularly critical due to the country's high economic instability and, in the second half of the 1990s, due to tight monetary control that hindered domestic demand. In addition, the implementation of a strict fiscal policy by the government considerably reduced the country's capacity to make much-needed investments in basic infrastructure. At a time when adequate conditions for competition were paramount, local companies also had to cope with critical bottlenecks in the Brazilian transport network, shortages of electricity, dysfunctional bureaucracy and, of no lesser importance, long-standing caveats in its education and health systems.

Top global companies based in the most developed economies, on the other hand, enjoyed a far more privileged position. These companies counted on long-established global presence, better-known brands, large investments in R&D, modern management practices, highly skilled human capital and easier access to credit. Finally, yet just as importantly, developed countries' capital markets, although not immune to crashes as recently shown by the 2008 economic crisis, are admittedly better equipped to cushion crises than the ones from emerging economies.

Despite this visible gap that separated the top global companies from the large Brazilian enterprises, in the early 1990s, Brazilian companies seemed willing to join in an opening-up process that would expose them to unprecedented levels of competition and could ultimately put their own businesses at risk. This is perhaps the most intriguing aspect of the Brazilian economic reforms. The support from part of the local entrepreneurial class for the opening up of the economy is a behaviour that would appear contradictory at first glance.[11] It implied the abandonment of the state-led development model that had given shape to the Brazilian industry and had been in place for nearly four decades. Local companies, since their foundation as part of a state-led programme of import substitution industrialisation, had relied on government support to get special privileges in the form of funding, incentives, subsidies and, in many cases, technology. Before the 1990s market-oriented reforms, the entrepreneurial class in Brazil was either protected by high import barriers or enjoyed a business environment that could be best described as one of controlled competition or co-existence with foreign multinational companies. The opening up of the Brazilian economy, on the other hand, meant the end of all this industry protection apparatus and forced local companies to join in a completely new business environment whose obstacles in many aspects were simply unknown.

In addition, the 1990s reforms led to a radical change in the 'tripartite system' that was at the core of the Brazilian industrialisation process: the *state-owned enterprises*, the *local private enterprises* and the *multinational corporations* (Evans 1979). Each one had for decades enjoyed a clear and distinct role. With the privatisation of the largest Brazilian state-owned enterprises, the opening up of the market and the rise in foreign investments, the participation of these three sectors in the economy was considerably reshaped. The changes in ownership structure of the top 500 companies in Brazil in the years that followed the opening up of the economy, as will be shown later in this work, convey a testimony to the strong impact that the economic reforms had on local business.

After two decades of economic reforms, what sectors have emerged as the most competitive in Brazil? What are Brazil's truly global firms? Have the Brazilian companies managed to take up a more dominant position in the newly formed global value chains? Were Brazil's opening up and the so-called modernisation of the economy translated into a real move up the technology ladder within its relatively diversified industrial sector? Or, alternatively, has the integration of Brazil into the world economy contributed even further to strengthening its dependence on basic commodities? What will this latter alternative mean for the future of Brazilian big business and for the role that the country is going to play in the world economy?

This book analyses the reasons that led Brazil to carry out the economic reforms of 1990s, the transition process and the impact of the opening up of the economy on some of its most important sectors. To best illustrate the profound changes that the opening up of the economy brought to Brazil, this work first makes an in-depth analysis of the theoretical background that gave support to the state-led development policies that were adopted by Brazil in previous decades, particularly in the post-war period. These were the years when Brazil built the foundations of its industrialisation process. This was a particularly prolific time of academic production on the part of Latin American and Brazilian scholars. Their propositions, in many respects, were largely divergent from the mainstream orthodoxy. At the very heart of their work was a critique of the trade relations between Latin America and, at that time, most developed economies. Under the claim that the Latin American economies were strongly dependent on primary commodities, most of the policies put forward by these economists called for the diversification of their economies and for massive investments in industrialisation.

The economic reforms of the 1990s in Brazil amounted to a profound change after the previous four decades of state-led development. They meant the end of a series of trade barriers on imports and drastically reduced the role of the state in the economy. This move aimed to bring new dynamism to the Brazilian economy. By moving away from allegedly inefficient sectors, the country would open its doors to a new business environment where market forces were set to make the economy more in tune with its real 'comparative advantages'. Last-decade economic reforms in Brazil very much echoed the neo-liberal trend embraced by most of the Latin American economies and followed the same recipe of capital market liberalisation, privatisation of state enterprises, stringent anti-inflation monetary policies and the relentless pursuit of a friendly environment for foreign investments. As support for the reforms reached a level of near consensus among policy makers in the region in the early 1990s, the question of their real consequences for the Brazilian economy now needs to be addressed. This is, in other words, the question of whether the choice of economic policies was in fact the most appropriate for the region at that time. The Argentinean crisis of 2001 and the shift to the left of the political agenda of countries like Bolivia, Venezuela and Ecuador are two signs that the orthodoxy of the reforms didn't take long to bring to the region a certain amount of popular discontent.

Brazil may not have been hit by an economic crisis of the same magnitude as that of Argentina in 2001 or gone through radical political changes like some of its neighbouring countries, but the consequences have been no less significant. The sudden rise of agribusiness and of the mining sector in the years that followed the economic reforms in Brazil is perhaps the most emblematic outcome. This move back to basic commodities is certainly an issue for concern, particularly after decades of state-led industrialisation and the fact that Brazil had already achieved a reasonably successful diversification of its economy. As previously mentioned, this is a period of great changes in the global market; any faulty move on the part of Brazil will surely affect the role the country is going to play in the world economy in the long term. Have the 1990s economic reforms contributed to making the Brazilian economy more competitive in the global arena, or have they otherwise helped to transform the country into a world supplier of basic commodities?

This book argues that the opening up of the Brazilian economy in the 1990s led to a rapid internationalisation of its industry which may eventually dent the capacity of its domestic companies to take a leading position in the most dynamic and technology-intensive sectors. This is an outcome that for many scholars would sound like a contradiction, but it is perfectly understandable when the latest changes in global business are taken into account. In the new global economy where businesses are becoming concentrated among a handful of global players and supply chains are being reshaped to accommodate tighter links between system integrators and a select number of first- and second-tier suppliers, to be in the upper end of the supply chain is, more than ever, of vital importance. With a few exceptions, most notably the case of the aircraft manufacturer Embraer, examples of Brazilian companies that have succeeded in becoming global system integrators are rare. Additionally, in the recently formed global supply chains, the vast majority of domestic companies have only found room as second- or third-tier suppliers. Only a few domestic companies have managed to emerge after the opening up of the Brazilian economy as true global players, and they are chiefly restricted to commodity-based sectors such as agribusiness, oil and mining. On the trade front, it was also the commodities sector that lay behind Brazil's trade surplus, which implied a growing dependence on basic commodities. This is an intriguing outcome for a country like Brazil whose reforms originally had the main aim of modernising the economy. This behaviour largely contrasts with that of other developing economies, most notably the South and East Asian countries, which are trying to combine their integration into the world economy with greater specialisation of their exports towards the higher end of the value chain.

This book is divided into four parts. The first is a brief account of the changes in the world economy in the last two decades and of the fast rise of neo-liberal practices in Latin American countries. It discusses Brazil's integration into the world economy and draws attention to the impressive rise in foreign trade as well as the growing relevance of the commodities sector for the Brazilian export economy. This first part also makes a comparison between Brazil and two other economies, South Korea and China. These two countries, in different phases of the world economy, have each outperformed Brazil's capacity to promote industrial development, South Korea in the state-interventionist post-war period and China in the recent move towards a more market-driven economy.

The second part of this work makes an in-depth analysis of two distinct currents of thought that strongly influenced the Latin American economic thinking in the years that followed the post-war period. The first, known as Structuralism, was particularly relevant to Latin America as it built, in the early 1950s, the intellectual framework that gave the basis for the economic diversification of the continent. Structuralist scholars challenged the prevailing neo-classical theory and supported the intervention of the state in the industrialisation of the Latin American economies. They claimed that the strong reliance of Latin America on basic commodities left the continent in a disadvantageous position in relation to the industrialised economies. For these scholars, without a comprehensive programme of industrialisation, the Latin American economies wouldn't be able to break away from their persistent state of underdevelopment. Structuralism enjoyed strong acceptance in Latin America, particularly among policy makers, but as its pro-industrialisation policies didn't show signs of delivering the expected leap of development, another current of thought gained strength in the region. The Dependency School had its most influential years in Latin America in the 1960s and 1970s and counted on the involvement of a large variety of local scholars, who joined in a vivid critique on the very basis of capitalism in the region. Dependency scholars addressed a large range of issues, which included, for instance, the continent's internal social formations, the appearance of new patterns of consumption, the dynamics of the region's own industrialisation process, the alleged downside features of foreign investment and the fast-growing presence of multinational corporations.

In many respects, what was claimed and prescribed by the Structuralist and Dependency scholars was in sound opposition to the neo-liberal reforms that were later implemented by the vast majority of Latin American economies in the early 1990s. Interestingly enough, it was one of Latin America's most celebrated Dependency scholars, Fernando Henrique Cardoso, who, decades later, while president of Brazil, led the country to a comprehensive pro-market reform.

Part III analyses the market-oriented reforms of the Brazilian economy in the 1990s and the support from an influential part of the local entrepreneurial class in the opening up of the economy. The backing of business leaders to the opening up of the Brazilian market is perhaps the most intriguing aspect of the last decade's economic reforms. By joining in a process of economic liberalisation, these leaders were about to expose their companies to an unprecedented degree of competition, which would ultimately put their own businesses at risk. The 1990s were a particularly dynamic period of the world economy when greater freedom of capital flow and reduction of trade barriers led to profound changes in the way business was carried out. The world industry was chiefly affected by an impressive surge in cross-border mergers and acquisitions, the growing concentration of businesses among a few global players and the reshuffle of global value chains to reflect, as previously mentioned, tighter links between system integrators and increasingly select groups of first- and second-tier suppliers. This was a global restructuring process, which by nature tended to favour the biggest and most competitive firms. Contradictory as it may look, Brazilian companies seemed willing to engage themselves in a market environment that was markedly ruled by global competition. This chapter sheds light on some of the reasons that motivated the local entrepreneurial class to abandon in the 1990s long-standing protectionist strategies and to embrace the neo-liberal agenda. It describes the measures that were actually taken by the Brazilian government to secure the country's transition to a more open economy and ends with an analysis of the change in perception of the Brazilian entrepreneurial class in the face of the first signs that a good number of the most traditional local companies seemed unprepared to compete with their foreign counterparts.

The fourth and final part of this book is dedicated to making an analysis of the inflow of foreign direct investments to Brazil in the years that followed the opening up of the economy and to examining the influence of trade liberalisation on the ownership structure of the largest companies in Brazil. The spectacular rise in foreign investments in the 1990s was followed by an equally impressive growth of cross-border mergers and acquisitions, which led to a fast internationalisation of the Brazilian economy. This chapter also compares the impact of the market-oriented reforms on two different industrial sectors: the aerospace and the automotive industries. While in the former, the Brazilian company Embraer found its way to become the world's third-largest aircraft manufacturer, in the latter, large domestic auto-part companies didn't survive foreign competition and were in their majority acquired by the global giants immediately after the liberalisation of the Brazilian market. The distinct trajectory of these two sectors sheds light on the importance of fostering big companies that can act as system integrators, as in the case of Embraer, and on the vulnerability of first- and second-tier suppliers in the face of the last decade's large-scale restructuring of global supply chains. At the end of this chapter, the analysis of the impact of trade liberalisation is extended to other sectors of the Brazilian economy—more specifically, food processing, steel, oil and petrochemicals, bio-fuels and ethanol, telecoms and telecom equipment industry. Along with the automotive and aerospace industries, these sectors were the ones most affected by the market-oriented reforms, the inflow of foreign investments and the recent surge of cross-border mergers and acquisitions.

This last part is followed by the final conclusions.

NOTES

1. According to the Brazilian Secretariat for Strategic Affairs, the per-capita income of Brazilian families rose on average by 3% a year between 2001 and 2011, jumping from US$257.71 to US$341.43; see www.sae.gov.br.
2. In July 2011, foreign direct investments into Brazil hit a new all-time record, with a twelve-month inflow of US$72.2bn. For the whole year of 2011, foreign investments into Brazil were of US$66.7bn, and this figure was nearly matched in 2012 (US$65bn) and in 2013 (US$63bn); see www.bacen.gov.br.
3. In the following two years, the numbers of mergers and acquisitions were, respectively, 816 and 796 (KPMG 2014).
4. Data from the Brazilian Central Bank, www4.bcb.gov.br/rex/CBE/Port/Res ultadoCBE2012p.pdf.
5. Data period from September 2006 to August 2007 (Sobeet 2007). The largest cross-border operation was the acquisition of Inco, the Canadian nickel producer, by the Brazilian miner Vale on September 2006 for US$17.4bn.
6. Data from the Brazilian Secretary for Strategic Issues, Secretaria de Assuntos Estratégicos—SAE, www.sae.gov.br/vozesdaclassemedia.
7. Data from the Brazilian Institute of Geography and Statistics, www.ibge.gov.br.
8. Data from the International Monetary Fund (IMF), www.imf.org.
9. Data from December 2013.
10. Data surveyed on Brazil's six largest metropolitan areas: São Paulo, Rio de Janeiro, Recife, Salvador, Belo Horizonte and Porto Alegre. Standard knowledge related to seasonality also applies, www.ibge.gov.br.
11. Evidence on the support of the Brazilian entrepreneurial class for the economic reforms will be given in Part III of this volume.

REFERENCES

Evans, Peter. *Dependent development: the alliance of multinational, state and local capital in Brazil.* Princeton: Princeton University Press, 1979.
Financial Times. "Brazil well-placed for the storm." London, 08 January 2009.

Goldman Sachs. "Dreaming with BRICs: the path to 2050." GS Global Economics, New York, 2003.

KPMG. "Mergers and acquisitions research 2014, 1st quarter: mirror of the transactions undertaken in Brazil." São Paulo, 2014.

KPMG. "Mergers and acquisitions research 2012, 4th quarter: mirror of transactions undertaken in Brazil." São Paulo, 2012.

Nolan, Peter. *China and the global business revolution.* Basingstoke: Palgrave, 2001.

Revista Exame Melhores e Maiores 2014. São Paulo: Editora Abril, June 2014.

Sobeet. "Internacionalização das empresas brasileiras foca países emergentes." São Paulo, 2007.

Valor Econômico. "Além do custo do crédito." Rio de Janeiro, 01 September 2011.

Part I
Economic Reforms in Brazil and the Lessons from South Korea and China

*Few concepts have gained more currency among
business people and politicians in recent years
than the idea of the BRICs—the giant, emerging economies
of Brazil, Russia, India and China, whose weight and influence is
supposedly changing economic and political realities.
Grouping the four, however, obscures a simple fact:
while the rise of China and India represents a real shift
in the power balance, Russia and Brazil are
marginal economies propped up by high commodity prices.*

—*Financial Times*, 04th December 2006

Brazil is to commodities what China is to manufactured goods.

—*The Economist*, 17th April 2008

*Twenty-five years ago, when South Korea's output
was $1,900 a head, Brazil's was $1,600. Now Brazil's has risen
to $7,000 while South Korea's is three times larger at $20,000.*

—*Financial Times*, 02nd May 2008

INTRODUCTION

The 1980s and 1990s were a period of profound changes in the global economy. State-led policies that for decades had set the rules for a considerable
part of the world economy showed, in the last two decades of the twentieth
century, clear signs of collapse. The developed economies were the first to
implement a series of measures that put an end to the state interventionism of the inter- and post-war periods. In the early 1980s the US, Japan
and Western Europe opened a new era in global business by joining efforts
to reduce the role of the state; abandon restrictions on capital flows; give
a new boost to the capital market (which thanks to the advent of Internet
technology managed to process a stunning amount of real-time cross-border
transactions at a low cost for the first time in history); privatise state-owned
enterprises in key sectors of the economy; lift trade barriers; and finally,

encourage their largest companies to pursue a leading position in the global market. This revival of the neo-liberal orthodoxy turned into a period of great capitalist expansion, which had an immediate impact on the then planned economies and on all developing capitalist countries.

This shift back to a more market-oriented economy quickly rippled throughout the world and forced entirely distinct economies to adjust themselves into what became a more competitive and globally integrated business environment. It witnessed the dramatic collapse of the former Soviet Bloc, influenced gradual changes in China and triggered off structural reforms in Latin America and in both South and South-east Asia. The reforms that were carried out in the West (particularly in the US and the UK) became, to a large extent, the model to be followed by other economies.

The Latin American economies were the ones that most enthusiastically embraced the wave of market-oriented reforms that sprouted in the Western developed world. Strongly affected by the debt crisis of the 1980s, the Latin American countries found themselves compelled to contest the effectiveness of the state in promoting growth and to abandon the very basis of their state-led model of development. This policy shift had a profound impact on the continent. It was in contrast to long-established beliefs and challenged the intellectual background that dominated the pro-development debate in the region during the post-war period, that is the need for a strong and controlling state committed to giving a 'big push' in their economies and propelling them into a new level of development. Leading Latin American economists were known, particularly in the mid-twentieth century, for supporting the premise that the state was the only force strong enough to diversify the continent's commodity-based economy and to sponsor the expensive process of industrialisation which could unleash its economy from a chronic status of underdevelopment.

The shift of Latin America back to a more market-oriented economy in the 1990s marked the end of a four-decade period of import substitution industrialisation (ISI) and of a business framework that was strongly driven by inward-looking development. This forced the Latin American economies to adapt themselves to a radically new business environment. Large state-owned enterprises were put on sale, and greater freedom of capital flows allowed the entry of a record amount of foreign investments. In addition, the lifting of trade barriers brought competition to a business environment that was until then mostly dominated by local companies. The main role left for the state after the reforms was one of ensuring macro-economic stability and the sound management of public accounts, a task that quite commonly involved the adoption of strict monetary policies. According to the neo-liberal discourse, once Latin America was finally freed from its excessive reliance on price controls and subsidies, the means of finding the best way to allocate its resources would be left to the market.

The promise of a new era of growth through the implementation of market-oriented reforms concealed, however, deep challenges. First, Latin

American companies were suddenly exposed to an unprecedented degree of competition, which in most cases came from the global giants. Second, there was the very condition of Latin America's poor macro-economic scenario, which, when compared to the stability of the developed economies, was not the most encouraging at that time to induce investments. Third was the continent's lack of expertise to deal with the new economic instability that came with the liberalisation of its capital market. Fourth was the region's chronic neglect of what turned out to be crucial elements of any economy willing to succeed in the global market like transport infrastructure, education and basic research (innovation capacity). And finally was the difficulty of implementing wide-ranging reforms when their own countries were going through periods of economic and political instabilities.

In reality, in the 1990s, the Latin American economies engaged in a process of global integration in which the developed economies had already reached a leading position. This new global business environment was not a playing field founded on equal opportunities. In almost every aspect, companies based in developed economies were in better position to compete. They had easier access to credit, better transport infrastructure, highly developed human capital, greater investments in R&D, long-established global presence and better-known brands. Once trade barriers were lifted, the chances of the Latin American companies to compete with the global leaders were markedly lower. This was, therefore, the beginning of a period of great changes for Latin America, whose prospects of creating global companies were relatively less promising. To make matters worse, the challenges brought about by the introduction of neo-liberal reforms were magnified by the fact that Latin America, as a late-industrialising continent, had always made use of some sort of industrial policy. This sudden shift from state-led development to one ruled by market-oriented global competition made the future of the continent's domestic industrial sector even more uncertain. This was a completely new business scenario for the Latin American countries whose policy tradition, as we have just seen, was at stake.

BRAZIL AND THE WORLD ECONOMY

Brazil was the last major economy in the region to catch the wagon of market-oriented reforms that had reached the Latin American railways so rapidly. Although the first steps to open up the economy were taken in the early 1990s, it was only in 1994 that the country begun to commit itself to a fully fledged programme of reforms. Of all Latin American economies, Brazil was the one with the most at stake. The Brazilian state had invested heavily during its phase of ISI and, over nearly forty years, managed to build a relatively diversified industrial sector. Brazil's industrialisation process was also unique in Latin America for managing to achieve a reasonable degree of vertical integration (notably in mining, auto and auto parts, aerospace and telecommunications).[1]

The opening up of the Brazilian economy in the 1990s brought about deep changes to the productive sector. It began with the implementation of a series of measures that were aimed at reducing the role of the state in the economy and the privatisation of several state-owned enterprises. Mining and steel were the first sectors to be privatised, which were followed by the whole set of state-owned petrochemical and fertilizer industries and the aerospace companies Celma and Embraer. In the service sector, the privatisation programme included the entire telecommunications network and part of the power generation and distribution systems, as well as railways and ports. All barriers against the entry of foreign capital were lifted, and global companies were allowed to invest in practically all segments of the Brazilian economy, including those that were traditionally kept as state monopolies like oil and oil refining, telecommunications and power generation. With the withdrawal of the state from core industries, the government shifted its focus of attention towards the creation of a regulatory framework. The main goal was to ensure the creation of a secure, reliable and friendly business environment for private investment, both foreign and local. Finally, the government carried out a wide-ranging cut on trade barriers. Practically all non-tariff barriers were lifted, and import tariffs were smashed from an average of 51% in 1987 to 14.2% in 1994.[2]

This quick opening up of the domestic market, which by itself entailed considerable challenges for the local economy, coincided with another equally decisive measure, the implementation of a monetary policy that made use of an 'exchange rate anchor' to keep inflation under control. This measure, strongly based on high interest rates, kept the Brazilian currency (*Real*) overvalued in the most critical period of Brazil's economic opening. Local exporters were therefore doubly hit with the opening up of the economy. Whereas the lift of trade barriers opened the doors for an unprecedented inflow of imports, the overvaluation of the local currency made imports more competitive at the same time that it considerably reduced the capacity of the Brazilian companies to sell abroad. The immediate result of Brazil's market-oriented reforms was a complete reversal of its trade balance and a drop of its current account. After an entire decade of annual average trade surpluses of US$12.7bn, the country witnessed from 1995 to 2000 an accumulated deficit of US$24bn.[3]

The introduction of market-oriented reforms brought about profound changes to domestic companies. First, there was an impressive growth of foreign direct investments, which jumped from a meagre US$731m in 1990 to US$32bn within just one decade. Second, there was the equally astonishing rise of mergers and acquisitions, which in the same period accounted for more than 2,000 transactions, the majority of them being cross border.

Third came the steady transfer of state-owned companies to private control. And finally was the complete restructuring of long-established supply chains, particularly in the automotive, food processing, mining, oil and oil refining industries, which after the market reforms gained a new but still undefined shape.

The 1990s were a decade of great uncertainties even to the biggest Brazilian companies. In almost every sector of the Brazilian economy, large local companies were severely affected by the new business environment that came about with the opening up of the economy. Despite the initial belief of the Brazilian business community that they were prepared to compete in a more open environment, the acquisition of leading traditional domestic companies by multinational corporations forced them to reconsider their initial optimism. Signs of vulnerability of the local companies in the face of foreign competition were clearly evident in the years following the reforms. In the Brazilian automotive sector, for instance, a vivid debate was raised when three of its largest domestic companies (Metal Leve, Cofap and Freios Varga) were sold to foreign groups.[4] In the food processing sector, one of the most affected sectors by the mid-1990s wave of mergers and acquisitions, Brazil witnessed its most traditional brands being acquired by global giants like Nestlé, Cargill, Sara Lee, ADM and Bunge foods. In telecom equipment manufacturing, after years of strong protectionism, two entrants (Nortel and Alcatel) were equally quick to acquire the star pupils of Brazil's infant industry promotion, Batik, Zetax and Promon. Even in the mining and steel industries, where participation in the privatisation process was initially restricted to domestic investors, as soon as barriers against foreign investment were lifted, global players like Arcelor (currently ArcelorMittal) and Nippon Steel moved quickly to consolidate their position in the Brazilian market.

Practically all sectors were hit by a wave of intense ownership restructuring.[5] The reform had a tremendous impact on big business in Brazil, which consequently brought several implications to the domestic economy as a whole. The end of state-led policies and the opening up of the economy transferred to private capital a leading role in the local economy that until then had been chiefly attributed to the state. As a consequence, the long-term strategies of the state were somewhat replaced by a new business environment that became more focused on the global rationality of large international corporations as well as on the most immediate demands of the market. This was a completely new business environment in which local companies back in the mid-1990s didn't have much expertise. Although those supporting the reforms were relentless in highlighting that the withdrawal of the state would make the economy less 'distorted' and therefore more in tune with its real 'comparative advantages', little was known about the long-term implications of such change to Brazil's relatively developed and diversified industrial sector.

INDUSTRIAL DEVELOPMENT AND FOREIGN TRADE

With the opening up of the Brazilian economy in the early 1990s, three key aspects of its move towards greater integration into the world economy were brought into light: first, the impressive growth of foreign investments; second, the sudden surge of cross-border mergers and acquisitions; and finally, the unprecedented rise in foreign trade. Whereas the first two changes are strongly interrelated and can only shed a dim light on the outward-looking objectives of the Brazilian economic reforms, the last one shows a radical shift in the way Brazil started to interact with other economies. It marked the end of ISI in Brazil, which until then had usually neglected the export sector, and rehearsed its first steps into intra-firm trade that came about with the wave of cross-border mergers and acquisitions in Brazil and with the recent consolidation of the global value chains.

After a whole decade of annual trade surpluses of more than US$10bn between 1985 and 1994 and an interval of sharp deficits from 1995 to 2000, Brazil's foreign trade has since reached a new all-time record. This impressive growth of foreign trade, which reached a new peak in 2011 with US$482.3bn in transactions, had a strong impact on the economy and opened a new phase in Brazil's development.[6] These changes (particularly the restructuring of long-established supply chains) had a decisive influence on Brazil's new portfolio of imports and exports. Brazil was suddenly forced to identify the sectors it seemed better prepared to compete in. Despite Brazil's diversified industrial sector and an almost four-decade-long programme of ISI, it was, however, the commodity-based products that secured Brazil's vast surpluses in the years following the opening up of the economy.

Aside from a few successful cases of high- and medium-high-technology-intensive sectors as the Brazilian aerospace and automotive industries, the exports that have led Brazil's recent expansion in foreign trade are still limited to basic commodities and labour-intensive manufactured products. In the new surge of global trade in the late 1990s and the early twenty-first century, it is predominantly in the low-value-added sectors that Brazil seems to have achieved its 'real comparative advantage' or, at least, enjoyed greater international recognition in the business media. 'Brazil is to agriculture what India is to business off-shoring and China to manufacturing: a power house whose size and efficiency few competitors can match. (. . .) Brazil has the largest agricultural trade surplus in the world, $34bn or 5 percent of national income last year [2004], an amount that was single-handedly responsible for putting the country's overall net trade in surplus' (*Financial Times* 2005). Brazil is 'the largest agricultural exporter among developing countries' (*Financial Times* 2001) and also has the world's biggest commercial herd of cattle (*Financial Times* 2003). This impressive expansion of Brazil's agribusiness sector in the late 1990s was even described by some analysts as a 'silent, green revolution' which, thanks to the 'diversity' of its 'soil and climates' and 'investment in sophisticated equipment and advanced agronomy techniques', turned the country into a truly 'leading agricultural nation' (*Financial Times* 2002). Brazil has 'emerged' over the last few decades as a 'global agricultural powerhouse'. 'The country is now the world's biggest exporter of a host of food commodities, including beef, chicken, orange juice, green coffee, sugar, ethanol, tobacco and the "soya complex" of beans, meal and oil, as well as its fourth biggest exporter of maize and pork' (*Financial Times* 2010).

Apart from agribusiness, mining is another commodity-based sector that has steadily expanded in the years following the opening up of the economy. This sector in Brazil, which is largely dominated by the Vale mining company (former CVRD), has been a key player in the world supply of iron ore. The company, which is the world's largest iron ore miner, is, along with the Anglo-Australians Rio Tinto and BHP Billiton, among the main leaders in the sector. Similarly to other resource-intensive industries in Brazil, Vale's output is chiefly destined for the foreign market, particularly China, Japan and Europe. In 2010, Vale overtook Petrobras as Brazil's biggest exporting company. Three years later, Vale was still Brazil's number-one exporter; its US$26.5bn in sales abroad were 92% higher than Petrobras. In 2013, these two companies alone accounted for nearly 16.6% of all Brazilian exports.[7]

The rising influence of commodities on Brazil's trade balance can be seen in Figure 1.1. This relative relevance of basic products has intensified over the last six years and reflects to a certain extent the country's growing reliance on resource-dependent economies like China. The rise of Brazil's exports to China, for instance, has been stunning. It grew forty-four-fold within only eleven years by jumping from US$1bn in 2000 to US$44.3bn in 2011, with nearly all exports to China being based on commodities (Valor Econômico 2012).[8] This gives an emblematic illustration of Brazil's integration into the world economy. Whereas Brazil's main exports to China over the last decade have been predominantly resource-based products, notably iron ore, soya and oil (81% of all Brazilian exports to China), its three main imports from China are, on the other hand, at the other end of the value chain, notably engines and electrical equipment, furnaces, nuclear reactors and chemicals (58.2% of all imports from China) (Observatório Brasil China 2011). This could be regarded as a minor issue if China had not become Brazil's biggest trading partner. Brazil faces the prospect of becoming a net exporter of commodities, whereas other large developing economies are consolidating their position as net suppliers of manufactured goods.

The dependence on low-value-added products remains a key aspect of Brazil's trade relations, as can be seen by the nature of its exports in the years that followed the opening up of the economy (Figure 1.2). From 2000 to 2013, the share of primary goods and low-technology-intensive products moved from 45.9% to 62.4% of all Brazilian exports. This reflects the growing influence of sectors related to agribusiness (mainly soybeans, cotton and sugar) as well as mining, steel, pulp and paper. Brazil's record of

Figure 1.1   Brazilian exports by value added, 1990–2013 (in %)
Source: Brazilian Ministry of Development, Industry and Foreign Trade (MDIC)/Secretary of Foreign Trade (SECEX)

medium- and high-technology goods, which together accounted for 36.3% of manufactured exports in 2010, is considerably below the world export average of 61%.[9] A quick comparison of Brazil with other developing economies that went through equivalent processes of 'infant industry' promotion or state-led industrialisation is enough to bring to light some of the deficiencies of Brazil's industrial competitiveness. The newly industrialised economies of East Asia managed to upgrade with greater success the technology content of their exports. According to estimates from the United Nations Industrial Development Organisations (UNIDO), in 2010, South Korea's share of mid-high- and high-technology products in manufactured exports was 75.8%, while in Taiwan it was 72.4%. Even the so-called 'second-tier' newly industrialised countries (NICs) of South-East Asia, which allegedly went through a more market-driven industrialisation process, outperform Brazil in terms of the technology structure of their exports. In 2010, nearly 63.5% of all Malaysia's manufactured exports were of complex products; in the Philippines, mid-high- and high-technology products accounted for 79.7% of all manufactured exports; and in Thailand, equally complex products represented 51.8%.[10] In all these countries, their share of manufactured exports in total exports was higher than in Brazil. Whereas in Brazil only 67.3% of all exports were of industrialised products, in the East Asian countries mentioned, nearly all of their exports were of manufactured goods, with South Korea accounting for 96.9%, Malaysia for 83.3%, the Philippines for 93.3%, Taiwan for 96% and Thailand for 83.9%.

When we compare Brazil's share of mid-high- and high-technology products in total manufacturing to data from these same economies, it is clear that Brazil's capacity to move up to the upper end of the value chain hasn't been as successful as the South-East Asian ones. According to UNIDO, between 1990 and 2010, the share of Brazil's most complex products in total manufacturing dropped from 44.1% to 35%. The performance of South-East Asian economies, on the other hand, tells the opposite story. Apart from Malaysia, all the economies mentioned managed to increase substantially the technology content of their manufactures. In that same twenty-year period, South Korea's mid- and high-tech content in total manufacturing moved from 41.6% to 53.4%, in the Philippines it jumped from 24.5% to 45.5%, in Taiwan from 37.4% to 61.9%, in Malaysia from 42.6% to 41.8% and in Thailand from 20.9% to 46.2%.[11] For all these economies, the share of manufacturing value added in GDP either increased or remained stagnant, whereas Brazil, on the other hand, witnessed a 20% drop from 16.7% to 13.5%.[12]

On the import side, Brazil's trade figures also show a worrying scenario. In recent years, Brazil seems to have consolidated its condition as a net

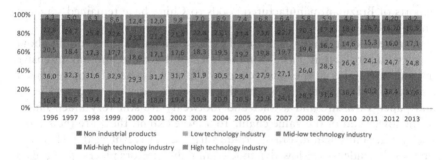

Figure 1.2   Brazilian exports by technology intensity, 1996–2013

Source: Brazilian Ministry of Development, Industry and Foreign Trade (MDIC)/Secretary of Foreign Trade (SECEX)

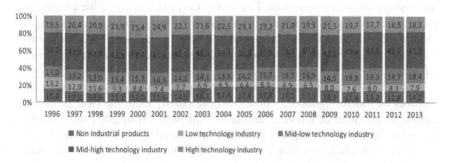

Figure 1.3   Brazilian imports by technology intensity, 1996–2013

Source: Brazilian Ministry of Development, Industry and Foreign Trade (MDIC)/Secretary of Foreign Trade (SECEX)

importer of complex, high-value-added products, as no less than 59.5% of its imports in 2013 were still among the medium- and high-technology manufactures (Figure 1.3). These imports were not restricted to capital goods that could lead to an immediate positive effect on productivity; a considerable amount was of consumer goods that were not produced locally or of a growing variety of imports which, due to the overvaluation of the local currency, flooded the Brazilian market.[13] The majority of those imports were fuel and oil, machinery, electronic equipment, auto and auto parts, chemicals and fertilisers, which in 2013 totalled US$158.3bn (66.1% of total imports). These are the sectors that are responsible for dragging down Brazil's trade balance. Some of Brazil's largest importers are multinational consumer goods giants. In 2013, Samsung was, for instance, Brazil's second-largest importer only behind the oil giant Petrobras.[14] On the import list was a long variety of consumer goods that ranged from LCD TV sets to mobile phones. A similar surge of imports of consumer goods from China is another striking trend. Imports of manufactured goods from the Asian giant grew at an impressive pace over the last decade, from US$1.8bn in 2003 to US$24.9bn in 2010. As a matter of comparison, in the same period, exports of Brazilian manufactured goods to China have remained stagnant on US$1.4bn.[15]

A more in-depth analysis of Brazil's trade balance leaves no doubt about the leading role that basic commodities and low-technology-intensive manufactures play in the local economy (Table 1.1). Brazil's top seven net exports (food and beverages, metallic minerals, agribusiness, steel, pulp and paper, furniture and leather and footwear) are still very much linked to the lower end of the value chain. To a large extent, these are the sectors that are actually behind Brazil's trade surpluses in recent years. This continuous dependence on low dynamic commodity sectors places, however, a strong hindrance on long-term economic development. Incapable of building a stronger position on the value chain, Brazil's trade balance remains uncomfortably sensitive to the ups and downs of commodity prices. On the other hand, Brazil's largest deficits are predominantly in medium- and high-technology-intensive products. The sector that leads Brazil's list of imports is chemical products, which are immediately followed by information technology (IT), electronics and medical equipment. Brazil remains a committed net importer of machinery, oil products, automotive vehicles and electrical equipment.

Nevertheless, Brazil's contribution to high-technology-intensive manufactures cannot be ignored. The most noteworthy example of a successful high-tech sector in Brazil is its aerospace industry. From 2001 to 2010, the Brazilian aerospace company Embraer accounted for US$35.7bn in sales to the foreign market, which corresponded to nearly 2.8% of Brazil's total exports.[16] However, this export performance is in a certain way overshadowed by the high import coefficient of this industry in Brazil. Although Embraer is one of Brazil's largest exporters, the company is also one of

Table 1.1 Brazil's trade balance by sector, 2010–2013 (in US$ millions)

Sector	2010	2011	2012	2013	2010–13
Food and beverages	32,726	38,771	36,084	36,045	143,626
Metallic minerals	29,134	42,146	32,425	33,749	137,454
Agribusiness	19,922	28,621	25,793	31,214	105,550
Steel	6,361	11,713	9,694	8,287	36,055
Pulp and paper	4,843	5,039	4,693	5,303	19,878
Furniture and other industries	3,943	5,101	5,263	2,225	16,532
Leather and footwear	2,618	2,492	2,229	2,548	9,887
Other vehicles	−183	151	845	6,881	7,694
Wood products (excl. furniture)	1,792	1,722	1,702	1,840	7,056
Tobacco products	50	51	3,160	3,194	6,455
Non-metallic minerals	396	332	−61	25	692
Logging	42	40	69	29	180
Publishing	−133	−186	−246	−266	−831
Fishing	−162	−207	−212	−351	−932
Non-metallic mineral products	143	−413	−497	−371	−1,138
Oil and gas	3,286	4,527	969	−10,053	−1,271
Textiles	−1,289	−1,376	−518	−1,513	−4,696
Clothing and apparel	−877	−1,505	−2,013	−2,236	−6,631
Metal products	−1,703	−2,228	−1,758	−2,760	−8,449
Rubber products	−2,670	−3,506	−2,867	−3,519	−12,562
Coal	−2,932	−4,295	−2,980	−2,455	−12,662
Electrical equipment	−4,493	−5,905	−5,362	−6,584	−22,344
Automotive vehicles	−4,916	−8,275	−8,288	−9,156	−30,635
Refined petroleum products	−9,976	−15,861	−11,252	−13,495	−50,584
Machines and equipment	−11,650	−13,883	−13,536	−16,456	−55,525
IT, electronic and optical equipment	−21,970	−24,900	−24,077	−26,096	−97,043
Chemicals	−22,036	−28,370	−29,846	−33,471	−113,723
Total	**20,266**	**29,796**	**19,413**	**2,558**	**72,033**

Source: Boletim Setorial Funcex (various issues).

Brazil's biggest importers. It is estimated that '[a]round 95% of the physical volume of inputs, raw material and components, turbines, aeronautic equipment, aeronautical aluminium and cabling used in Embraer's production process come from the international market' (Bernardes 2003, p. 15).

At the firm level, the role of Brazil among the companies with greatest investments in technology is also very timid. Only eight Brazilian companies—Vale (mining), Petrobras (oil), Embraer (aerospace), Tutvs (IT), CPFL Energia (energy), Weg (industrial engineering), Braskem (chemicals) and Itautec (IT)—are currently listed among the top 2,000 global companies by research and development (R&D) spending (IRI 2013). These eight companies account for only 0.4% of the total list, a far cry from the position granted by the leading economies of the US (32.6% of the companies listed), Japan (17.6%) and Germany (6.5%). According to the same ranking, Brazil lags well behind even other developing economies like China mainland (4.6%), India (1.1%), South Korea (2.8%) and Taiwan (4.05%) (ibid.). In terms of firm size, the participation of Brazilian companies in the select group of the world's largest corporations is still relatively small. In 2013, no more than three Brazilian non-financial institutions (Ambev[17], Petrobras and Vale) were among the *Financial Times* (FT) top 500 companies ranked by market capitalisation,[18] and only four non-financial institutions (Petrobras, Vale, JBS and Ultrapar) were listed in *Fortune*'s top global 500 companies ranked by sales revenues.

LESSONS FROM SOUTH KOREA AND CHINA

Brazil's economic development can be roughly split into two distinct phases in terms of industrial policy orientation. The first lasted from the 1930s to the late 1980s and was largely marked by the strong intervention of the state in the economy. The second and current one began in the early 1990s and has been built over more market-driven pillars. In each of these two phases, Brazil's capacity to foster its own industrial development was in some way outperformed by other developing economies. In the first phase, Brazil's industrial sector was overshadowed by the competitive capacity of the East Asian newly industrialised economies, and in the current phase, with the shift of Brazil towards greater integration into the world economy, the country seems unable to keep pace with the recent spectacular growth of the manufacturing capacity of the large economies of India and China. Along with the normally heated academic debate that has been raised about the 1990s transition of Brazil from a state-led to a market-driven economy, a parallel discussion is also commonly carried out about the performance of Brazil within each one of these phases when compared with other developing economies. Although the focus of this work is on the market-oriented reforms of the last two decades, a quick comparative analysis of Brazil's state-led development experience can shed some light on the path taken by Brazil during its transition process to a more open economy.

Brazil and South Korea

Of the four East Asian newly industrialised countries, South Korea is certainly the one whose economic conditions in the first half of the twentieth century most resembled those found in Brazil. Still solely dependent on their natural resources or on their commodity sector, both economies engaged themselves in wide-ranging industrialisation processes as a way to diversify and upgrade their economic activities and prop up economic growth. Although these two economies followed different state-led industrialisation paths, they shared the same goal of building vertically integrated systems and, to a certain extent, of catching up with the more developed economies.

In contrast to Brazil's inward-looking ISI of the 1960s and 1970s, South Korea structured its development around an outward-looking agenda. The participation of the state was key in the design of several five-year economic and social development plans that rapidly transformed a backward agrarian economy of the late 1950s into one of the most developed Asian economies by the turn of the century. Korea's industrialisation process contrasted, from the start, with the Latin American one with its mid- and long-term objectives of catching up to international standards. By making use of a wide variety of incentives, subsidies and special finance programmes, the government made deliberate use of its discretionary power to select the most strategic sectors of the economy. Another aspect in which Korea stood out from the Latin American economies was the former's support in the creation of a series of large and usually family-owned conglomerates. As part of a general programme of export-oriented development, these large, diversified conglomerates, also known as *chaebols*, became the main engine of the country's economic growth. Initially created to substitute imports, these firms became, over the years, internationally competitive.

Korea's fast upgrade from low-value-added to high-tech industries was not possible without large investments in education and, in the later stage, in home-based research and development. This area, which was notably neglected in Brazil during its post-war industrialisation process, was decisive in guaranteeing Korea's migration into the more sophisticated industries.[19] Among the largest *chaebols*, Samsung, LG, Hyundai and SK Business Group have a participation in medium- and high-technology sectors like IT equipment manufacturing, telecommunications, semiconductors, petrochemicals and shipbuilding.

Despite the economic crisis of 1997, which exposed the frailties of its industrial de-regulation and the vulnerable financial situation of several *chaebols*, South Korea managed during its entire industrialisation process to secure a leading position among the newly industrialised economies. In 2013, Korean companies were ranked eighth in the global top 2,000 companies by R&D spending; the country was only behind the US, Japan, Germany, the UK, China, Taiwan and France (IRI 2013). Korea's share of 2.8% of global spending in R&D was, for instance, seven times higher than the total amount invested by Brazilian companies in that same year (ibid.). This disparity of R&D investments between Korea and Brazil is nevertheless reflected in the technology structure of their exports. Korea's share of medium- and high-technology products in manufactured exports of 75.8% in 2010 was twice as high as the Brazilian one.[20]

Unlike Brazil, Korea followed a more gradual trade liberalisation process, with its first steps towards industrial deregulation being taken in the late 1980s. The pace of reforms was only speeded up with the Asian crisis of 1997. Under guidance from international lending institutions, the Korean government put forward a 'crisis management package', which included a series of measures to make the country's financial system more accountable.[21] At the heart of the pro-market reforms was the restructuring of its long-established state-banks-*chaebols* tripod. This was no trivial measure, as it challenged the very basis of Korea's catching-up system. Under new corporate policies, the *chaebols* were forced to drastically cut their debt-equity ratio and to concentrate on their core business by reducing their level of diversification (Shin 2004, p. 134). The implications of such changes were vast and forced Korea to adapt to a new business scenario in which it had to counterbalance 'financial prudence' with 'industrial catch-up' (ibid., p. 149). Even so, despite losses in employment and a certain increase in social inequality, the Korean economy managed to have a reasonably quick recovery from the 1997 economic crisis.

Brazil and China

Although any comparison between China and Brazil may at first be tempted to merely highlight their large differences in terms of scale, mode of industrial development and degree of rural–urban migration, a more in-depth analysis reveals that these two countries can in fact be united by the challenges they both have to face as a result of their growing integration into the world economy. In the last decades, China and Brazil, like other major developing economies, had to find ways to adapt themselves to the rules and risks of a world business scenario marked by rampant international competition, sweeping takeovers, increasing industrial concentration and, most importantly, by the prospect of having their industries completely restructured as their markets were gradually opened. This was a period of economic transition that brought about profound changes in the way their governments had to relate both to the private and to their own state sectors, to conduct their industrial policies, to deal with foreign investments, to plan their economic targets and to set their social priorities.

The path taken by China towards its greater integration into the world economy is in deep contrast to those taken by most developing economies. Unlike Russia and the Eastern European countries that followed the 'transition orthodoxy' of fast withdrawal of the state from the economy or the debt-ridden Latin American economies that followed the Washington Consensus's comprehensive package of 'structural adjustments' as the only feasible way to economic stability and growth, China opted for a more independent approach of plotting its course towards integration.[22] Drastic 'one cut of the knife' reforms that dominated the economic agenda of the transition economies in the 1990s were rejected straight away by the Chinese government. Instead, the country followed, under strong criticism of leading Western analysts, the slow course of an 'incremental' and gradual reform (Nolan 1994). China's decision to conduct the reforms through careful planning was also a strategy to protect itself from the uncertainties inherent in any major transition process and to guarantee that the reforms would not result in any disruption of the country's social and political stability.[23] For the Chinese government, long-term planning was fundamental in ensuring the desired 'evolution' of its process of integration into the world economy. In real terms, the controlling stance of the state in the opening-up process of the economy was aimed at the achievement of a key strategic goal: the guarantee that Chinese industry would be able to adapt to the growing presence of market forces and also survive to the adverse environment of international competition (Nolan 1995).

China's integration into the world economy stood in contrast to the main policies preached by the orthodox view. It resisted international pressure for a quick opening up of the economy. It allowed prices to be liberalised in a careful manner, which was carried out through the use of a dual-track system in which state-controlled prices were gradually replaced by free-floating prices. It made use of incentives and subsidies to promote exports and made sure that imports were organised 'according to needs'. It avoided drastic cuts of import tariffs and permitted competition to be carried out first between domestic companies. It defended a cautious position when it came to the opening up of its capital market. It encouraged the entry of long-term foreign investments, which flowed into the country primarily by means of joint ventures with local companies, while it maintained, on the other hand, strict barriers to short-term speculative capital. Finally and equally important, it refrained from launching, unlike most transition economies, a comprehensive campaign to privatise its largest state enterprises. The 'commanding heights of the economy' remained 'firmly under state control' (Kynge 2006, p. xv).

The privatisation of large state-owned enterprises (SOEs), which was put as top priority by the 'transition orthodoxy' in the list of reforms to be carried out by former Stalinist economies, didn't find an echo in China. Western economists believed that a wide-ranging divestiture of SOEs was a bitter but necessary medicine that all transition economies should inevitably have to take. Besides expected gains in productivity, their belief was that, with the privatisation of large enterprises, the transition economies would show commitment to the reforms and set foot in a new virtuous cycle of development. The guarantee of a market-friendly environment was considered vital to attract the investments needed to accelerate the modernisation of the means of production and to ensure the entry of their companies into the highly competitive and newly formed global value chains. Any move towards modernisation in this case was solely attributed to the private initiative, either foreign or local.

The position of China was, however, a distinct one. Instead of carrying out a straightforward privatisation programme, the country decided to restructure its largest enterprises. As a consequence, whereas most developing economies were abandoning their industrial policies and handing over to the market the responsibility for short- and long-term strategic decisions, China was instead investing in an ambitious plan of building 'national champions' to compete with global corporations. Fast access to foreign technology, which for the 'transition orthodoxy' came as a by-product of privatisation, was in the case of China mostly sought out through joint ventures with large Western corporations. Like no other developing economy, China made use of its extraordinary bargaining power to negotiate trade-offs with foreign companies that were trying to gain access into its highly promising domestic market.

On the firm level, the central government tackled efficiency-related problems by granting, among other measures, greater autonomy to its state enterprises. China's large SOEs were encouraged to have their management dissociated from government control, and state monopolies were broken to foster the creation of a business environment ruled by competition. Many enterprises reached their 'managerial autonomy' by means of 'contract responsibility systems', which consisted of a new mechanism by which the state, in return for an 'agreed amount of profits and taxes', allowed large companies to enjoy greater independence in the management of their own finances (Nolan and Xiaoqiang 1999, p. 186). In the mid-1990s, this management strategy was gradually replaced by a 'system of joint-stock companies'. This sharing of ownership among several distinct institutions allowed enterprises to stop being solely linked to a 'particular ministry' or 'local government'. This change was fundamental in giving greater autonomy to the shareholding institutions and consequently freeing China's large enterprises from direct government intervention. With the opening of the country to foreign investments, the quick rise of Sino-foreign joint stock companies contributed to the expansion once again of a new form of ownership structure.

China's positive attitude towards the entry of foreign direct investment (FDI) strongly contrasted with its strict policies over portfolio capital. For several years, the country remained protected from the influx of speculative capital. In reality, the participation of foreign investment in public offerings was allowed only fifteen years after the reforms were launched, when in 1993 a group of selected large SOEs was listed. These first public offerings didn't take place in Shanghai but in the more developed stock markets of Hong Kong and New York (ibid., p. 188).

China's cautious decision in the 1990s of not conceding to the pressure from international institutions to rapidly liberalise its capital market prevented it from being, to a large extent, seriously hit by the Asian financial crisis of 1997 and by the Russian crisis of 1998. Given China's long-standing record of high growth and the fact that the country was already a top recipient of FDI, the fast liberalisation of its capital market could have put the country into a vulnerable position by making it an easy target for highly volatile capital. Instead, in the 1990s, China took the prudent option of first working towards the improvement of its still-incipient financial and capital markets. This decision, which was largely criticised by Western analysts, who saw in China's spectacular growth a unique opportunity for short-term investment, allowed the country, on the other hand, to emerge practically unscathed from the Asian and Russian crises (Stiglitz 2002, pp. 59–67). If China had suffered a financial crisis of equivalent magnitude, the consequences could have been disastrous for the country, with unpredictable implications to its social and political stability. Like nearly all developing economies, China didn't have a sophisticated 'safety net to soften the impact' in case of an eventual collapse of its banking or financial system (ibid., p. 65).

China's integration into the world economy has been marked by an impressive economic expansion. In the last three decades, since the beginning of the economic reforms in 1978, the country has been the world's fastest-growing economy. China's staggering average annual growth of 9.8% from 1978 to 2013 is far ahead of the rate reached by any former planned economy (notably Russia and the Eastern European countries) and by the developing economies of Latin America and East Asia. In just thirty-five years, China's nominal GDP rose sixty-two-fold, from US$147.3 billion in 1978 to US$9.2 trillion in 2013. This same period was also marked by a staggering growth in foreign trade, from US$20.6 billion to US$4.16 trillion. China's exports skyrocketed from US$9.75bn to US$2.21tn, and its imports jumped from US$10.89bn to US$1.95tn. In 2009, manufactured goods accounted for no less than 96.3% of all China's exports. From 1995 to 2010, China's share in the world's total manufactured exports jumped from 3.4% to 14.1%, which places the country as the world's top exporter of manufactured products, ahead of other very competitive economies like the US (8%), Japan (6.5%) and Germany (10.2%).[24] China's efforts to build globally competitive companies have recently drawn world attention to several potential 'national champions'—companies that are emerging from totally different industrial sectors like, for instance, telecom equipment (Hauwei), personal computers (Lenovo), white goods (Haier), TVs and electronics (TCL), auto parts (Wanxiang), cars (SAIC), steel (Baosteel), aluminium (Chalco) and oil and gas (PetroChina, Sinopec, CNOOC) (*The Economist* 2005). In 2013, China had ten non-financial institutions among the FT Global 500 companies by market value and sixty-six non-financial institutions in *Fortune's* 500 top global companies by sales revenues. Both figures represent the largest amount of top global companies of any developing economy. The great majority of these companies are controlled by the state.

China's growing influence in the world economy is an unarguable trend, which has become even more visible among developing economies. In Latin America, for instance, China has already overtaken Brazil as the main supplier of manufactured products to the region. From 1990 to 2004, for instance, the share of Chinese imports to Latin America grew ten-fold from 0.7% to 7.8%, whereas the share of Brazilian imports had a timid growth from 5.3% to 6.5% (Valor Econômico 2006). In 2011, China's bilateral trade with Latin America reached US$241.7bn (*China Daily* 2012). From 2005 to 2011, China's state banks lent more than US$75bn to Latin American countries and, more staggeringly, in 2010, China gave to the region more than the World Bank, the Inter-American Development Bank and the US Export-Import Bank combined (FT.com 2012). Perhaps the most emblematic example of China's interest in Latin America is the talks over a rail link in northern Colombia to run as an alternative route to the Panama Canal. The estimated US$7.6bn project would be funded by the Chinese Development Bank and operated by China Railway Group (FT.com 2011). This link between Colombia's Pacific and Atlantic coasts could improve even further China's already fast-growing trade with Latin America.

In Africa, where China is already the biggest trading partner (*The Economist* 2011), a new era in terms of foreign investments has emerged. China's fast-growing economic links with Africa have even set the stage for a new political agenda in the continent. In November 2005, an unprecedented summit meeting gathered forty-eight African leaders in Beijing. Alongside trade negotiations, there was also the promise of US$5.5bn in aid to the African nations (*The Economist* 2007). An impressive amount has also taken the form of loans and direct investments. It is estimated that between 2005 and 2010, Chinese investments to Sub-Saharan Africa reached US$43.6bn (*The Economist* 2011). China now operates oil facilities in Gabon and Sudan, mining companies in Zimbabwe and Zambia, railways in Angola, roads in Ghana, textile manufactures in South Africa and countless infrastructure projects in a dozen other countries. In Asia, China's vigorous economic expansion has lured the entry of several companies from neighbouring economies, most notably Taiwan and Japan, into its own borders. 'Trade within East Asia has grown even faster than the region's trade with the rest of the world', and for many East and South-East Asian countries, China has also become their major trading partner (*The Economist* 2007, p. 11). These two phenomena, migration of companies from neighbouring countries and the growth of trade with these economies, may suggest that China is in fact at the very centre of a regional process of intra-firm 'specialisation' and 'integration' (ibid.).

Despite reaching considerable achievements in carrying out a gradual integration into the world economy, China is far from having overtaken some of its major challenges. Most Chinese companies are still not in condition to compete with the global giants or haven't achieved a leading position in the new global value chains.[25] These apparent competitiveness problems are, however, just part of an even more problematic scenario. China still has to find ways to tackle problems that could eventually harm its social stability. Urgent measures are needed to solve the country's persistent rural poverty, massive urban migration and growing social inequality. In addition to these domestic issues, in the coming years, China will also face problems of deep international interest like, for instance, the world concern about China's environmental policies and the international pressure to rapidly liberalise its financial system.

Although the obstacles faced by China in the near future are of great complexity, the country has so far shown an incredible capacity to deal with the challenges that have emerged with the recent changes in the world economy. More importantly, China seems to have been able to set its own development path. This was not an easy task, which implied making critical decisions that very often have stood up against the traditional orthodoxy. Given China's recent outstanding growth record, one major issue is worthy of careful attention. If successful integration into the world economy already looks challenging for China in the near future, it might look even more problematic for the other more fragile and less dynamic developing economies, like for instance the Latin American ones.

CONCLUSIONS

No concept better describes the changes Brazil went through in the 1990s than that of 'transition'. Such a claim can be made not only due to the impressive scale of the reforms but also due to the completely new business environment that Brazil suddenly had to deal with. For the first time in decades, the Brazilian state found itself in the situation of having to ensure the creation of a business environment in which its rationale was not restricted to the interests of local entrepreneurs but was *equally* open to international interests. This was a profound change. It implied the creation of new pro-market regulations, the abandonment of state intervention in the form of special subsidies and incentives, the lift of trade barriers and the integration of the country into the global economy. These reforms also drove Brazil into the complex task of having to conciliate a strict economic stabilisation programme with contentious measures to liberalise its still-incipient capital market.

The reforms carried out by Brazil echoed the economic liberalisation process that was in full swing in Latin America in the early 1990s. In general, they were characterised by a certain lack of long-term planning and by the near absence of tailor-made measures. The policies implemented by Brazil didn't differ in essence from those adopted by neighbouring economies. The most visible difference probably incurred at the pace and degree of economic openness implemented by each economy, with Argentina and Bolivia being perhaps the most radical examples. Another common aspect between Brazil and the other Latin American economies was their lack of expertise in dealing with the complexities inherent in every step of the economic reform and, more intriguingly, their general lack of knowledge about its long-term implications.

The impact of the reforms was immediate. The changes in the local business environment became clearly evident with the impressive growth of foreign investments, the unprecedented surge in mergers and acquisitions, the rearrangement of the local value chains and the fast growth of foreign trade. Brazil's integration into the world economy was soon marked by the rapid expansion of its commodities sector and the growing relevance of its role as a world supplier of commodity-based products. The opening up of the Brazilian economy seems to have given new leeway for the strengthening of its already vigorous agribusiness (particularly soybeans, orange juice, sugar, cotton, beef and poultry), iron ore and steel sectors, and the pulp and paper industry. Moreover, Brazil was also caught at the forefront of a new economic frontier in the energy sector with the growing world demand for 'green' fuels like bio-diesel and ethanol. It was mostly due to the commodity-based products that Brazil managed to ensure its large trade surpluses in the years following the opening up of the economy. The implications of this shift to a newly opened economy are vast. In the new surge in global trade of the late 1990s and of the early twenty-first century, it is predominantly in the low-value-added sectors that Brazil seems to have achieved its 'real comparative advantage'.

The expansion of basic commodities in Brazil after the reforms may indicate that the country is at risk of having primary and low-value-added goods gaining weight over the technology-intensive industry. This would be a surprising outcome, particularly after a long period of state-led industrialisation in which large investments were made in areas like aerospace, auto parts and telecom equipment manufacturing. The growth of the commodities sector in Brazil could also bring serious implications in the country's integration into the world economy. This eventual move back to basic commodities largely contrasts with the tendency followed by other developing economies, particularly those of South and South-East Asia, where the shift toward a greater integration into the world economy was more strategically focused on technology upgrading.

Any comparison between Brazil and other successful developing economies is not complete without revealing deficiencies in the two most important phases of its economic development, the period of state-led import substitution industrialisation and the recent process of economic liberalisation. Despite the impressive growth of Brazil during its state-led development period, the country was not able to avoid a series of problems (like persistent inflationary pressures, economic instability and the loss of investment power from the part of the government) that contributed to the alleged exhaustion of its inward-looking industrialisation. On the other hand, the recent modernisation effort of the Brazilian economy by means of market opening was not as anticipated. Although the opening of the economy resulted in much-needed gains in productivity, the reforms did not seem sufficient enough to prop up the innovative capacity of the Brazilian industry and place it in a more comfortable position in the newly formed global value chains.

In many sectors, Brazilian industry was not able to catch up with the fast expansion of major developing economies and may even have fallen behind. This is in deep contrast to other developing economies that made use of this period of transition to strengthen their industry. The most notable example is perhaps China, which, by means of a gradual opening and more strategic integration into the world economy, managed to achieve astonishing growth rates.

This is a period of profound changes in the world economy, where every move could have long-lasting effects, and it is therefore crucial for Brazil to secure an active role in the new global business scenario. Recent events show, however, a distinct picture. Apart from a few exceptions like the high-tech aerospace industry, it is mainly in the commodity-based sectors that Brazil has experienced its most significant growth and its companies enjoyed larger international recognition. Whereas the move towards greater integration into the world economy promoted in China an impressive growth in manufacturing, it may eventually cause in Brazil an unexpected move back to basic commodities. This is an intriguing outcome for a country like Brazil, whose set of reforms originally had the main aim of modernising the economy.

NOTES

1. A paper by Armando C. Pinheiro and Fabio Giambiagi (Brazilian privatisation in the 1990s 1994, pp. 737–9) provides a brief description of the direct participation of the state in key sectors of the economy in the early 1990s, particularly in oil and oil refining, petrochemical, chemical, mining and public utilities like telecommunications, power generation and sanitation. 'In industry, federal SOEs dominate the mining sector, with 88.6% of gross revenues, 85.7% of net worth and 83.3% of net fixed assets; (main companies: Petrobras and CVRD). (. . .) The metallurgy sector, with nine of the 56 largest federal SOEs accounting in 1990 for nearly two-thirds of the revenues and net-worth, and almost 90% of the net fixed assets. (. . .) In chemicals, the 11 largest federal SOEs accounted for about one-fourth of the revenues, two-fifths of the net worth and a third of the net fixed assets. (. . .) The public utilities sector (power, water and sanitation) is totally dominated by the state, with 25 SOEs out of the total 27 companies accounting for almost all sales, net worth and net fixed assets'.

2. Data from Werner Baer (The Brazilian economy: growth and development 2001, p. 184).
3. Data from the Brazilian Central Bank, www.bacen.gov.br.
4. Metal Leve, Brazil's largest manufacturer of pistons, rings and bearings, was usually hailed by analysts as an 'island of excellence', an 'example of quality and productivity' and a 'model of labour relations' (Revista Exame 1996). One of the most 'admired Brazilian companies', Metal Leve was regarded by many as an 'unshakeable asset' (ibid.). However, despite the widespread belief among the business community in Brazil of the company's capacity to compete in a more open environment, Metal Leve was suddenly sold in 1996 to the German group Mahle. This unexpected acquisition of a successful and relatively globally integrated company like Metal Leve raised concerns within the Brazilian business community. The main issue, as brought up by the Brazilian economist Antônio Barros de Castro, was not particularly the reasons that led to the sale of Metal Leve but more importantly the implications of a more complex question: If the new market-oriented environment in Brazil didn't seem to give room for a company like Metal Leve, what would the chances be for other Brazilian companies to succeed in a truly open economy (Folha de São Paulo 1996)?
5. According to a study by the KPMG consulting group, from 1994 to 2013, a total of 9,003 mergers and acquisitions (M&As) was carried out in Brazil. Top of the list was the IT sector with 886 transactions, which was followed by food, beverages and tobacco with 776 M&As. The following ten most dynamic sectors were: telecommunications and media (463 M&A), financial institutions (455), energy companies (435), company services (365), advertising and publishing houses (373), metallurgy and steel (317), oil and gas (312), chemical and petrochemical products (302), insurance (279) and real estate (262), (KPMG 2014).
6. In the following years of 2012 and 2013, Brazil's foreign trade was respectively US$465.8bn and US$481.8bn. Data from the Brazilian Ministry of Development, Industry and Foreign Trade, www.desenvolvimento.gov.br.
7. Data from the Brazilian Ministry of Development, Industry and Foreign Trade, www.desenvolvimento.gov.br.
8. In 2013, Brazilian exports to China reached a new record with US$46bn in sales.
9. Data from the United Nations Industrial Development Organisations (UNIDO 2013).
10. Data from the United Nations Industrial Development Organisations, www.unido.org/data1/Statistics/Research/cip.html.
11. Ibid.
12. Ibid.
13. In 2006, for instance, the substitution of domestically produced consumer goods by imported ones reached at that time a new peak. In September of that year, imports of durable consumer goods recorded a twelve-monthly increase of 74%. Imports of automotive vehicles had a record increase of 200% in the first quarter of 2006 and a total increase of 109% in the first two quarters. Above-average increases were also observed in the segments of white and brown goods. In the first two quarters of 2006, these two sectors recorded growths of, respectively, 50% and 60% when compared to the same period in the previous year. On the other hand, exports of consumer durables in the twelve-month period ending in September 2006 grew by only 6%. In contrast to the spectacular growth of car imports, exports of automotive vehicles grew by only 12% in the first quarter of 2006. With regard to white goods, exports in this segment registered a drop of 4.6% in the first two quarters of 2006

(Valor Econômico 2006). This rapid growth of consumer goods imports and the poor performance of Brazil's traditional manufacturing exports raised a vivid debate about the possibility of Brazil being affected by the so-called Dutch disease (Boletim Setorial Funcex 2006). According to some analysts, Brazil's booming commodity sector (mainly agribusiness and mining) could be drawing the economy into a similar process of deindustrialisation faced by the 'suddenly-oil-rich' Netherlands of the 1970s, the loss of competitiveness of the local industry brought about by the sudden rise of the commodity export sector and the consequent overvaluation of the local currency.

A more in-depth analysis of different sources of industrialisation and the manifestation of the Dutch disease in Brazil and in other Latin American economies can be found in Palma (2004). Differently from the traditional source of the 'disease' based on a sudden 'surge of primary-commodity exports', the author claims that the kind of Dutch disease that affected Latin America in the 1990s comes from a distinct strain. According to his work, the deindustrialisation faced by Latin America was mainly caused by the 'drastic switch of the economic policy regime' and the 'sharp reversal of ISI policies' (ibid., p. 19). This 'shift in the "police regime" (mostly implemented after the 1982 debt crisis) brought about the end of industrial and trade policies and, in particular, changes in relative prices, in real exchange rates, in the institutional framework of the economies, in the structure of property rights and in market incentives in general. This shift led [the Latin American economies] to abandon their industrialisation agenda, bringing them back to their "natural Ricardian position"; i.e., a position associated with comparative advantages more in accordance with their traditional resource endowment' (ibid., p. 34)—in this case, Latin America's vast supplies of natural resources.

14. In 2013, Samsung was ranked 211th on the list of Brazil's top exporters. Only 2% of the company's total sales were for abroad. Data from the Brazilian Ministry of Development, Industry and Commerce, www.mdic.gov.br/, and Revista Exame Melhores e Maiores (2014).

15. Data from Federação das Indústrias do Estado de São Paulo, www.fiesp.com.br/noticias/brasil-registra-deficit-comercial-com-a-china-de-us-235-bilhoes-em-manufaturados/.

16. Data from Embraer, www.embraer.com.

17. Although the Brazilian beverage company Ambev merged with the Belgian brewer Interbrew in 2002, both companies were treated as separate entities in the FT Global 500 Companies 2013.

18. Four Brazilian financial institutions were in the FT Global 500 companies, namely Itaú Unibanco, Bradesco, Banco do Brasil and Itaú S.A.

19. In the year 2000, South Korea's school enrolment in tertiary education was, for instance, nearly 4.5 times higher than in Brazil. While in South Korea tertiary education reached up to 72.6% of the population in the corresponding age group, in Brazil this ratio was of only 16.1%, www.worldbank.org.

20. Data from the United Nations Industrial Development Organisation, www.unido.org/data1/Statistics/Research/cip.html.

21. A large debate was raised about the origins of Korea's economic crisis. Contrary to the mainstream view that by and large put the blame on the alleged exhaustion of the state-banks-chaebols catching-up system, some analysts like Ha-Joon Chang (2004) and Jang-Sup Shin (2004) claimed that the economic crisis had its origin in the very process of market opening. For these authors, Korea's economic reform was comprised by an ill-advised industrial deregulation process which helped to create an excessive overcapacity in a number of sectors that were previously controlled by the state and, more importantly, by the liberalisation of the financial market which was carried out without a

'commensurate upgrading in the financial supervision system', (ibid., p. 106). In their view, this hasty liberalisation of a still-emergent financial system left the Korean economy exceptionally vulnerable to the speculative attack that followed the outbreak of the Asian crisis in 1997.

22. China's strategy towards economic reforms, which strongly challenged the predominant guidelines of the 'Washington Consensus', began being called by some analysts the 'Beijing Consensus' (Ramo 2004). This alternative approach to economic transition drew attention to key issues of trade and market liberalisation where the Washington-based precepts in many developing economies had drastically failed, particularly in those aspects regarding the achievement of an equitable and sustainable development. For the so-called Beijing Consensus, the 'best path for modernisation' was through a gradual and experimental process ('groping the stones to cross the river') instead of the 'one-big, shock-therapy leap' advocated by the transition orthodoxy (ibid., p. 4).

23. China's decision to maintain its political structure of a one-party system was in profound contrast to the main precepts of the 'transition orthodoxy'. For the orthodox Western economists, the shift towards economic liberalisation by the transition economies would need to come in tandem with an equivalent process of political liberalisation.

24. Data from the United Nations Industrial Development Organisation, www.unido.org.

25. 'After more than two decades of rapid growth, there is still a wide development gap between China and the high-income countries (. . .). China's national income is only one-fifth, and national income per person is only 16 per cent, of that of the high income countries. It has just nine firms in the G1,400 list of companies [by R&D spending] and none in the top 100. Its household wealth is only 4 percent of that of the high-income countries' (Nolan 2012, p. 66).

REFERENCES

Baer, Werner. *The Brazilian economy: growth and development*. 5th edition. Westport: Praeger Publishers, 2001.

Bernardes, Roberto. "Passive innovation system and local learning: a case study of Embraer in Brazil." *1st Globelics Conference: Innovation Systems and Development Strategies for the Third Millennium*. Rio de Janeiro, 2003.

Boletim Setorial Funcex. "'Dutch Disease' no Brasil? Analogia incorreta para um fato preocupante." January 2006.

Chang, Ha-Joon. "The 1997 Korean Crisis: causes and consequences." In *Brazil and South Korea: economic crisis and restructuring*, by Edmund Amann and Ha-Joon Chang, 105–22. London: Institute of Latin American Studies, 2004.

China Daily. "Deeper Sino-Latin American trade cooperation urged." 18 October 2012. http://usa.chinadaily.com.cn/business/2012-10/18/content_15827101.htm.

The Economist. "A special report on China and its region." London, 31 March 2007.

———. "China's top companies." London, 06 January 2005.

———. "The Chinese in Africa: trying to pull together." London, 20 April 2011.

Financial Times. "Brazil looks to Doha for progress on fairer farm trade." London, 06 November 2001.

———. "Brazilian farms sow seeds of openness." London, 14 April 2010.

———. "China fever drives Brazil's exporters to frenzied activity." London, 11 November 2003.

———. "Farms buck downward trend." London, 03 July 2002.

———. "Top of the crops: Brazil's huge heartland is yielding farms that can feed the world." London, 23 June 2005.

Folha de São Paulo. "Mudando o diagnóstico." São Paulo, 26 June 1996.

FT.com. "Brazil's import substitution industrialisation 2.0." 02 January 2012. http://blogs.ft.com/beyond-brics/2012/01/02/12-for-2012-brazils-import-substi tution-2-0/.

———. "China in talks over Panama Canal rival." 13 February 2011. www.ft.com/ intl/cms/s/0/7e14756c-37a9-11e0-b91a-00144feabdc0.html#axzz3QQOq5fVS.

IRI. *EU R&D Scoreboard: the 2013 EU industrial R&D investment scoreboard.* European Commission, Luxembourg: Publications Office of the European Union, 2013.

KPMG. "Mergers and acquisitions research 2014, 1st quarter: mirror of the transactions undertaken in Brazil." São Paulo, 2014.

Kynge, James. *China shakes the world.* New York: Houghton Mifflin Company, 2006.

Nolan, Peter. *China's rise, Russia's fall.* New York: St. Martin's Press, 1995.

———. *Is China buying the world?* Cambridge: Polity Press, 2012.

Nolan, Peter. "The China puzzle: 'touching the stones to cross the river.'" *Challenge.* Vol. 37 (1994): 25–31.

Nolan, Peter, and Wang Xiaoqiang. "Beyond privatisation: institutional innovation and growth in China's large state-owned enterprises." *World Development.* Vol. 27 (1999): 169–200.

Observatório Brasil China. "Participação da China no comércio exterior Brasileiro é a maior nos últimos 10 anos." *Informativo da Confederação Nacional da Indústria.* Rio de Janeiro, March 2011.

Palma, Gabriel. "Four sources of 'de-industrialisation' a new concept of the 'Dutch disease.'" *UNU-INTECH Research Seminar.* Maastricht, 19 May 2004.

Pinheiro, Armando Castelar and Giambiagi, Fabio. "Brazilian privatisation in the 1990s." *World Development.* Vol. 22 (1994): 737–53.

Ramo, Joshua Cooper. *The Beijing Consensus.* London: The Foreign Policy Centre, 2004.

Revista Exame. "Como a Metal Leve perdeu o passo." São Paulo: Editora Abril, 03 July 1996. 74–6.

Revista Exame Melhores e Maiores 2014. São Paulo: Editora Abril, June 2014.

Shin, Jang-Sup. "Globalisation and industrial restructuring: the case of South Korea." In *Brazil and South Korea: economic crisis and restructuring,* by Edmund Amann and Ha-Joon Chang, 123–51. Institute of Latin American Studies, 2004.

Stiglitz, Joseph. *Globalisation and its discontents.* London: Penguin Books, 2002.

UNIDO. "Industrial development report 2013." United Nations Industrial Development Organisations, Vienna, 2013.

Valor Econômico. "China passa Brasil na venda de manufaturados para a América Latina." Rio de Janeiro, 07 August 2006.

———. "Importação de bens duráveis cresce 93% no terceiro trimestre." Rio de Janeiro, 20 October 2006.

———. "Para governo superávit comercial pode cair para até US$10bi neste ano." Rio de Janeiro, 10 February 2012.

Part II
The Public, the Private and the Multinationals
Brazil's Long Road from Structuralism to Neo-Liberalism

By development, in this context, we mean 'capitalist development'. This form of development, in the periphery as well as in the centre, produces as it evolves, in a cyclical way, wealth and poverty, accumulation and shortage of capital, employment for some and unemployment for others. So, we do not mean by the notion of 'development' the achievement of a more egalitarian or more just society. These are not consequences expected from capitalist development, especially in peripheral economies.

—Fernando H. Cardoso and Enzo Faletto
'Dependency and development in
Latin America', 1979

To reform the state does not mean to dismantle it. On the contrary, reform could never entail destruction of the administrative and political decision making systems, much less lead to a lessening of the state's regulatory capacity or of its power to steer the process of change and to set its course. To change the state means, above all, to set aside visions of the past, visions of paternalistic welfare state—a state that, due to circumstances, focused largely on direct intervention in production of goods and services. Today, all are well aware that the production of goods and services can and should be handed over to the society, to private enterprise, with substantial gains to efficiency and lower costs to consumers.

—Former President of Brazil Fernando H. Cardoso (1995–2003)
Foreword to 'Reforming the state: managerial public
administration in Latin America', 1999

INTRODUCTION

The integration of Brazil into the world economy gained speed with the structural reforms carried out in the last two decades and brought new challenges to several sectors of its industrial economy. This is a country in transition not only because of the recent withdrawal of the state from key sectors of the economy but also due to the complete rearrangement of its local production that came about as a result of an equally recent and comprehensive market liberalisation programme. These changes affected the country's most relevant industrial sectors and redefined the role of the state in its main public utilities. Although they are commonly explained by a large variety of motivations, the recent economic reforms can be roughly summarised as being stimulated by a range of interconnected internal and external factors: first, as a way of reducing the country's mounting debt by exerting control on its fiscal accounts and of creating a new regulatory environment more attractive to private and foreign investments; and second, as a response to the pressures of the recent changes (most notably, those of the last two decades) in the global economy which were characterised by an impressive number of cross-border mergers and acquisitions, the concentration of production among a few global players and a complete rearrangement of the global value chain.

The consequences of this process for the Brazilian economy are striking. It brought new elements into an environment that was intrinsically inward looking and triggered the rupture from an industrial model that was strongly based on state intervention and market protection. More importantly, the recent wave of reforms has imposed a complete reshuffle of the three entities that since the beginning of Brazil's industrialisation have been crucial for the definition of the country's development policies. As a result, *state enterprises*, *local private enterprises* and *multinational corporations* were forced to rapidly redefine their roles. This is a key process. The prevalence of interests from any of these three entities, as well as the role that they are allowed or willing to play, will set the conditions and perspectives for the country's future participation in the global economy.

Big business in Brazil has been traditionally shaped by the synergies among these three entities. Each one had enjoyed for decades a clear and distinct role (Evans 1979). Although the state was present in several sectors of the economy, the lion's share of Brazil's industrial output was actually controlled by private enterprises. The relationship between the *state* and the *local private* and *foreign capitals* followed an apparent underlying principle of common interests (Evans, 1979). In this division of functions, the *state* was responsible for providing the necessary incentives for local private companies and the required infrastructure for the entry and participation of foreign investments. This was by no means a uniform practice, and the participation of the *state*, the *local private enterprises* and the *multinationals* would vary according to each industrial sector. The *state* could, for instance, act as a supplier of basic inputs (steel) as in the case of the then-infant Brazilian automotive industry, or it could take a more up-front position as in the case of the aerospace industry. The central role of the state was nevertheless conspicuous. Since the beginning of Brazil's industrialisation, the state had concentrated its efforts on maintaining a presence in those sectors that either were considered to be strategic, under-invested and incipient or that dealt with the country's main non-renewable resources. The oil, steel and iron ore sectors in the 1950s and 1960s and the aerospace, chemicals and electronics industries in the 1970s are the most obvious examples where the participation of the state was decisive. In terms of basic infrastructure, this same period also witnessed a strong presence of the state in the main public utilities, such as 'telecommunications, gas and electricity, water and sanitation, railways and public transport' (Goldstein and Schneider 2000, p. 8).

Local private entrepreneurship, on the other hand, had to follow a different path. Brazilian domestic companies, which were more vulnerable to market conditions, had to find their way through a variety of obstacles and opportunities that could be summed up as their ability to deal with political uncertainties, face economic instabilities, raise capital, lobby for government support and finally identify niche markets. Industrial entrepreneurship in Brazil started in the first quarter of the twentieth century in the initially less technology- and capital-intensive sectors (such as textile and food processing) and evolved over the following decades to more complex consumer durables and a certain range of capital goods to finally reach a large and diversified industrial park in the 1990s. This was the largest in Latin America and one of the largest in any developing country. Local entrepreneurship did not flourish in an independent fashion, and its expansion was closely linked with the pro-industrialisation policies put forward by the Brazilian government.

Finally, the *multinational corporations*, which were strongly attracted by the highly protected Brazilian market, were usually associated with (a) the most dynamic and capital intensive industries or (b) those sectors in which Brazil had not developed any indigenous capability. Their decision to transfer production to Brazil was mainly a way of bypassing the protective barriers that were in practice in the early years of the country's industrialisation process. A limited amount of transference of technology was expected by the Brazilian government and, in those cases where conditions were convenient, these foreign companies would engage in the formation of joint ventures with local capital.

Despite all its shortcomings, as will be discussed later in this chapter, Brazil's process of late industrialisation managed to attain a considerable degree of local content and a fairly diversified economic environment. With the end of the second boom of Brazil's industrialisation in the mid-1970s, the move from an agrarian to an industrial economy was already consolidated. In 1973, the industry share of the GDP was nearly four times greater than that of the agricultural sector, and the distribution of manufacturing activities had considerably moved to intermediate and capital goods, which respectively represented 41.5% and 19.1% of the total industrial output (Tyler 1981). In 1989, of the top 500 companies, 44% were private domestic enterprises, 30.8% were foreign multinational corporations and 25.2% were actually composed of state-owned enterprises (Revista Exame Melhores e Maiores 2012).

The recent opening up of Brazil's economy has been powerful enough to destabilise this arrangement and shape a new one in which the role of the state is smaller and the presence of foreign investment is more pronounced. The Brazilian industrial economy has now reached a different arrangement in which the *state* has considerably reduced its manufacturing activities, the *local private enterprises* have become more exposed to foreign competition and the *multinational corporations* have rearranged their local production so as to be more in tune with their global rationality. In addition, the local companies had to adapt themselves to the course of events that has made them move from being inherently inward looking to becoming more exposed and integrated into the global economy.

Before a more detailed analysis of the integration of Brazil into the world economy is carried out, a brief overview of the first stages of Brazil's industrialisation may be helpful in order to understand the conflicts, discrepancies and contradictions that have given shape to the diversification of the Brazilian economy. This long process of transition from an agrarian economy to a diversified industrial economy in the late 1970s can be analysed through the different economic schools of thought that have interpreted the Brazilian and Latin American economies throughout the second half of the twentieth century, namely the United Nations Economic Commission for Latin America's (ECLA's) 'Structuralism' and 'Dependency Theory'. Although they were constantly criticised by neoclassical and orthodox scholars, these currents of thought were in fact two comprehensive contributions from Latin American scholars towards the incipient post-war debate on development economics. Despite local constraints, the participation of the Latin American countries in the debate was not small. The need for an inner interpretation of the economic problems seemed to be evident: although the focus of attention was on underdeveloped economies, the development debate had until then been mainly carried on among economists based in developed countries. 'Structuralism' and 'Dependency Theory' were fundamental in the condemnation of the economic practices that prevailed in Latin America and in indicating, in their own way, alternative policies for the development of the region. Both schools had a long-lasting effect on the Latin American mindset and are still referenced by the international business media (FT.com 2012).

Apart from giving a brief overview of these schools of economic thinking, this chapter also aims to extract an example from the Brazilian industrialisation process that can well illustrate the influence of each of these theories. The first example is an account of the relevance of the coffee sector to the beginning of the Brazilian industrialisation process, and the second is an account of the development of the petrochemical and pharmaceutical sectors in Brazil in the 1970s.

Finally, a detailed analysis of these initial years of development thinking in Latin America might shed some light on the effectiveness of the current neo-liberal policies in which free market, monetary orthodoxy and industrial deregulation are expected to form the necessary conditions for economic growth and long-term sustainable development. This chapter also aims to comment on the recent changes in the world economy and the impact of global business on the industrialisation of developing countries. The growing concentration of production among a few global companies (mostly based in developed countries) and the recent restructuring of their corresponding global supply chains certainly add new complexity to the development debate. Within this context, a detailed analysis of the recent consolidation of global big business might provide a comparable or even 'a more appropriate intellectual framework than the conventional trade' argument constantly used by Structuralism and Dependency scholars to explain the peripheral role that is left to the developing countries.

FROM RURAL TO URBAN—THE FIRST LATIN AMERICAN INDUSTRIALIZATION EFFORT

Free market, state retrenchment and large-scale integration into global production were not usually part of the main policies put forward by Brazilian or, to a large extent, Latin American economists. These scholars had learnt to be sceptical about any *laissez faire* doctrine on trade and industrial promotion. Until the early twentieth century, foreign trade in Latin America, when not performed under mercantilist practices, was mainly depicted as unfavourable; production (mostly agrarian) was strongly concentrated in the hands of a few; and society was incapable of building any solid political institutions, let alone of building any sort of comprehensive means of social justice. Compared to the then-developed European economies, Latin America was a backward[1] region.

Attempts to understand the origins of the region's economic backwardness and the subsequent formation of development policies started to emerge in Latin America in the third quarter of the twentieth century and were highly influenced by studies that were carried out in ECLA, a development agency that was created in Santiago del Chile in 1948. Not restricted to the theoretical understanding of the economic agents in play, ECLA also had a pragmatic role in proposing policies that were later adopted by the great majority of Latin American countries. A whole generation of economists was formed under its premises, and the project of developing a region-concerned school of economic thinking became the norm.[2]

The creation of ECLA was a landmark for Latin American economic thinking in the post-war period. The importance of this research institution can be measured not only by the fact that it constituted the first attempt in Latin America to establish a forum among local economists dedicated to the continent's development issues but also by the fact that its policies quickly came to represent a distinct voice in the prevailing debate on development economics. From its early years, ECLA's writings aimed to challenge the predominant neo-classical theory that gave emphasis to the 'comparative advantage' argument that had allegedly kept the Latin American economies strongly reliant on agrarian production. In an innovative way, ECLA engendered the intellectual framework that provided the basis for the economic diversification and industrialisation of Latin American countries. Following the premise that the exclusive and historical dependence on agrarian activities had been harmful to the overall development of the continent, ECLA pointed to the fact that the 'distribution of gains' in international trade tended to be skewed to the benefit of the developed economies. ECLA was fundamental in the attempt to shed light on the participation of the Latin American countries in foreign trade and in identifying the role of these economies as 'peripheral' in the global capitalist rationality.

According to ECLA, the development path of Latin American economies was intrinsically different from the one taken by developed countries, as these latter economies had not faced, in the earlier stages of their development, the same trade conditions and divisions of labour that the developing Latin American countries were then experiencing. The assumptions that were valid for the developed economies were not present in the developing economies and, as a consequence, many of the models that were put forward by the developed economies were not applicable to the then economic condition of the developing countries. ECLA also opposed the common view that development had to be achieved in stages and that developing countries would, as a consequence, eventually reach higher standards of development.

ECLA's early studies were strongly concerned in analysing the Latin American economy from a social-historic perspective, an approach which was notoriously advocated by its first director, the Argentinean economist Raúl Prebisch. From Prebisch's first writings in the United Nations' Commission, it is possible to observe a concern that would be constant in his future works and would influence many other scholars. It was a call for the interpretation of the Latin American reality through its own local perspective, a perception that would be, in many cases, in conflict with the thinking supported by the developed economies.

> Admittedly much remains to be done in the Latin American countries, both in learning the facts and in their proper theoretical interpretation. Though many of the problems of these countries are similar, no common effort has ever been made even to examine and elucidate them. It is not surprising, therefore, that the studies published on the economy of Latin American countries often reflect the points of view or the experience of the great centres of the world economy. Those studies cannot be expected to solve problems of direct concern to Latin America. The case of the Latin American countries must therefore be presented clearly, so that their interests, aspirations and opportunities, bearing in mind, of course, the individual differences and characteristics, may

be adequately integrated within the general framework of international economic cooperation.

(Prebisch 1950, p. 2)

In a sub-continent that was constantly polarized by antagonistic economic thinking, ECLA was commonly criticised by both left- and right-wing scholars. The first, as it was mentioned in a study carried out by Gabriel Palma (1978, p. 907), condemned the agency 'for failing to denounce sufficiently the mechanisms of exploitation within the capitalist system, and for criticizing the conventional theory of international trade only from "within"', whereas the right wing considered ECLA's attitude as 'totally heretical from the point of view of conventional theory, and threatened the political interests of significant sectors' (ibid.).[3]

ECLA had, however, an undeniable influence on Latin American thinking. Apart from providing an interpretation of the region's underdevelopment, the agency also contributed, as was expressed by Bresser-Pereira (2001, p. 20), to the presentation of a 'coherent strategy of development'. Backwardness in Latin America was not to be investigated as an isolated fact; it had to be inserted in a structural context in which a better understanding of the different functions taken by developed and underdeveloped economies could be given. This concern in providing a major perspective for the analysis of the object under investigation was in tune with a broader school of thought known as Structuralism.[4] ECLA would then make use of characteristics related to developed and underdeveloped economies, as well as their trade relations, to explain the disadvantageous condition of the latter ones.

THE LATIN AMERICAN STRUCTURALIST SCHOOL

For an initial comprehension of Latin American economic Structuralism, two preliminary concepts need to be understood: the 'centre' and the 'periphery'. The first made reference to those countries that had a diversified economy and whose production was mainly composed of manufactured goods. At the opposite end, the 'periphery' was composed of economies that had a low diversification of production and relied, in many cases, on a few agricultural products.[5] These latter economies also differed from the ones of the 'centre' by presenting a lack of developed institutional organizations (work unions, social representatives and labour regulations), a feature that would be perceived as crucial for the distribution of production gains and, as a consequence, influential in the relation between 'centre' and 'periphery'.

The relation between centre and periphery was, in its essence, asymmetric. Productivity gains, although perceived by both in their distinct areas of production, tended to be more skewed towards the centre, a phenomenon that had its roots in the way that trade, capital accumulation and income distribution were organized.

In the periphery, imports were mainly of manufactured goods, a trade that tended to grow as real income in the periphery increased. On the other hand, the centre was mainly an importer of primary goods, products whose low elasticity prevented an equivalent growth in demand. This high elasticity of manufactured goods, in contrast with the low elasticity of primary goods, created a discrepancy that benefited the centre. Production gains in the periphery would be eventually converted into a higher demand for products imported from the centre. This transference of gains, however, was not reciprocated by the centre; an increase of real income in the centre did not echo into a comparable increase of imports from the periphery.[6]

Production gains in the periphery, apart from generating a higher demand for imported goods, were also responsible for promoting an expansion of the production of exportable primary goods. From the perspective of the periphery, the higher demand for manufactured products, combined with a larger production of agricultural goods, resulted in an appreciation on the price of imports and a depreciation on the price of exports, factors that were identified as crucial for a continuous deterioration of the 'terms of trade'[7] of the periphery. As Singer illustrated:

> The industrialised countries have had the best of both worlds, both as consumers of primary commodities and as producers of manufactured articles, whereas the underdeveloped countries had the worst of both worlds, as consumers of manufactures and producers of raw materials.
>
> (Singer 1950, p. 478)

Under the Prebisch-Singer perspective, the most efficient way for the periphery to start to accumulate gains and be less harmed by foreign trade would be through a process of industrialisation. Only then would the so-called periphery be less dependent on income-elastic manufactured imports and, eventually, even be able to export products that had a higher elasticity of demand. Industrial promotion began to be regarded as a necessary path that Latin America should take to break away from its periphery condition and move towards the centre level of development.[8]

The claim of the 'deterioration in the terms of trade' of the periphery to the benefit of the centre countries that was argued by ECLA's economists was not put forward without strong opposition from neoclassical scholars, who were commonly based in the developed world (Kay 1989, p. 8). What was probably one of the most virulent critiques came from Peter Bauer in his review of the import substitution proposition published by UNCTAD in 1964. The UNCTAD (1964) document titled *Towards a New Trade Policy for Development* was not only a reassessment of Prebisch's previous works at ECLA, but it also re-endorsed many of his claims regarding international trade. In a strong critique of the UNCTAD document, Peter Bauer argued that the 'conceptual, analytical and empirical bases of [the deterioration in the terms of trade] allegations [we]re invalid' (Bauer 1971, p. 245). According to the author, 'the allegation of a long-run decline of the terms of trade of primary producers or of underdeveloped countries [we]re untrue' (ibid., p. 255). Peter Bauer not only condemned UNCTAD's claim of alleged 'deteriorations in the terms of trade' but also criticised its policies, more specifically, the need for the underdeveloped countries to diversify and industrialise their economies. As the author wrote in the concluding part of his critique of UNCTAD, 'in the conditions of most underdeveloped countries agricultural production for the market is likely to be more effective for the development of the changes in attitudes and skills required for material progress than is subsidised manufacturing' (ibid., p. 267).

Peter Bauer's efforts to criticise the claim of 'deterioration in the terms of trade' overlooked, however, a major issue: namely ECLA's fundamental premise that it was actually due to industrialisation and economic diversification that the centre countries had achieved higher standards of development. Bauer's disregard of the benefits that industrialisation could bring even to a few large underdeveloped economies was therefore a 'crucial omission'.

The author did provide a real contribution to the debate when he pointed to an issue that was largely ignored by ECLA and should indeed be more carefully addressed by its scholars. This was the fact that the *factoral terms of trade* as opposed to *commodity terms of trade* could provide a more accurate measure of the gains and losses in the trade between primary and manufacture-producing countries. However, the attempt by the author to disqualify Prebisch's original claims by means of allegations of methodological problems, due to the fact that those claims were based only on high aggregate data, had a negative implication for the practicability of Bauer's own counter-argument. Any analysis of foreign trade can reach even more methodological constraints when variables related to factoral terms of trade are also taken into account. In consequence, although Bauer argued that when *factoral terms of trade are taken under consideration* there is no evidence of the alleged deterioration, his argument was never fully empirically illustrated or tested and basically remained in the realm of theoretical assumptions.[9] Even so, if both of his main allegations were correct, that is that (a) '[e]xcept for very short periods the factoral terms of trade normally improve for all or most trading partners' and that (b) '[e]ven if factoral terms of trade, corrected for quality changes, have deteriorated, the economic welfare of people in exporting countries can still improve if there is a large increase in total trade' (ibid., p. 246), the author seemed to have once again ignored one of the premises of the UNCTAD report. Bauer overlooked the fact that it was exactly to avoid unforeseeable conditions like the one just stated and that had hit the agrarian economies in the 1930s and in the World War II period that the Structuralist scholars were suggesting the industrial diversification of the peripheral economies.

In addition, with regard to the underlying issue of low income elasticity of primary products, also one of the main points of Bauer's critique, his counter-argument was considerably based on biased examples. An evident case is, for instance, his example of oil as a commodity whose demand increased according to the rises of income in the developed economies. Although oil, as Bauer himself pointed out, represented almost 50% of all exports from underdeveloped countries, the author seemed to have ignored two key issues. First, oil production was not representative of the activities carried out by the great majority of the underdeveloped economies. Among the Latin American countries, where ECLA's propositions were the focus of concern, only two economies were oil exporters, Mexico and Venezuela. Second, oil (like steel and mining) shows anomalous behaviour when compared to agrarian products, as these former commodities do demonstrate a demand that is more in tune with the rises of income of the centre economies. Even so, the recommendations of ECLA for these primary commodities of higher elasticity consisted of adding value to these products locally and therefore giving rise to domestic intermediate and durable-goods sectors.

Bauer, however, raised doubts about the capability of developing countries to reach a more autonomous industrialisation process. The call for greater integration and cooperation among developing countries that emerged in the UNCTAD discussions was, for instance, strongly criticised by the author. The creation of trade blocs among developing economies, as put forward by UNCTAD, came as an attempt for the formation of new markets and a response to barriers imposed by the already industrialised economies against manufactured products from underdeveloped economies. The author tried to disqualify any effort towards this aim by stating that '[t]here is a tendency to exaggerate the benefits to be expected from common markets among underdeveloped countries' and concluded his argument by making what is, to say the least, an intriguing remark: '[a] collection of poor people does not add up to a rich society' (ibid., p. 265). Needless to mention, it was exactly in order to suggest alternatives to this kind of orthodox interpretation of development that the Latin American Structuralist scholars developed their work.

A much more effective critique of the strengths and weaknesses of the ECLA's understandings and perceptions of underdevelopment in the peripheral economies can be found in a review compiled by Fernando Henrique Cardoso. In an attempt to address ECLA's theory of 'deterioration in the terms of trade' through the lenses of contemporary scholars from different economic traditions, the author built up a comprehensive analysis that compared the views of three different groups: the 'orthodox' scholars (such as Haberler and Viner), the 'heterodox' liberals (such as Myrdal, Nurkse, Roseinstein-Rodan and Hirschman) and the Marxists (such as Baran and Dobb). Cardoso's analysis of ECLA's economic formulations provides a better understanding of the contributions and contradictions of the propositions that characterised these initial efforts to address development issues in Latin America. With regard to the weaknesses of the ECLA's propositions, the author drew attention to the fact that the agency avoided developing any detailed examination of the mechanisms of exploitation of the periphery by the centre (Cardoso, Originality of the copy: ECLA and the idea of development 1977, p. 10), as well as not providing any 'explicit analysis of the role and nature of economic cycles, and the distinction between such cycles and tendencies towards constant deterioration' (ibid., p. 16). More importantly, another issue that was constantly ignored by ECLA was related to the irrational use of the economic surplus by the peripheral countries. This characteristic, which is intrinsically connected with the way that internal agents were organized in these economies, brings implications for the way that capital is accumulated to the benefit of a small minority. As a consequence, in accordance with what was observed by Cardoso and many other scholars, the modernisation process introduced with industrialisation instead of reducing underdevelopment in the periphery could paradoxically result and actually did result in higher inequality.

In terms of policy making, the propositions put forward by ECLA were in clear conflict with the neo-liberal practices and the interests of the centre economies. Many of ECLA's policies were 'laid on the need for "programmed" industrialisation' in tandem with the adoption of controlling mechanisms of foreign exchange. In addition, under the pretext of shifting the centre of decision to the periphery, the 'decision-making and regulating capacity of the state' had to be strengthened (ibid., p. 27). Given the interventionist character of the measures advocated by the Latin American Economic Commission, it comes as no surprise that the agency was constantly criticised by more 'liberal-conservative' scholars. As Cardoso pointed out, '[e]ven without exacerbating the "social question", [ECLA]'s ideas were [already] disturbing' (ibid., p. 27). It is misleading however to believe, as many critics would argue, that ECLA was in favour of more comprehensive state intervention in the economy. Cardoso highlighted the fact that Prebisch himself was very much in favour of competition and distrusted the Soviet-style form of state control (ibid., p. 28). This concern with free-market rules became more evident during ECLA's reassessment of its own policies in the early 1960s, when the agency focused on the creation of a common market among Latin American countries. This trade bloc, apart from giving scalability to the small economies, would also 'offer resistance', in a competitive fashion, to the interests of the centre (ibid.).

Cardoso concluded his analysis of ECLA's intellectual legacy by calling attention to two issues that should be handled more carefully in the agency's agenda. First was the fact that at the same time that ECLA was developing its studies of foreign trade and carrying out its analysis of the impact of industrialisation in Latin America, a different form of 'international movement of capital' was starting to gain shape. The growing importance of multinational corporations (MNCs) in the industrialisation process of the continent introduced new variables to the form in which the relation between centre and periphery was traditionally carried out. Although the participation of foreign investors was perceived as a solution for the immediate necessity of capital and technology, the mid- and long-term consequences of this interference of foreign capital were, at that time, highly arguable and demanded further investigation.

Second was the fact that the equalising 'trickle-down' effect of investment and industrial modernisation was not achieved as expected and that development came to be characterised in Latin America as being 'concentrative and exclusive' (ibid., p. 27). Although ECLA had succeeded in making a sound critique of 'neoclassical theories of international trade', the problems that were pertinent to underdevelopment in Latin America required the adoption of a more multidisciplinary investigation. This forum, which became known as Dependency Theory, will be analysed in more detail later in this chapter and had in Cardoso himself one of its most prolific scholars.

Import Substitution Industrialization

Although policies regarding industrial promotion gained unprecedented relevance in the early 1950s due to the influence of ECLA, the first attempts towards import substitution industrialization (ISI) in Latin America date back to the 1930s. The Great Depression and the subsequent price fall of primary commodities 'left Latin Americans with little foreign exchange to spend on imports, forcing them to produce substitutes for imported essentials' (Cardoso and Helwege 1995, p. 84). This first wave of industrialization was followed by a second during World War II due to the inability of industrialized countries to meet the international demand for manufactured products. Once again, less developed economies were forced to expand their industrial capacities. Although this industrial expansion was limited in both periods and mainly counted on labour-intensive manufacturing, these efforts strongly contributed to the initial creation of an urban and politically engaged entrepreneurial class.[10]

Any attempt to promote industrialisation in less developed economies would inevitably meet several constraints, which were mainly related to the shortage of domestic private capital, low incentives for entrepreneurial activities and a complete lack of adequate infrastructure facilities, as in the case of energy generation, production supply and access to credit. The costs of turning an economy based on primary commodities into a more diversified industrial one were high. As was soon realised by the Latin American economists, the initial stages of this transition process could only be possible as long as there was the strong participation of the state. This would require a major effort to divert returns from exportable primary goods into incipient industrial capabilities.[11]

The commitment of the state to ISI policies becomes evident when a close look is taken at the several measures that demanded a considerable amount of public intervention. This intervention could be carried out in many ways and would vary from the definition of a protectionist regulatory environment to the direct control of manufacturing activities. In summary, the less developed economies that embarked on a process of late industrialisation made use of several mechanisms, which included, among other instruments, (a) the definition of licensing schemes to control the inflow of imported products; (b) the creation of trade barriers by means of tariffs; (c) the maintenance of an overvalued exchange rate; (d) investment in infrastructure such as rail, motorways, ports and power generation; (e) the provision of easy access to credit with low interest rates for some selected sectors; (f) the use of state procurement; and finally (g) the direct control of production through state-owned enterprises in key sectors of the economy, as in the case of public utilities and heavy industries such as steel, mining and petrochemicals (ibid., p. 90).

These mechanisms had the goal of creating a highly protected domestic market in which the new local companies would be able to flourish without the risks of uneven external competition. As a result, such barriers would underpin the rise of an indigenous industrial entrepreneurial class. This was the initial step towards a self-reliant, inward-looking process through which the outcome of the first industrial activities would bring the necessary investments for a larger and more capital-intensive industrial sector.

> As could have been expected, import substitution proceeded in waves, affecting first the more basic industrial branches from the point of view of capital visibility, availability of manpower with the required skills and access to technology: textiles and clothing, and food-processing. Then it reached other consumer goods, intermediate goods and, only after a long maturation and often with the involvement of foreign capital, consumer durables goods and capital goods.
>
> (Cardenas, Ocampo and Thorp 2000, p. 163)

Attempts across the Latin American economies to reduce imports were marked by uneven levels of success. As was mentioned in a study carried out by ECLA on the outcomes of the first two decades of import substitution policies, it is possible to observe that the large Latin American economies, such as Argentina, Brazil and Mexico, were the ones that had more effectively reduced the domestic demand for imported manufactures, whereas medium and small-size economies had developed restricted and in some cases still incipient industrial growth. Whereas larger economies were able, within the time span of two decades, to reduce their dependency on imported goods by more than 50%, other countries were only able to promote small reductions in their import coefficients (Ayza, Fichet and Gonzáles 1975).

A similar discrepancy was also noticed in the industrial sectors in which the Latin American countries were more successful—in this case, the traditional labour-intensive goods (textiles, shoes, leather, food and beverages) to the detriment of expansions in intermediate and capital goods. In addition, lack of technological capabilities kept preventing these economies from engaging in more complex and higher-return activities.

This limited expansion of import substitution in some economies can be explained by their small market size and the average low purchasing power of the population. In consequence, companies were obliged to operate under conditions of large overcapacity, which were usually reflected in high end costs. Investments were not directly translated into returns, and considerable amounts of subsidies were commonly provided by the state. Unable to compete with foreign products, industrial output was mainly destined for the domestic market, the same market that, as was just mentioned, did not offer ideal conditions for these industries to reach a process of self-sufficiency or even of further expansion.

In those economies in which import substitution industrialisation was more efficiently attained, some results were not as had been initially expected. Import substitution ended up paradoxically generating a higher demand for new types of imports, a fact that brought undeniable consequences for the deterioration in the balance of payments. The reason for this surge in imports was described by Ayza and colleagues (1975) as the congruence of several factors, which included (a) new patterns of consumption of imports that were generated by the upper strata of the population whose income rose during the industrialisation process; (b) the need to import parts for final assembly; (c) the lifting of tariff barriers for capital goods; (d) the increase in inter-regional trade; and finally (e) the easy access to foreign finance for the acquisition of equipment.

Another problem that was attributed to the process of industrialisation was related to the comparatively low absorption of the labour force by the new industrial sector. 'The technology available to the underdeveloped countries was that developed in the advanced nations where labour was expensive and capital relatively cheap. In the Third World, on the contrary, cheap labour was abundant and capital expensive. The technologies available tended to involve massive outlays on capital, and employed very few people' (Roxborough 1979, p. 34). In addition, neglect of the agricultural sector in favour of investments in industrialisation contributed to massive rural migrations to the main urban areas. This disorderly migration, combined with the inability of the industry to accommodate such demand for employment, resulted in high coefficients of labour surplus, which brought negative implications to the rise of the average living standard of the population.

In addition, the creation of trade barriers to curb the inflow of imported goods had the inverse effect of promoting a surge of MNCs, an outcome that was not in tune with the initial efforts to promote the development of indigenous companies. Although multinational corporations contributed to the transference of technology, such gains were not achieved if they were not closely regulated by the state. Finally, it is necessary to analyse the sources of funding that these less developed countries commonly employed to finance their industrialisation process. Largely based on international loans, these economies were soon hit by mounting debts.

By the late 1960s, much had already been discussed about the alleged exhaustion of import substitution policies in Latin America. After two decades of government-planned import substitution industrialisation, a considerable part of the population was still excluded from the gains of the industrial growth, the social gap had widened, the demand for imports was diverted to more capital-intensive products, the transference of technology had been low and, in most economies, their balance of payments was still under pressure. It was evident that the model needed to be revised, and this process started from ECLA itself. Prebisch, who had already warned about 'the limits of industrialisation' in his early writings, published in the early 1970s a detailed re-assessment of the import substitution policies (Prebisch 1971). Efforts should have been made to reduce the discrepancies relating to the highly uneven income distribution, rising unemployment, lack of technological innovation and the 'insufficient dynamism' of the industrial sector. A set of measures was proposed which included, among other features, the coexistence of agricultural activities with industrial manufacturing, greater specialisation on a few selected industrial products, the development of an exporting economy and, finally, the creation of a free-trade area for the Latin American economies.[12]

Many of these objectives were never fully achieved, and the Latin American economies kept presenting unsatisfactory improvements in living standards, a feature that gave rise to new theories that attempted to explain the origins of this persistent underdevelopment.

ISI and Brazil's Industrialisation

Contradictory as this may seem, the beginning of Brazil's industrialisation during the first quarter of the twentieth century is strongly related to the expansion of its main agrarian export, which had reached its peak in the same period: coffee beans. Coffee growing in Brazil began in the first half of the nineteenth century and had its production expanded rapidly to become, later in that century, the most important product of the Brazilian economy. In 1891, coffee had already become Brazil's top economic activity and represented 63% of the country's exports (Baer 2001, p. 17). In that same period, according to Furtado (Furtado 2001, p. 178), three-quarters of the world's exports of coffee had their origin in Brazil. If Brazil has ever enjoyed a quasi-monopoly position in a single sector of the world economy, then coffee has definitely been the only case so far.

The coffee cycle in Brazil differed from the previous economic cycles, most notably sugar cane (seventeenth and eighteenth centuries) and gold-mining (eighteenth century), due to the fact that its production was not controlled by the country's former Portuguese colonial ruler but, instead, the control of its production was decentralised among the autonomous states of the newly proclaimed federal republic.[13] In practical terms, this change represented higher leverage for coffee growers, as it allowed them to become 'more intimately linked to the commercial end of their sector' (Baer 2001, p. 18). Moreover, the relatively large scale of coffee production helped, in an indirect way, to build an environment that would be propitious for an initial process of industrialisation in Brazil. Apart from the export capital that coffee growers had managed to raise, the coffee cycle was also responsible for introducing changes to the use of a slave workforce and for giving a strong boost to the infrastructure of railways and ports in the areas involved in its production. With regard to the ending of slave work, in addition to the use of free workers, coffee growers were the ones who most enthusiastically collaborated with the large influx of European immigrants who came to work in the plantations. In consequence, the slave workforce, which did not take part in the local economy, started to give way to an emergent class of salaried workers and, more importantly, potential consumers. Another feature of the coffee activity was related to its then unquestionable central position in the country's economic affairs that was fundamental in the shifting of the economic centre of Brazil from the Northeast to the Southeast region, more precisely to the São Paulo area, the same region that would later become Brazil's main industrial area.

Although coffee growing had indirectly contributed to setting the conditions for the beginning of the industrialisation process in Brazil, the prevailing government priorities were entirely focused on the interests of the agro-export sector. This arrangement could not have been otherwise, as the central government was actually composed of or closely linked with the coffee growers' oligarchies. Efforts towards economic diversification were therefore limited, and any measure towards a more comprehensive industrialisation effort would inevitably come into conflict with the leading outward-oriented agrarian policies. This export-oriented view was commonly justified by the country's natural 'agrarian inclination'.

The move from an agrarian to an industrial economy only started to take shape effectively in the 1930s. This shift came as a direct result of the Great Depression and its damaging consequences for coffee production in Brazil. Decades of continuous re-investments in the sector resulted in a production capacity that was far beyond real demand. When the crisis of the late 1920s struck, coffee production was overheated and stockpiles were high, so that in consequence, the sharp fall in exports and the continuous fall of coffee prices constituted a severe blow to coffee growers in Brazil. This was the beginning of a steady fall after a long period of the economic and political dominance of coffee activity in Brazil. 'The price of coffee in

1931 was at one-third of the average price in the years 1925–29 and the country's terms of trade had fallen by 50 percent. In addition to the decline of exports receipts, the entrance of foreign capital had come to almost a complete halt by 1932' (Baer 2001, p. 35). In that year, the country had registered US$180.6 million in exports, less than a half of the total amount of US$445.9 million in 1929 (ibid.).

The 1930s represented a turning point for coffee growing in Brazil and sparked the awareness of the need to make the economy less vulnerable to a single agrarian activity. Although some measures such as investments in steel mills and the cement industry started to be taken, it was only after World War II that a comprehensive industrial programme came to be fully part of the government agenda. By the 1950s, '[industrialisation] had become the principal method for the government to modernize and raise the rate of growth of the economy. Policymakers had become convinced that Brazil could no longer rely on the exportation of its primary products to attain its developmental ambitions' (ibid., p. 47). As pointed out by Joel Bergsman (1970) in his work on the industrialisation of Brazil, the Great Depression of 1929 and the two world wars were decisive in imprinting in the country the urgency of a profound change in the economy.

> The difficulties of importing manufactured goods caused by the two world wars and by several drastic declines in Brazil's export earnings, abetted by some protection and other state support, especially to textiles, joined with Brazil's now larger market and natural advantages in ferrous metals and metal products to create a significant manufacturing sector. By the end of the second world war, manufacturing already accounted for some 20 per cent of [Brazil's] GDP
>
> (Bergsman 1970, p. 24).

The move from an outward-oriented agrarian activity to an inward-oriented industrial economy in Brazil endorsed ECLA's argument about the necessity of diversifying the economy and making the country less dependent on manufactured imports. On the other hand, the way the industrialisation process was carried out also contributed to shedding light on some of its main weaknesses. Such limitations became more evident by the way that new problems started to appear—more specifically, problems related to rural–urban migration, accentuation of inequalities and the over-concentration of economic power in the area of São Paulo, which resulted in strong regional imbalances. In addition, the beginning of Brazil's industrialisation was constantly marked by pressures in the country's balance of payments. This growing deficit in the balance of payments was due to the inward characteristics of ISI, which became patent with the neglect of the exporting sector, and to the fact that the industrialisation process was largely financed through foreign investments and international loans.

DEPENDENCY THEORY

The poor performance of capitalist development in Latin America, which became more evident with the unsatisfactory results of the policies put forward by Structuralist scholars, gave room for the emergence of new efforts to understand the origins of the region's persistent social and economic problems. It was an intensive debate that evolved into what came to be known as the Dependency School and whose main concern lay in identifying the reasons behind the region's continuous underdevelopment and sluggish growth.[14] The Dependency Theory is chiefly a critique of the capitalist mode of development that was exercised by the underdeveloped economies.

The main idea that permeated the Dependency School was that the development of the centre would necessarily require the underdevelopment of the periphery. This latter would be then confined to a condition in which many of the '*dependentistas*'[15] would describe as 'subservient' and, in consequence, opposed to any attempt to reach higher standards of development. If no measures were taken to reverse this situation, the condition of being a dependent economy would only result in even more dependency (Marini 2000).

The Dependency School was always characterised by a plurality of propositions. As highlighted by Gabriel Palma (1978), the dependency debate would range from those of more Marxist-driven beliefs who postulated that the only way for Latin America to reach better standards of living was through a rupture with the existent economic model (Baran 1957;[16] Frank 1969; 1970) to those who accepted the capitalist means of production but condemned its dynamics (Cardoso and Faletto 1970). A separate branch would include ECLA economists who were engaged in re-evaluating the policies that were implemented by the UN economic commission (Furtado 1964; Sunkel 1973).[17]

The debates carried out by the Dependency School were very broad and dealt with issues related to the interactions between internal and external factors, the role of the local elites, income distribution, divisions of labour, the increasing influence of multi-national corporations, the transference of technology and, above all, a deep understanding of the reasons, even in those cases in which economic growth was reached, it was not followed by an overall improvement in the standards of living (Lall 1975).[18]

Some of the concepts developed by Structuralist scholars were also adopted by the *dependentistas*. The key perception of the centre and periphery economies was maintained; however, it was expanded to express an inter-relational dynamic that was no longer limited to the initial abstraction of national geographic boundaries. The development–underdevelopment dichotomy, which some *dependentistas* would describe as a *metropolis–satellite* relation, could also be observed within a single region. According to this functional relation, even areas that present a satellite status can, in other spheres, take the role of a metropolis. In consequence, a provincial capital can, for instance, act as the metropolis of its countryside region and as a satellite for an external economy. 'A whole chain of constellations of metropoles and satellites relates all parts of the whole system from its metropolitan centre in Europe or the United States to the farthest outpost in the Latin American countryside' (Frank 1969, p. 6). This abstraction (i) is helpful in explaining the reasons underdevelopment cannot only be reduced to deteriorations in the terms of trade and (ii) leaves room for the identification of other conditions that contribute to the state of backwardness of the Latin American economies. Dependence, as was pointed out by Theotônio dos Santos (1973), in a view shared by many other scholars, was not only the result of the 'external factor' which lies behind ECLA's arguments of 'deterioration in the terms of trade'. According to most Dependency scholars, it is actually the historical characteristics of a nation and its internal structures which 'determine the effect of international situations upon the national reality' (ibid., p. 72).[19]

Although the initial period of import substitution had brought growth to some of the Latin American countries, many of these economic gains were not fully shared by the great majority of the population. Capital accumulation was not followed by an equivalent income distribution. In certain cases, economic growth served mostly to widen the social gap and helped even to '[aggravate] the existential, social, and economic problems of the majority of the population' (F. H. Cardoso 1976, pp. 12a–13). This was a phenomenon that, according to some scholars, had its roots in the way the local social strata in Latin America had been originally formed (ibid., p. 10). The dominant elites, in an attempt to perpetuate their leading condition, would, in most cases, be more in tune with their international links than with the needs of the lower classes (Palma 1978, p. 900).

The interpretation of the interaction between internal and external forces, which were mainly represented by local dominant groups and foreign hegemonic structures, as the rationale that had shaped the condition of underdevelopment in the Latin American countries was one of the arguments of the branch of the Dependency School that had in Fernando Henrique Cardoso as its most influential scholar. According to Cardoso's "The Consumption of Dependency Theory in the United States" (1977, p. 13), the state, although 'formally sovereign and ready to be an answer to the interests of the "nation"', would 'simultaneously and contradictorily' act as 'the instrument of international economic domination'. Underdevelopment cannot only be explained by the influence of the centre economies; local groups were decisive in internalising external conditions that turned into 'outward-directed relations' which benefited leading local groups and hindered any attempt towards more even social development (Cardoso and Faletto 1970, p. 17).

The role of local elites was extensively analysed by Cardoso and, in an examination of his work co-authored with Faletto (ibid.), it is possible to identify two distinct periods of transition in Latin America in which dominant groups had to adjust themselves in order to secure their leading political position.[20] The first took place in the early nineteenth century and was associated with the decolonisation of the Latin American economies and their subsequent integration into the world economy, and the second occurred in the mid-twentieth century with the shift of political influence from the agrarian oligarchies to the emergent urban industrial and bureaucratic bourgeoisies. Whereas the former period culminated in an emphasis on outward primary production, the latter was characterised by a more diversified, inward-driven industrial manufacturing that counted on a strong participation by the state. In both situations, the relationship between the local and external groups was decisive in giving shape to the ongoing process of *dependent development*.

Although 'internal' conditions are constantly mentioned in Cardoso's writings as a way of explaining the origins of underdevelopment in Latin America, the region's mode of production and division of labour were in fact strongly shaped by 'external forces', that is its bond with the centre economies, that, since the period of colonisation, had contributed to moulding a process of development that through the Latin American perspective would be described as 'dependent'. The existence of the 'economic periphery cannot be understood without reference to the economic drive of advanced capitalist economies, which were responsible for the formation of a capitalist periphery and for the integration of traditional non-capitalist economies into the world' (Cardoso and Faletto 1979, p. xvii). 'Underdevelopment then comes to be seen not merely as a process which is a concomitant of the expansion of mercantile capitalism and recurs under industrial capitalism, but it is actually generated by them' (F.H. Cardoso, "The Consumption of Dependency Theory in the United States" 1977, p. 13). In consequence, the initial assumption that the periphery countries could achieve the development stages of the centre ones was misleading, the main allegation was that 'historical conditions' that determined the development of the centre and periphery countries had been intrinsically 'different' for each of them (Cardoso and Faletto 1979, p. 24). In the same way that capitalism shifted from mercantile to industrial in the centre economies, the Latin American ones moved from the status of a colonial situation to that of dependent states.[21]

The post-colonial period was marked by the appearance of new local dominant groups, which were mainly formed of emerging agricultural oligarchies that were able to establish a closer link with the centre economies. This was also a period of relative economic expansion, as many of the Latin American countries started to have access to new stocks of foreign capital. Much of this capital was employed in improving their basic infrastructure, which had remained highly neglected during the colonial period. Investments in transport, port facilities and even power generation and distribution were mainly financed by British capital in the form of loans.

The expansion of the agricultural sector contributed to the creation of a bureaucratic middle class and provided the financial incentive for the formation of an urban industrial bourgeoisie (ibid., p. 75). This initial industrialisation was later intensified by the economic crisis of 1929 and the subsequent fall in the price of primary commodities. Lack of foreign exchange commonly generated by agricultural exports resulted in a corresponding decrease in imports. In consequence, labour-intensive low-technology manufactures started to be produced locally, which contributed to the consolidation of the domestic urban market and the 'partial breakdown [of the] agricultural oligarchic domination' (ibid., p. 101). The influence of this incipient industrial sector was intensified during World War II and was responsible for political changes of the role of the governing elites. The state that had so far mainly 'express[ed] the interests of [agro-]exporters and landholders' started to present a more industrialist stance with a shift towards actions which were more designed 'to set up protective tariffs, transfer the income from the export to the domestic sector, and to create the infrastructure needed to support the import-substitution industrialisation' (ibid., p. 129). This was a process that made room for an unprecedented surge in foreign investments and, due to its protectionist features, led to the appearance of multinational corporations.

The effort towards industrialisation, which 'was previously seen as an anti-imperialist struggle', was actually financed by foreign investment, a feature that suggested a real possibility of development, even though dependent, in the periphery. In other words, this was a clear indication that dependency and industrialisation ceased to be contradictory (Palma 1978, p. 909). This latter view, however, turned out to be short lived. The benefits of industrialisation in Latin America had not been as initially expected, and economic growth in the region would later be revealed as unsustainable and partially influenced by the period of global expansion of the post-war period. The transition from agrarian to industrial production introduced new forms of 'dependent situations' for the periphery economies. Within a socio-historical perspective, this new industrialisation would also reflect the role of the leading groups in monopolising the gains obtained from the new opportunities. Production was biased in order to meet the needs of the high-income classes;[22] manufacturing had a propensity for the adoption of capital-intensive technologies which were inappropriate for economies affected by high unemployment rates, increasing reliance on foreign capital, intensive urban migration and high concentration of incomes.

Cardoso acknowledged that industrialisation and trans-nationalisation of production had changed the relationship between the centre and the periphery, but he criticised the pessimism that lay behind the stagnant-driven view of most Dependency scholars. According to the author, although it was perceptible that the advent of foreign-financed industrialisation had introduced new situations of dependency for the periphery, the reason for the modest contribution of industrialisation towards long-term sustained development in the region is not related to the concept of capitalist industrialisation per se but is related essentially to its specific dynamics in the peripheral economies.[23] The persistent discrepancy between centre and periphery economies could be explained in many ways, and the form that this divergence would present had itself evolved over time. The author finally concludes that the focus of investigation should be directed towards the structure of Latin American society, with less emphasis on the imposing influence of the centre economies. If centre economies have so far been able to keep an advantageous position, this was mainly possible due to the implicit support of local groups in the periphery, a constant dispute of interests between foreign and local groups that was by no means straightforward.

Bearing in mind that social structures are not static phenomena and constitute mechanisms that can mould themselves according to different historical periods, the industrialisation process in Latin America served then to illustrate a new and distinct situation of dependence.[24] This situation of dependent development would go beyond the 'traditional dichotomy between the terms "development" and "dependence"' as it permits a real increase in development while it 'maintain[s] and redefine[s] new links of dependency' (Cardoso and Faletto 1979, p. 175). In this new scenario, some aspects could already be identified: (a) the configuration of the US as the leading economic capitalist power and (b) the stronger influence of multinational corporations which resulted in a complete restructuring of the process of production and an increasing reliance on foreign technology.

The rapid emergence of multinational corporations in the periphery economies turned into a key issue in the Dependency debate and, as a consequence, an extensive literature began to be produced among Dependency scholars as an attempt to investigate the rationality behind this new form of intervention by foreign capital. In this new forum of debate, Osvaldo Sunkel, in his work titled *Big Business and "Dependencia"*, published in the early 1970s, helped to anticipate much of the discussion that dominated the debate among Latin American scholars. For the author, the growing influence of foreign groups in the local economy was, once again, a way to create, establish and reinforce new patterns of dependency. Sunkel strongly criticised the way ISI was carried out in Latin America and pointed out some of its weaknesses. The project of the creation of a 'national entrepreneurial class' that should have come in tandem with the development of the industrial sector had in fact lost ground to the growing influence of foreign groups represented by the multinational corporations. In addition, the quick growth that was observed in the industrial sector as the result of the rise of foreign subsidiaries operating in the Latin American countries was challenged by the author as responsible for introducing an uneven form of development (Sunkel 1972).

According to the author, the industrialisation effort that was supposed to free the Latin American economies from their 'heavy reliance on primary exports, foreign capital and technology' had in reality helped to aggravate 'the situation and nature of "dependencia"' (ibid., p. 518). The author claimed that the growing presence of multinational corporations was in contradiction with the effort of building an indigenous industry.

As can be observed, on several issues, Cardoso's conciliatory perception that put the emphasis on the interactions among social groups and that claimed that the expansion of capitalism in the periphery could eventually lead to higher degrees of development did not represent a consensus among Dependency authors.[25] For many other Dependency scholars, such as, for instance, Paul Baran and Andre Gunder Frank, the dynamics of capitalism could only generate more conditions of underdevelopment in the periphery. For this branch of Dependency scholars, only a rupture with the capitalist mode of production could bring an end to the vicious cycle of underdevelopment in Latin America. The authors' theses were based on the arguments that the means of production in the continent had their origins in feudal or semi-feudal structures and their expansion was carried out under the continuous exploitative behaviour of the capitalist mode of production kept by the 'centre' economies.

In Frank's writings, 'dependent development' was replaced by the notion of 'satellite development'. This latter concept rejects the view that economic expansion in underdeveloped areas can be generated by capital or incentives from their corresponding metropoles. According to the author, experience has shown that in those cases in which satellite economies benefited due to closer links with the metropoles, development was characterised merely by illusory and short-lived cycles of economic expansion, a pattern of development that was neither 'self-generating' nor 'self-perpetuating' (Frank 1970, p. 8) and, in consequence, incapable of meeting the necessary conditions for continuous economic expansion.

Three main hypotheses were used by Frank to explain the advantageous position of the metropoles in relation to their satellite counterparts. The first made reference to the antagonistic dynamism between metropolis and satellite economies—that is, whereas the former tended to 'develop', the latter were more inclined to 'underdevelop'. The second hypothesis claimed that development had been greater in satellite economies exactly on those occasions where ties with the metropolis were weaker. And the third hypothesis was based on the argument that the regions that had become more underdeveloped were the ones that had kept closer links with the metropoles in the past (ibid., pp. 9–13). These three hypotheses completely contradicted the widely held view, even among Dependency scholars, that the expansion of capitalism to the periphery could bring, even though in limited terms, some sort of development, in this case dependent development.

According to Frank, however, the underdevelopment of the periphery was a consequence of the continuous dominance of the 'centre' economies, whose trade and industrial policies would mainly serve to perpetuate, to an even greater extent, their leading position. In order to ensure this position, the concentration of economic surplus in the 'metropolitan centres' had been achieved at the expense of the underdevelopment of the 'peripheral satellites' (Frank 1969, p. 27). In other words, the satellite economies had remained underdeveloped due to the 'lack of access to their own surplus' (ibid., p. 33). Ruy Marini, in his analysis of dependent development in Latin America, went even further in this respect to build up a detailed argument claiming that the continent's underdeveloped conditions were originally linked to the way that labour relations were carried out by the peripheral economies. The author's main argument rests on an attempt to shift the focus of the 'deterioration in the terms of trade' debate *from* the international market sphere *to* the internal contradictions that shaped labour conditions in the Latin American countries. The role of Latin America in providing raw materials primarily to England and then to the other industrialising European countries in the nineteenth century was fundamental to allow these latter countries (i.e. Western Europe) not only to shift to the production of manufactured goods but also to reduce the value of their labour power. The 'deterioration in the terms of trade' which was also recognised by Marini took a perverse dimension in Latin America, however, as it forced primary-good producers to transfer the costs of diminishing profits to their workforce.

According to the author, there were three forms in which this attempt to recover losses and increase the absolute and relative surplus values were more pronounced in the peripheral rural economies: 'the increase in the intensity of work, the expansion of the working day and the retention of part of the income destined to the worker's own subsistence' (Marini 2000, p. 124). This 'over-exploitation' of labour, as it was named by the author, was the real detrimental factor in the Latin American trade relations and the source of surplus value to the industrialised economies. Whereas for the latter, reductions of labour value allowed the real increase of workers' income and the consequent expansion of the internal market, in the former, the continuous suppression of the workers' gains had adverse effects on capital formation. In other words, whereas in the latter a virtuous circle between production and consumption was clearly established, in the former, this relationship between production and consumption was broken to fuel the demands of an economy based on agricultural exports. In the underdeveloped countries, wages were kept low, as the internal market was then not relevant for the accumulation of capital. According to the author, the move from an agrarian to an industrial economy in Latin America did not bring any substantial change in the way the accumulation of capital was locally realized. If, from one side, production tended to satisfy the demands of upper-income groups, from the other side, the realisation of capital was not very much dependent on the consumption of a substantial number of low-income workers. When this mid- to high-income segment of the local market reached saturation, production moved again to exports, in this case of manufactured products. Marini concluded his analysis by pointing to the growing presence of the multinational corporations and the new division of labour that this phenomenon intrinsically implied, that is the use of cheap labour for domestic and export production. According to the author, this scenario of continuous uneven access to capital accumulation reached its ultimate format with the widespread rise of authoritarian governments in the majority of the largest Latin American economies in the later 1960s and the early 1970s.

In this setting, where Western capitalism was imperative, the role of the periphery was basically confined to guaranteeing that the centre's leading position would be maintained.[26] This more radical perception was contemporary with as well as being politically challenged by the outbreak of the Cuban Revolution (Frank 1977). This event contributed to the intensification of the discussion of the role of the periphery economies and helped to establish the foundations of an eventual socialist movement in other Latin American countries. In addition, this branch of Dependency Theory also gained relative sympathy even among some North American scholars, who made use of its intrinsic anti-imperialist content to intensify the debate on US foreign policy, which at that time was very much under scrutiny.

The over-exposure of this branch of Dependency Theory, both in Latin America and in the US, led to a vivid debate that pointed out some of its main weaknesses. Critics claimed that the understanding of capitalist expansion to the periphery by some Dependency authors, such as Baran and Gunder Frank, was usually over-simplistic, with excessive emphasis on issues of imperialism and external economic conditioning. Sanjaya Lall (1975) in his analysis of 'dependence' as a 'useful concept' for understanding 'underdevelopment' points out the harm of generalising the negative consequences of the expansion of capitalism towards the periphery; this view was also shared by Bill Warren (1980) when the author drew attention to an actual rise of an 'indigenous capitalism system' in the underdeveloped economies. The author suggested that the development of capitalist structures in the periphery would eventually result in the reformulation of their relationship with the leading economies. Philip O'Brian (1974, pp. 14–15) in his 'critique of Latin American theories of dependency' argued that the Dependency theoretical propositions were 'undoubtedly here to stay', but he criticised the inability of Dependency scholars to reach an agreement about the 'essential characteristics of dependency' and pointed to the problems that such a lack of consensus projected when it came to the definition of policies. This was an issue that tended to be treated in fairly generic terms by Dependency scholars.

Big Business and Dependent Development: The Petrochemical and Pharmaceutical Industries in Brazil in the 1970s

As industrial production in Latin America evolved, in the second half of the twentieth century, *from* labour-intensive sectors (such as textile and food processing) *to* complex consumer durables and capital-intensive products, the theoretical formulations related to the concept of 'dependent development' were also re-evaluated to also include the new challenges that came with industrialisation. As previously mentioned, the growing influence of foreign capital in the industrial sector by means of multinational corporations laid the foundations of a new development path that came to be widely investigated by Dependency scholars. An impressive contribution on this subject can be found in the work by Peter Evans (1979), who produced an in-depth analysis of the 'alliance of multinational, state, and local capital' with specific reference to Brazil. In the author's assessment of the motivations of foreign groups to invest and interact with the state and local private companies in Brazil, it is possible to observe much of the rationality underlying the then growing presence of multinational corporations.

According to the author, the alliance among *state, private* and *foreign* capitals was far from following a single and pre-defined model; the alleged success or failure of this kind of partnership strongly relied on the interests of the different parties, which were, however, not necessarily in tune with the immediate needs of the local population as a whole. Although Evans illustrated his argument through the use of several case studies, his insights on the early years of the petrochemical and pharmaceutical industries in Brazil were particularly illustrative of two opposite experiences in which the participation of foreign groups took a completely distinct rationality. Whereas in the petrochemical sector, the alliance among state, local private and foreign capital was organised according to an arrangement of interests in which the Brazilian government enjoyed a privileged position, in the pharmaceutical sector, the largest share of bargaining power was actually in the hands of the multinational corporations.

The distinct paths that the petrochemical and pharmaceutical industries took in Brazil in the 1970s are clear illustrations of the equally different types of goals, concerns and priorities that are intrinsic to each of the three forms of *state, local* and *foreign* capitals. Although these three players were allegedly interacting under the same set of market rules, the role that each ended up having was not necessarily bonded into the same bloc of converging interests. The privileged position that the state enjoyed in the petrochemical sector due to having the state-owned company Petrobras as the main supplier of raw materials was key for the government to enjoy strong bargaining power. The Brazilian government managed not only to build an alliance with the local private and foreign capitals but also to invest in an entire development project whose goals could be better explained as an effort on the part of the government to stimulate growth in an underdeveloped region in Brazil (in this case the Northeast region) than to the raw observance of pure economic practices. The privileged position of the state in this sector did not result, as many critics suggested, in the government becoming the sole player in the sector. On the contrary, it allowed more even interaction with foreign capital and represented a unique opportunity for local private entrepreneurs to also enter the petrochemical industry.

In the case of the pharmaceutical industry, however, the results were quite different (ibid.). The attempt of the Brazilian government to build a domestic pharmaceutical industry in the 1970s clashed with the interests of dominant multinational corporations. Foreign companies, having already dominated the market, did not find any reason to build alliances with local capital, and their opposition to the Brazilian government programme for the production of low-cost medicine clearly indicated that they were not willing to have their dominant position under menace, even if this risk were posed in a fairly unthreatening way or were simply considered non-existent. As the state didn't have strong bargaining power in this sector, the prospects of local capital reaching any kind of alliance with multinational companies were dismal. Unable to compete or establish links with the dominant foreign enterprises, the local companies were left to play a secondary role.

Although the literature has strongly emphasized the importance of foreign investment and transference of technology from the MNCs as two efficient strategies to reduce the technological gap that characterises late-industrialising countries, the extraordinary speed with which this new kind of foreign intervention started to engulf larger shares of local businesses in the periphery countries forced local scholars to also look at the negative effects that such policy could bring. Instead of complementing and giving new stimulus to the formation of local capabilities, as some groups had initially argued, the participation of foreign investment, in many cases, ended up producing the reverse effect of inhibiting 'the creation and mobilization of indigenous enterprise, management, technology and savings' (Streeten 1975, p. 393). In this market environment, where foreign investment frequently stops being complementary and shifts to a more competitive stance, it was 'generally recognized' according to the author 'that resource transfer often amounts not to a net addition to, but only to a displacement of, domestic efforts' (ibid.). On innumerable occasions, the growing influence of the multinational corporations had clearly been in conflict with local efforts to build indigenous capabilities. Given the unbalanced conditions in which the foreign, state and local private capitals normally interact, it is not surprising that the multinational corporations had quickly taken, whether desirably or not, a leading position in the industrialisation process of periphery economies.

CONCLUSIONS

Any attempt to summarise the debate on the development policies that were marked by the influence of Latin American Structuralism and Dependency Theory is fated to invariably incur problems of over-simplification, omission and lack of accuracy. This was a particularly prolific period of academic production in which a lengthy and pioneering literature dealing with the continent's development issues was produced by a large variety of scholars from different and sometimes even opposite economic traditions. If the academic discussion engendered its own frictions and elaborations, the social context in which many of these propositions were put forward was fundamental to add even more complexity and tensions to the debate. On the political ground, this was a singular moment in Latin American history, as the continent became visibly marked by recurrent situations of social unrest, disruption of civil rights and constant threats to its already precarious democratic institutions. The work of these authors in attempting to reflect the dramatic changes that characterised the world economy after World War II was equally helpful in grasping the uncertainties that much of this period implied.

Sensitive to the changes of the world economy and aware of the limitations of their own policies and propositions, the analytical framework of both Structuralist and Dependency scholars managed to evolve over time to constantly include new elements and variables. From the incipient investigation of the limitations faced by economies based solely on primary exports to a more comprehensive analysis of the internal and external factors that led to the underdevelopment of the Latin American region, both these currents of thought were forced to address a large number of issues which had simply never been investigated through a local perspective.

Probably the most relevant contribution that both Structuralist and Dependency scholars managed to offer lies precisely in their principal objective of raising awareness of the continent's own interpretation of its specific problems. Although such an achievement may look somewhat modest, at first glance, it entailed a genuine challenge to the precepts of the prevailing mainstream orthodoxy. This was not an easy task. The conflict of interests that had historically characterised the relation between the Latin American and the more developed economies was also present in an equivalent way in the academic arena. Any rupture with the economic ties that had shaped the relation between those two groups of countries necessarily had to deal with the very theoretical framework on which such bonds were based. Both Structuralist and Dependency scholars were fundamental not only in shedding light on a myriad of local issues, which was in itself a major achievement, but they were also instrumental in providing a counter-view, analysis and interpretation to the dominant literature on development.

In addition to providing the intellectual background for the diversification of the predominant Latin American agrarian economies, Structuralism and Dependency also contributed to delivering the required analytical apparatus for an in-depth investigation of the economic drive of advanced capitalism on the continent. Although the centre-periphery division of trade was never fully accredited by more orthodox scholars and the mainstream literature, it is not possible to deny that the allegation of such a division did manage to draw attention to the different rationalities according to which the same capitalist structures were able to act in both more and less developed economies. More importantly, the model constituted an intrinsic challenge to the evolutionary character of capitalism and the belief that development could be achieved through stages.

It was through the lenses of Structuralism and Dependency that many of the Latin American scholars found ground to reassess the continent's internal social formations; to scrutinise the origins and consequences of new patterns of consumption; to re-examine the continent's own industrialisation process; and to point to the downside features of foreign investment and the fast-growing presence of the multinational corporations. Opposition to many of their accounts, however, was also ripe. Structuralist scholars were constantly accused of being over-simplistic in the theoretical formulation of their arguments and too optimistic in the prescription of their policies. *Dependentistas* were commonly criticised for their lack of consensus, for their misunderstanding of both capitalist and communist modes of production and finally for their inability to address a more pragmatic policy programme.

What critics failed to grasp, however, was the unique and independent understanding that the Structuralist and Dependency scholars managed to develop of the Latin American region. The more region-based it was, the more acute were its findings. Not surprisingly, the initial optimism of the Structuralist scholars towards the industrialisation process of the Latin American region was completely overshadowed by the pessimism with which the Dependency scholars started to treat the first, even apparently successful, outcomes of the region's economic transition. This concern proved to be well founded and became even more evident with the economic collapse that the region faced in the early 1980s.

Structuralism and Dependency were a period of intermission in the development debate in the Latin American countries that had their most affluent years from the early 1950s to the mid 1970s. In the late 1970s, most of these economies had already moved back to more orthodox practices, a process that was undeniably consolidated in the 1990s, when all the Latin American countries adopted comprehensive projects of economic liberalisation. The globalisation drive that the region has subsequently embraced is, in its essence, in sound opposition to what was claimed and prescribed by Structuralist and Dependency scholars.

NOTES

1. To make use of a term that was constantly used by development scholars in the post-war period, as was noted by Gunnar Myrdal in his work 'Economic Theory and Under-Developed Regions' (1957, p. 7). A notable example of the use of the term 'backward' can also be observed in the works of Peter Bauer, '[m]any of the societies whose position is a principal theme of this volume ["Dissent on Development"] have at various times been referred to

as materially primitive, backward, poor, underdeveloped, developing and less developed. The last three expressions are clearly euphemisms, induced in part by political considerations but mainly by the emergence and extension of feelings of guilt in industrialised western society. Poor, or materially backward, are the most appropriate expressions: they best describe the condition which serves as a basis of classification; they best convey the fact that distinction is a matter of degree; and they are neutral, in the sense that they do not suggest that the condition described is abnormal or reprehensive' (Bauer 1971, p. 24). A more detailed analysis of the usage of the term 'backward' as a way of interpreting the social economic conditions of under-developed economies can also be found in an essay by Hla Myint, 'An Interpretation of Economic Backwardness' (1979).

2. For discussions on the relevance of ECLA for the creation of Latin America regional economic thinking see: (Hirschman 1961; Di Marco 1972; Furtado 1985).

3. A similar comparison was also made by Fernando Henrique Cardoso in his analysis of the theoretical contribution of ECLA to the understanding of Latin America's underdevelopment. In his work published in 1977, 'The Originality of the Copy: ECLA and the Idea of Development', Cardoso equally contrasts the general views of left- and right-wing scholars on the propositions put forward by ECLA in the 1950s and 1960s. 'The Left criticized [ECLA] because, once again, there was no explicitation of the mechanisms by which the two goals—capital accumulation and improvement of popular living standards—would be made compatible; the Right criticized it because it did not see in the Latin American Manifesto [ECLA's original proposal] (. . .) any more than a accusation of the rich countries and a declaration of international distributivism which failed to take seriously the need to form capital funds and increase productivity' (Cardoso 1977, p. 25).

4. According to Palma (1987, p. 528), 'the principal characteristic of Structuralism is that it takes as its object of investigation a "system", that is, the reciprocal relations among parts of a whole, rather than the study of the different parts in isolation'. This 'method of enquiry' was commonly 'found in literary criticism, linguistics, aesthetics and social sciences'.

5. There is a comprehensive literature on the conceptualisation of centre and periphery. However, most of these works were originally based on the writings of Raúl Prebisch (1950) and Hans W. Singer (1950). Although they were independently published in different documents, the congruence of their ideas formed what would later come to be known as the 'Prebisch-Singer Thesis'.

6. The low elasticity of demand of primary goods as one of the reasons for the alleged deterioration of the terms of trade between developed and underdeveloped countries was also shared by Gunnar Myrdal in his book *The Challenge of the World Poverty* when the author stated, '[i]n the present era, primary commodities that are more directly going into consumption, such as various kinds of food and beverages but also textiles and their raw materials, tend, as a general rule, to have a rather low income elasticity and often to lag behind increases in income levels in the developed countries which are the main importers' (Myrdal 1970, p. 286). Although the author had equally made clear in previous writings that trade could be characterised as operating with a 'fundamental bias in favour of the richer and progressive regions against the other regions' (Myrdal 1957, p. 28), Gunnar Myrdal also believed that the theory of international trade was not sufficient to explain 'the reality of economic under-development and development' (ibid., p. 9). The author called attention to the existence of 'non-economic factors' that tend to lead to

causal chains' which are normally not accounted for in the 'theoretical analysis of the play of market forces'. Gunnar Myrdal points to two tendencies that can be observed in the interrelation between developed and underdeveloped areas, the 'backwash effect' and the 'spread effect'. The first is a reference to movements of labour, capital, goods and services that tend to have an upward cumulative effect in richer areas and an opposite downward effect in poorer areas. The second is a reference to the 'expansionary momentum from the centres of economic expansion to other regions' (ibid., p. 31). Although these are contrasting processes, their forces are not supposed to reach equilibrium. 'Spread effects' to underdeveloped countries are usually unsustainable, and they are not strong enough to neutralise the downward trend of the 'backwash effect'.

7. The empirical data that gave evidence of the deterioration in the terms of trade claimed by Prebisch and Singer came from a piece of research that had been previously developed by the United Nations. This study conducted an analysis of prices of primary goods vis-à-vis manufactured goods throughout a period of seven decades, from 1879 to 1947.

8. Contemporary to the Prebisch-Singer thesis but making use of a different approach, Arthur Lewis also called the attention of scholars to the possibilities of deterioration in the terms of trade between industrialised and agrarian economies. According to the author, 'capital importing' agrarian countries with an 'unlimited supply of labour' had a tendency to export their productivity gains to the benefit of the 'foreign consumer'. Although the author did not make use of the terms 'centre' and 'periphery' to identify these two types of economies, these two distinct regions were represented in his work as 'capital exporting', 'labour scarce' and 'temperate' regions in contrast to 'capital importing', 'surplus labour' and 'tropical' regions (Lewis, "Economic Development with Unlimited Supplies of Labour" 1983; Lewis, "Aspects of Tropical Trade" 1983).

9. According to the author's argument, 'factoral terms of trade' differ from 'commodity terms of trade' due to the fact that the former also take into consideration eventual reductions in the production costs of primary goods. '(. . . [A] fall in export prices compared to import prices is compatible with an improvement in the factoral terms of trade, if the cost of production of exports has fallen more than the price of imports' (ibid., p. 246). In consequence, eventual deteriorations in the commodity terms of trade could be counter-balanced by even further reductions in the cost of production of primary goods.

10. With regard to the creation of urban elites, Brazil is probably the clearest example among Latin American countries. The so-called Revolution of the 1930s in Brazil was essentially an urban uprising against the then-dominant agricultural oligarchies. The newly appointed president, Mr. Vargas, was a strong advocate of industrialisation, and during his mandate, an extensive legislation was put forward to regulate labour work.

11. This more intensive participation of the state to the detriment of the logic of market forces was, however, strongly criticised by neoclassical economists. According to Ian Little (1982, p. 120), 'Planning was, by and large, a failure, and sometimes a disaster. Big pushes, where they occurred, resulted in much wasted investment and piling up of debt and inflation. (. . .) Less developed country governments were not always benevolent and almost nowhere showed much concern for the welfare of the poorest sections of the society'.

12. The creation of a free-trade area for the Latin American countries was largely reiterated by Prebisch (1973). This proposal was prescribed as a solution to

the constraints which were mainly related to the small size of some Latin American economies. Support for more integrated trade among Latin American countries can be also observed in writings by several other Latin American economists who were highly engaged in the creation of this free-trade area, such as Enrique Iglesias (1973) and Alberto Solá (1973).

13. Although Brazil had gained its formal political independence from Portugal in 1822, the country was kept under a monarchic regime that was actually ruled by the son of Portugal's emperor. The transition from monarchy to republic was only carried out in 1889, when a military coup ousted the ruling royal family and established a more decentralised federal government.

14. Dos Santos, in his critique of the forms of development theory that dominated the Latin American academic scene in the 1950s and 1960s, produced an analysis of the several aspects that contributed to the alleged exhaustion of the continent's industrialisation drive. The author concluded his critique by joining the chorus of other Latin American scholars in favour of the construction of an alternative approach to the understanding of underdevelopment in the continent. 'This crisis of the model of development (and of the project it implied) which has dominated social science in the continent has thrown that very science into a crisis. The very notion of development and underdevelopment and the explanatory power of these concepts have lost credibility. In this situation the concept of dependence has appeared to offer a possible, if partial, explanation of these paradoxes, seeking to explain why Latin American development has differed from that of today's advanced countries' (Dos Santos 1973, p. 71).

15. The Spanish term '*Dependentista*' makes reference to those scholars who were associated with the Dependency School. The term is largely used in the literature to denote the Latin American origins of this theoretical thought.

16. For a concise and equally influential illustration of Baran's interpretation of capitalist development in Latin America, his earlier essay 'On the Political Economy of Backwardness' (Baran 1979) is his most representative work.

17. The diversity of propositions put forward by Dependency theorists has also allowed some other authors to categorize the Dependency debate into distinct branches. Like Palma (1978), Bath and James (1976) have also identified three distinct approaches to the Dependency debate: a 'conservative' one headed by ECLA economists, a 'moderate' approach influenced by 'Furtado, Sunkel, and Dos Santos' and a 'radical' approach that had Gunder Frank as its main leader. In addition, a distinct division was also described by Cardoso (1977). In his analysis of 'the consumption of the Dependency Theory in the United States', the author identified two basic divergent groups: one that claimed that the expansion of capitalism from the centre to the periphery would mainly result in 'stagnation and a kind of constant reproduction of underdevelopment' and an opposite group which believed that the expansion of capitalism could indeed bring development, although dependent, to the periphery (ibid., p. 19).

18. An issue that was pointed out by Cristóbal Kay (1989) and has to be taken account of in the Dependency debate is related to the historical imbalance which is pertinent to the consumption of the 'Dependency Theory' by non–Spanish-Portuguese speakers. English-speaking scholars tended to focus their understanding of the Dependency debate on the literature that was available in English and, in consequence, were strongly influenced by the writings of Andre G. Frank. A very large 'Dependency' literature produced in Latin America was therefore ignored by many of the scholars and critics based in the developed world.

19. An exception must therefore be made with regard to some scholars, like Baran and Gunder Frank, who argue that the underdevelopment in the peripheral economies was strongly, almost indeed solely, built on the detrimental role of the developed economies.

20. An early study that was carried out by Fernando H. Cardoso on the role of the new type of entrepreneurial class that emerged in Latin America as a result of the continent's industrialisation process can be found in his work 'The Industrial Elite in Latin America', which was originally published in 1967. Although this work does not present his influential formulations on 'concrete situations of dependent development', some of his initial concerns regarding the shift of 'control of the state machinery' from the old traditional agro-exporter sector to the newly formed and similarly oligopolistic urban industrial groups can already be observed in this preliminary essay. A reprint of this work can also be found in Cardoso (F. H. Cardoso, "The Industrial Elite in Latin America" 1973).

21. Cardoso and Faletto's analysis of Latin America is structured on a cross-country 'socio-historical interpretation' of different types of 'dependent situations'. This analysis makes reference to a general division of Latin American countries that experienced distinct conditions of market integration after the colonial period: (a) those economies where production came to be dominated by local entrepreneurs (e.g., Argentina, Brazil, Uruguay) and (b) those where exports were mainly controlled by foreign capital, the so-called enclave economies (e.g., Chile, Mexico, Venezuela). This proposed division would reflect different degrees of political autonomy and the way that the leading elites interact with local and external groups.

22. Celso Furtado in his revision of the ECLA's policies towards ISI considerably shifted his previous structuralist analytical focus on the deterioration in the terms of trade to give more emphasis to the creation of new patterns of consumption as the underlying cause that was responsible for the origin of underdevelopment in Latin America. According to the author, the additional surplus obtained with the modernisation of agrarian and industrial capabilities in the peripheral countries tended to be either 'appropriated from outside' or used domestically to 'finance a rapid diversification in the consumption habits of the ruling classes through the import of new products. Furtado concluded that '[i]t was this particular use of the additional surplus that gave rise to the social formations that we now identify as underdeveloped economies' (Furtado 1973, p. 2). It is important to notice that in this analysis, Furtado made use of the concepts of 'internal' and 'external' forces that were introduced by Fernando H. Cardoso. 'Underdevelopment is rooted in a specific connexion, created in a particular historical setting, between an internal process of exploitation and an external process of dependence. The more intense the inflow of new patterns of consumption, the more concentrated income tends to become. Thus if external dependence increases, the internal rate of exploitation has also to go up. Higher rates of economic growth tend to imply aggravation of both external dependence and internal exploitation. Therefore, higher rates of growth, far from reducing underdevelopment, tend to make it more acute, as it entails increasing social inequalities' (ibid., p. 17).

23. Although it was not restricted to the Latin American context, the author's view of the industrialisation in the periphery which was published in the early 1980s serves to reinforce his initial perception of dependent development. '(. . .) even though it is true that much has been said since, say, 1945 about the ills and distortions of industrial civilisation, most of it consists of half-truths,

starting with the very target of criticism, industrial society, as though it existed as an entity independent of the interests of men, groups, classes, states and nations. As we move from general to more specific problems (hunger in Bangladesh or infant mortality in São Paulo, for example) it becomes apparent that is not industrialisation itself which causes the problems, but rather the (often interrelated) interests of minorities in different countries that offer the ghostly appearance of a civilisation of Molochs which devours its own fruits' (F. H. Cardoso 1981, p. 297).

24. A distinction between the terms 'dependence' and 'dependency' is found in (Caporaso and Zare 1981, p. 44). According to the authors, the first makes reference to 'external reliance', and the second is 'the process by which less developed countries are incorporated into the global capitalist system'. The authors also point out the overlap between the two concepts.

25. For a larger debate on the contribution of Cardoso and Faletto to the Dependency analysis in Latin America, see the papers published in the symposium to celebrate the tenth anniversary of the publication of their book *Dependencia y desarrollo en América Latina* (Cavarozzi 1982; Halperín-Donghi 1982; Packenham 1982; Chase-Dunn 1982).

26. Marxist Dependency scholars like Andre G. Frank, Theotônio dos Santos and Ruy M. Marini made use of this argument in an attempt to provide new insights into the concept of 'imperialism', which therefore would also take into consideration the point of view of the peripheral economies.

REFERENCES

Ayza, Juan, Gérard Fichet, and Norberto Gonzáles. *Integración económica y sustitución de importaciones en América Latina*. Mexico City: Fondo de Cultura Económica, 1975.

Baer, Werner. *The Brazilian economy: growth and development*. 5th edition. Westport: Praeger Publishers, 2001.

Baran, Paul. "On the political economy of backwardness." In *The economics of underdevelopment*, by A. N. Agarwala and S. P. Singh. Oxford: Oxford University Press, 1979.

———. *The political economy of growth*. New York: Monthly Review Press, 1957.

Bath, C. Richard, and Dilmus D. James. "Dependency analysis of Latin America: some criticisms and suggestions." *Latin American Research Review*. Vol. 11 (1976): 3–54.

Bauer, Peter T. *Dissent and development: studies and debates in development economics*. London: Weidenfeld and Nicolson Publishers, 1971.

Bergsman, Joel. *Brazil: industrialisation and trade policies*. Oxford University Press: London, 1970.

Bresser-Pereira, Luiz Carlos. "Método e paixão em Celso Furtado." In *A grande esperança em Celso Furtado: ensaios em homenagem aos seus 80 anos*, by Luiz Carlos Bresser-Pereira and José Marcio Rego, 19–43. São Paulo: Editora 34, 2001.

Caporaso, James A., and Behrouz Zare. "An interpretation and evaluation of Dependency Theory." In *From dependency to development: strategies to overcome underdevelopment and inequality*, by Heraldo Muñoz, 43–56. Boulder: Westview Press, 1981.

Cardenas, Enrique, Jose Antonio Ocampo, and Rosemary Thorp. *An economic history of twentieth-century Latin America. Volume 3. Industrialisation and the state in Latin America: the postwar years*. Oxford: Palgrave, 2000.

Cardoso, Eliana, and Ann Helwege. *Latin America's economy: diversity, trends and conflicts.* Cambridge: MIT Press, 1995.

Cardoso, Fernando Henrique. "The industrial elite in Latin America." In *Underdevelopment and development: and third world today*, by Henry Bernstein, 191–204. Harmondsworth: Penguin Books, 1973.

———. *Capitalist development and the state: bases and alternatives.* Paper presented at The State and Economic Development in Latin America. Cambridge: Centre for Latin American Studies, University of Cambridge, 1976.

———. "The consumption of Dependency Theory in the United States." *Latin American Research Review* (1977): 7–24.

———. "Originality of the copy: ECLA and the idea of development." *Working Paper 17.* Cambridge: Centre for Latin American Studies, 1977.

———. "Towards another development." In *From dependency to development: strategies to overcome underdevelopment and inequality*, by Heraldo Muñoz, 295–313. Boulder: Westview Press, 1981.

———. "Foreword." In *Reforming the state: managerial public administration in Latin America*, by Luiz Carlos Bresser-Pereira and Peter Spink, vii–ix. London: Lynne Rienner, 1999.

Cardoso, Fernando Henrique, and Enzo Faletto. *Dependência e desenvolvimento na América Latina.* Rio de Janeiro: Zahar Editores, 1970.

———. *Dependency and development in Latin America.* Berkeley: University of California Press, 1979.

Cavarozzi, Marcelo. "El 'desarrollismo' y las relaciones entre democracia y capitalismo dependiente en 'dependencia y desarrollo en América Latina.'" *Latin American Research Review.* Vol. 17 (1982): 152–65.

Chase-Dunn, Christopher K. "A world-system perspective on dependency and development in Latin America." *Latin America Research Review.* Vol. 17 (1982): 166–71.

Di Marco, Luis Eugenio. "The impact of Prebisch's ideas on modern economic analysis." In *International economics and development: essays in honour of Raúl Prebisch*, by Luis Eugenio Di Marco, 15–34. New York: Academic Press, 1972.

Dos Santos, Theotônio. "The crisis of development theory and the problem of dependence in Latin America." In *Underdevelopment and development: the third world today*, by Henry Bernstein, 57–80. Harmondsworth: Penguin Books, 1973.

Evans, Peter. *Dependent development: the alliance of multinational, state and local capital in Brazil.* Princeton: Princeton University Press, 1979.

Frank, Andre Gunder. *Capitalism and underdevelopment in Latin America.* New York: Monthly Review Press, 1969.

———. *Latin America: underdevelopment or revolution.* New York: Monthly Review Press, 1970.

———. "Dependence is dead, long live dependence and the class struggle: an answer to critics." *World Development.* Vol. 5 (1977): 355–70.

FT.com. "Brazil's import substitution industrialisation 2.0." 02 January 2012. http://blogs.ft.com/beyond-brics/2012/01/02/12-for-2012-brazils-import-substitution-2-0/.

Furtado, Celso. *Development and underdevelopment.* Berkeley: University of California Press, 1964.

———. "Underdevelopment and dependence: a fundamental connection." *Working Paper 17.* Cambridge: Centre for Latin American Studies: University of Cambridge, 1973.

———. *A fantasia organizada.* 4th Edition. Editora Paz e Terra, Rio de Janeiro, RJ, 1985.

———. *Formação Econômica do Brasil.* 30th edition. São Paulo: Companhia Editora Nacional, 2001.

Goldstein, Andrea, and Ben Ross Schneider. *Big business in Brazil: states and markets in the corporate reorganisation of the 1990s.* Paper presented at Workshop on Brazil and South Korea Institute of Latin American Studies, University of London, 7–8 December, 2000.

Halperín-Donghi, Tulio. "'Dependency Theory' and Latin American historiography." *Latin American Research Review.* Vol. 17 (1982): 115–29.

Hirschman, Albert Otto. "Ideologies of economic development in Latin America." In *Latin American issues: essays and comments,* by Albert Otto Hirschman, 3–42. New York: The Twentieth Century Fund, 1961.

Iglesias, Enrique. "La integración económica en la planificación nacional del desarrollo." In *La integración latino-americana en una etapa de decisiones,* by Eric Wyndham-White, 29–45. Buenos Aires: Instituto para la Integración de América Latina, Banco Interamericano del Desarrollo (BID), 1973.

Kay, Cristóbal. *Latin American theories of development and underdevelopment.* London: Routledge, 1989.

Lall, Sanjaya. "Is 'dependence' a useful concept in analysing underdevelopment?" *World Development.* Vol. 3 (1975): 799–810.

Lewis, William Arthur. "Aspects of tropical trade." In *Selected economic writings of W. Arthur Lewis,* by Mark Gersovitz, 8–53. New York: New York University Press, 1983.

———. "Economic development with unlimited supplies of labour." In *Selected economic writings of W. Arthur Lewis,* by Mark Gersovitz, 139–91. New York: New York University Press, 1983.

Little, Ian A. D. *Economic development: theory, policy and international relations.* New York: Basic Books Inc. Publishers, 1982.

Marini, Ruy Mauro. *Dialética da dependência.* Petrópolis: Editora Vozes, 2000.

Myint, Hla. "An interpretation of economic backwardness." In *The economics of underdevelopment,* by A. N. Agarwala and S. P. Singh. Oxford: Oxford University Press, 1979.

Myrdal, Gunnar. *Economic theory and under-developed regions.* London: Gerald Duckwarth & Co, 1957.

———. *The challenge of world poverty.* London: The Penguin Press, 1970.

O'Brian, Philip. "A critique of Latin American theories of dependency." *Occasional Paper 12.* Glasgow: Institute of Latin American Studies, University of Glasgow, 1974.

Packenham, Robert A. "Plus ça change . . .: the English edition of Cardoso and Faletto's 'Dependencia y desarrollo en América Latina.'" *Latin American Research Review.* Vol. 17 (1982): 131–51.

Palma, Gabriel. "Dependency: a formal theory of underdevelopment or a methodology for the analysis of concrete situations of underdevelopment?" *World Development.* Vol. 6 (1978): 881–924.

Palma, Gabriel. *Structuralism.* Vol. IV, in *The New Palgrave: a dictionary of economics,* 528–31. Palgrave, 1987.

Prebisch, Raúl. *The economic development of Latin America and its principal problems.* New York: United Nations Department of Economic Affairs, 1950. http://archivo.cepal.org/pdfs/cdPrebisch/002.pdf.

———. *Change and development. Latin America's great task: report submitted to the Inter-American Development Bank.* New York: Praeger Publishers, 1971.

———. "La integración económica en América Latina." In *La integración latino-americana en una etapa de decisiones,* by Eric Wyndham-White, 29–45. Buenos Aires: Instituto para la Integración de América Latina, Banco Interamericano de Desarrollo (BID), 1973.

Revista Exame Melhores e Maiores 2012. São Paulo: Editora Abril, July 2012.

Roxborough, Ian. *Theories of underdevelopment.* London: Macmillan, 1979.

Singer, Hans W. "The distribution of gains between investing and borrowing countries." *The American Economic Review.* Vol. 40 (1950): 473–85.

Solá, Alberto. "Visión crítica de la ALALC." In *La integración latino-americana en una etapa de decisiones*, by Eric Wyndham-White, 126–30. Buenos Aires: Instituto para la integración de América Latina, Banco Interamericano de Desarrollo (BID), 1973.

Streeten, Paul. "Policies towards multinationals." *World Development*. Vol. 3 (1975): 393–97.

Sunkel, Osvaldo. "Big business and 'dependencia': a Latin American view." *Foreign Affairs*. Vol. 50 (1972): 517–31.

———. "The pattern of Latin American dependence." In *Latin America in the international economy*, by Victor Urquidi and Rosemary Thorp, 3–25. London: Macmillan Press, 1973.

Tyler, William G. *The Brazilian industrial economy*. Toronto: Lexington Books, 1981.

UNCTAD. "Towards a new trade policy for development." Report, Secretary General of the United Nations Conference on Trade and Development, New York, 1964.

Warren, Bill. *Imperialism: pioneer of capitalism*. London: Verso Editions, 1980.

Part III
The Shift towards Market Reforms in Brazil in the 1990s

We live, in principal, in a capitalist system.
But Brazilian capitalism is more controlled
by the state than in any other country,
except for those under communist regimes.

—Mr Eugênio Gudin, Brazilian Finance Minister in 1974
quoted in Pinheiro and Giambiagi 1999

INTRODUCTION

The 1990s were a period of major economic changes in Brazil. The country that started the decade relying on the strong participation of the state in key sectors of the economy, as in the case of the petrochemical, mining, manufacturing and public utilities sectors, entered this new century by conducting a massive privatisation programme that raised more than US$100bn in proceeds. During this period, state monopolies were broken, the divestiture of large state-owned enterprises (SOEs) was undertaken and barriers against foreign investment were completely eliminated. Although the consequences of Brazil's attempt to integrate itself into the world economy will only be fully understood in the medium and long terms, some of its effects are already evident. This recent period of 'economic liberalisation' in Brazil has shown an impressive surge in foreign direct investments (FDIs), an unprecedented number of acquisitions of local companies by foreign investors and a complete restructuring of the local supply chain. Economic indicators such as consumer price and foreign exchange rates have finally reached stability. The trade balance went to positive figures after five years, from 1996 to 2000, in the red.[1] Economic growth is still an issue of concern. GDP growth from 1990 to 2002 registered an annual average of 1.98%, while GDP per capita in the same period was marked by a low average annual figure of only 0.37% (Vernengo 2003). In the eight years of Luiz Inácio Lula da Silva's administration, from 2003 to 2010, both GDP and GDP per capita recorded annual growths of, respectively, 4% and 2.9%. According to data from the IMF, the first three years of Dilma Rousseff's administration were marked by a dismal annual GDP growth of 2%.

Following the purpose of 'modernising the economy', many of the local means of production, labour rights and public investments in key sectors of the economy were put at stake. Economic stabilisation had become the main goal, which, once accomplished, would deliver the necessary conditions for the economy to grow at last. The path that was set to lead Brazil towards greater integration into the world economy was shaped by well-known practices that ranged from the lifting of trade tariffs and greater freedom of capital flows to the withdrawal of the state from core production activities. The country that emerged after this decade of reforms is intrinsically different, in both economic and political terms, from the one that rehearsed its first steps towards economic liberalisation in the early nineties. Within a short period, Brazilian companies were exposed to a highly competitive environment which was itself experiencing a worldwide transformation. In the global sphere, the number of mergers and acquisitions reached record highs; production in many industrial sectors became even more concentrated among a few big players; and supply chains were reshaped to reflect tighter links between system integrators and a select group of first- and second-tier suppliers (Nolan 2001). This was a 'revolutionary' process in 'global business', which was powerful enough to give a new shape to the landscape of the world's most successful firms (ibid.).

In the midst of this global restructuring process, which was very much created by the logic of competition and in many cases disproportionate competition, the Brazilian companies had to find a way to get themselves integrated into the world economy. This was by no means an easy or straightforward process, and what brought even more complexity to the Brazilian case is that this was an economy that, after a long period of state-led industrialisation, had reached a fair level of diversification and had internalised a large number of core technologies. The fast pace at which the reforms were carried out in Brazil in the 1990s was in stark contrast to any long-term industrial policy that the country had previously implemented and produced a large number of challenges and uncertainties for local companies.[2]

Although it was to be expected that the changes in the world economy in the late 1980s and throughout the 1990s would inevitably take their toll on the way big business was traditionally run in Brazil, the magnitude and fast pace of the reforms far exceeded initial predictions. They triggered the complete dismantling of a long-established model of state-led industrialisation, expanded in an unprecedented way the participation of foreign companies in local capital formation and contested previous efforts to internalise production and build vertically integrated systems across all the sectors of the economy. Bearing in mind that reforms on such a scale could only go through once they had the necessary endorsement of the local entrepreneurial class, it is therefore crucial to understand the reasons these companies gave their support to a liberalisation process that was bound to expose these same companies to an unparalleled degree of competition, bring about a good deal of uncertainty and, in many cases, ultimately put their businesses at risk.

Not only should the challenges that the entrepreneurial class in Brazil was about to experience in the face of international competition have been at the centre of their concerns, but also the fact that such challenges would be magnified by the country's poor macroeconomic environment in the period during which the whole liberalisation process was carried out. Whether plagued by high economic instability in its first years or under tight monetary control in its final years, the local business scenario was not in any sense propitious for domestic companies to either take risks or engage in head-to-head competition with their larger global counterparts.

In many respects, the obstacles that the local companies were going to face as a result of their greater integration into the world economy were completely unknown. Any previous experience of a more consistent fully fledged open-market environment was simply unheard of in post-industrial Brazil. Local companies, since their foundation as part of a state-led programme of import substitution industrialisation, had constantly relied on government support to obtain privileges in the form of loans, incentives, infrastructure, subsides and, in many cases, technology. In the domestic market, the entrepreneurial class either was protected by high import barriers or enjoyed a business environment that could be better described as one of controlled competition or coexistence with foreign multinational companies. In the most intensive period of import substitution industrialisation in the late 1960s and early 1970s, it was up to the federal government to provide licenses for any multinational corporation that was willing to set up operations in Brazil and, in many sectors, like the petrochemical, automotive, aerospace and electro-electronic sectors, foreign companies were only allowed in through alliances with the local entrepreneurial class.

The Brazilian state-led industrialisation programme, although successful in shifting local production from being highly reliant on primary goods and raw materials to becoming a diversified industrial economy, was, however, not immune to creating its own pitfalls. The mismanagement of the Brazilian economy toward the end of the 1970s and the government's failure to deal with the decade's two oil crises, which ultimately led to the debt crisis of the 1980s, are notable examples. Seriously compromised by unsustainable foreign debts and constantly hit by economic crises, the country went in the 1980s through a decade of dismal growth in which inflation rose rampantly, the investment power of the state was reduced to basic operational levels and long-term strategic planning faltered under constant political uncertainties and economic instabilities.

It is impossible to deny that the crisis of the 1980s, as well as the economic stagnation the country plunged into, did have a long-lasting effect on the change of attitude of some of the local industrialists towards the role of the state in the economy. However, the willingness of the Brazilian entrepreneurial class to abandon its links with the state and to opt for a more open economy remains an intriguing phenomenon. After a long history of protectionism and a whole decade of meagre investments and dismal growth, the prospect of Brazilian companies being able to compete on an equal basis with foreign enterprises was simply impracticable. Even so, local companies seemed willing to take the risks that greater integration into the global economy and market liberalisation inherently entailed. Examples of pressure towards structural reforms could in fact also be found within Brazil's most affluent industrial class.

'FREE TO GROW: A PROPOSAL FOR A MODERN BRAZIL'

In 1990, the Federation of Industries of the State of São Paulo, *FIESP—Federação das Indústrias do Estado de São Paulo*, Brazil's most powerful association of industries, released a detailed report which expressed the organisation's view on the set of measures that should be taken to restore the country's economic growth. The report itself is worthy of attention due to the fact that FIESP alone commanded nearly 50% of the country's industrial GDP and the state of São Paulo hosted the highest number of both local and foreign industrial subsidiaries in Brazil. The document, titled 'Free to Grow: a proposal for a Modern Brazil', was a comprehensive analysis of Brazil's economic stagnation in the eighties and consisted of an elaborate manifesto for neo-liberal reforms (FIESP 1990). According to the document, by promoting market-oriented reforms, FIESP endorsed a 'modern Brazil', 'efficient and competitive, mature and non-paternalistic', 'inserted into the *First World*' and respectful of 'the fundamental values of the international community' (ibid., p. 16, emphasis added). The main argument of the report was the need to carry out a complete restructuring of the role of the state in the economy. According to FIESP, economic activity in Brazil should be entirely handed over to the 'free initiative', whereas the state should have its activities reduced to the 'social areas'.

The document was a very intriguing piece of work, first due to the assertive way it embraced the neo-liberal agenda and second because of the impressive magnitude of the reforms being proposed, which also included a comprehensive liberalisation of labour and capital markets. Any intervention by the state in the economy (either in the form of taxes, subsidies, incentives or price and salary controls) was described as a 'distortion' and therefore expected to bring negative implications for the market's ability to best allocate resources. There was no middle road; Brazil was either to follow the path that would inevitably lead to a complete liberation of the local economy or it was to continue, unaltered, on the current path of state intervention.[3] If reforms were to be launched, they had to be comprehensive and fully committed to reducing the role of the state in the economy.

> The strong participation of the State in the Brazilian economy still stirs conflicting opinions. For some, the development of the Brazilian economy shall remain dependent on the public sector whose actions must

even be intensified to ensure the recovery of growth within a framework of reducing social inequalities. For others, the entrepreneurial capacity of the public sector is exhausted and therefore there is an urgent necessity to bring about private investments and market competition.

In the first option, efforts are meant to preserve the State-Owned Enterprises, expand the participation of the state in health, education and infrastructure; and give greater priority to the domestic market. Whereas in the second, efforts are for the withdrawal of the government from the productive sector; privatization of a considerable part of the State-Owned Enterprises; *the internationalisation of the economy*; and the efficient concentration of public resources in infrastructure and social areas. The present document ['*Free to Grow: a proposal for a Modern Brazil*'] supports this latter vision of the role of the State.

(FIESP, p. 225–6, translated from Portuguese by the author, emphasis added)

The report claimed that the inward-looking rationality of the Brazilian economy had moved the country considerably away from its 'comparative advantages'. Brazil's protectionist strategy, which was strongly based on barriers against both imports and foreign competition, was held to be responsible for the country's poor records in 'allocation efficiency, income distribution and economic growth' (ibid., p. 47). The study also criticized the government's past developmentalist policies and extolled the benefits that greater integration of Brazil into the world economy could eventually bring. According to FIESP, Brazil's industrial protectionism had turned the country into an excessively autarkic economy with negative implications in terms of foreign trade, product innovation and access to state-of-the-art technology. This scenario should therefore be reversed with the opening up of Brazil's economy to foreign capital and products. As mentioned in the report,

[t]he liberalisation of imports and the higher inflow of capital and foreign technology are indispensable measures for the rise of competitiveness, modernisation and diversification of the country's productive activity which, as a consequence, can be translated into higher rates of export growth: only a greater opening of the country will give access to the gains in efficiency and productivity which are needed to restore economic growth.

(ibid., p. 53, translated from Portuguese by the author)

In addition to calling for the reduction of the participation of the state in the productive sector of the economy, the lifting of trade barriers and the abandonment of Brazil's long-standing system of subsidies and industrial incentives, the document released by the confederation of the industries of the state of São Paulo was equally liberal when it came to defining policies related to regulating the participation of foreign capital in the Brazilian economy. In an attempt to make the country more attractive to foreign capital, FIESP's report called for the implementation of a comprehensive set of policies which were to include, among other measures, tax cuts on remittance to other countries, lower restrictions on financial applications made by non-residents and, more importantly, the proposal to extend to foreign investors the same rights enjoyed by the domestic private sector. Moreover, the opening up of the Brazilian economy to foreign capital should not be restricted only to long-term forms of foreign investments but should also give room for the more volatile portfolio capital. The liberalisation of highly volatile capital flows was justified by the fact that this constituted, according to the study, 'the most dynamic and promising segment of the international financial market' (ibid., p. 208).[4] The risks and potentially negative implications linked to this kind of volatile capital in less developed and poorly regulated capital markets, as in the case of Brazil, were, however, ignored by the authors.

Probably the most striking feature of the FIESP report is that although it was released by a federation of industries, the document did not make any comment on the impact that greater liberalisation of the Brazilian economy could have on the country's own domestic companies. The challenges local firms would face in a more competitive scenario as well as the transformations that were taking place in global business were simply ignored throughout the document. The report based its argument on the harms the excessive influence and regulation of the Brazilian state had caused to the economy and claimed that only a committed transition to a market-oriented economy could restore sustainable economic growth. Any loss the Brazilian industrial sector could experience in this initial period of transition would later be compensated by expected growth in productivity and gains in efficiency. For the companies that would eventually not survive in the new open-market environment, the view of the report is limited to a single comment: '[the companies] that are going to break, were going to break sooner or later' (ibid., p. 258, translated from Portuguese by the author).

Although the opening up of the Brazilian economy was in clear conflict with the traditional strategies of the great majority of the local companies, the support for a more competitive and less state-interventionist economy seemed to have become more widely accepted by the local business class. This support from part of the entrepreneurial class of a developing economy like Brazil for a shift from a regime strongly structured on import barriers, subsidies and governmental incentives to an environment led by global competition could be described by many scholars as no less than contradictory. However, this was the path that an influential part of Brazilian industry was willing to take.

It is important to note that business–state relations in Brazil are usually carried out through complex arrangements and negotiations. Frequently, lobbying activities are hindered due to lack of coordination within both parties. On the companies' side, there is a common belief among businesspeople that they can be more effective when acting alone than collectively through their industry associations. On the state side, the problem rests with the Brazilian electoral system, which does not encourage legislators to follow the collective decisions of their political parties. The excessive autonomy of Brazilian members of Congress forces business associations to practically lobby on an individual basis (Schneider 1997). This scenario was particularly evident when the FIESP report was published in 1990, as it coincided with the end of a long process of political liberalisation in Brazil. Mechanisms of political representation were fully restored in 1989 with the direct election of the first civilian president after an interval of almost three decades. The re-democratisation of Brazil led to the emergence of new political leaderships and the subsequent reshuffle of the old business–state coalitions that had been built during military rule.

This was also a period of changes for FIESP itself as it witnessed the emergence from its own ranks of two dissident organisations, PNBE (Pensamento Nacional das Bases Empresariais) and IEDI (Instituto de Estudos para o Desenvolvimento Empresarial). These two organisations were created by business leaders as a response to the alleged insularity of FIESP. Among their complaints was the issue of misrepresentation, as the federation adopted a voting system that allowed small industry associations to be over-represented in the decision boards. Under the FIESP representative structure, a modest sector like that of toys could enjoy the same voting power as the influential auto parts industry. There was also the claim that the FIESP leadership was heavily dominated by the old corporatist elite. Both dissident organisations had different business groups and goals. The first was mostly formed by young entrepreneurs whose agenda dealt with broad social and political issues; the second was a select group of influential business leaders engaged in the revival of a certain degree of industrial policy (Kingstone 1999; Schneider 1997). Although both organisations were welcomed with enthusiasm by the national press, their long-term contribution of providing alternative routes of communication between business and state proved to be somewhat limited.

Any analysis of the reforms of the Brazilian economy in the 1990s must therefore take into consideration the reasons that motivated a branch of the local business class to act in favour of the liberalisation of the local market. Were the Brazilian companies fully aware of the challenges that they were going to confront? Were the expected benefits compelling enough to compensate for the risks that such radical transition to a more open economy inherently implied? Should the reforms be taken as a circumstantial imperative that resulted from the failure of Brazil's former state-led model of development? This chapter hopes to shed light on some of the reasons that motivated the local entrepreneurial class to abandon long-standing protectionist strategies and to embrace a neo-liberal agenda that, in their belief, would bring back economic stability, modernise the local means of production and restore economic growth. This reforming agenda will be then contrasted with the actual measures that were taken by the Brazilian government during this period of transition towards a more open market environment.

Economic Crisis

The support for structural reforms was, above all, a strong reaction from part of the business class to two major concerns: First, the sharp deterioration of the Brazilian economy throughout the 1980s and second, the failure of all the economic stabilisation plans put forward by the Brazilian government to restore the country's economic growth.

Throughout the 1980s, the Brazilian government had shown unquestionable signs of poorly managing the economy. The country's GDP growth, which reached record highs in the first half of the 1970s, suddenly dropped into record lows in the first part of the following decade.[5] Inflation spun out of control, with rates skyrocketing to unbearable levels in the second half of the 1980s.[6] In 1989 alone, Brazil's consumer price index reached the annual figure of 1,636%. To make matters even worse, Brazil's economic and financial worries were deeply aggravated by a high and fast-growing foreign debt, with figures jumping from US$6.2bn in 1970 to US$115.5bn in 1989. The Brazilian default of 1987 turned an economy already thirsty for capital into an economy completely cut off from any form of foreign investments or loans. Brazil's strong reliance on foreign loans (particularly after the oil crises of 1972 and 1979) finally proved unsustainable.[7] Drowned in foreign debt, high inflation and economic crises, the investment power of the state was reduced to basic operational levels.[8]

The low capacity of the Brazilian government to invest in its own productive sector was a major blow to an economy that was very much reliant on the entrepreneurial capacity of the state. Unable to invest and cut off from foreign sources of finance, the Brazilian government witnessed a gradual deterioration of its state enterprises. The perverse implications of the deep Brazilian economic crisis of the 1980s were amplified by the fact that it came immediately after Brazil's most impressive period of growth.

In addition to widespread discontent related to the sharp deterioration of the economy in the 1980s, the discredit of the Brazilian entrepreneurial class in the central role of the state became even more acute after successive failures on the part of the federal government to restore economic stability.[9] In the second half of the 1980s, Brazil witnessed no fewer than five major economic stabilisation plans put forth by the federal government to curb inflation. In a scenario of growing economic instability, the failure of one economic plan was followed by another one, which generated even more disastrous consequences. The chaotic economic situation that the country slipped into and the urgent need for immediate solutions can be measured, for instance, by the constant reshuffles of the head of the Finance

Ministry—basically a new minister for each economic plan, a worrying sign of the discontinuity of the measures being implemented.[10]

The entrepreneurial class was particularly dissatisfied with the unpredictability and the authoritarian manner that marked the launching of all the anti-inflation shocks that were put forward by the Brazilian government. To make matters worse, the ingredients of each of these economic stabilisation recipes were also the object of widespread criticism. In reality, the government's unsuccessful agenda of price freezes and tax rises helped only to gradually undermine the support of the entrepreneurial sector. For the industrial class, the government had repeatedly failed, in all its anti-inflation plans, to tackle the real source of the country's economic collapse: the loose and excessive spending capacity of the state. In other words, this was a clear indication that, in their view, the government itself was one of the key sources of the long-standing economic crisis of the 1980s.[11]

As dissatisfaction with the government's policies became rampant, reaction from the local entrepreneurial class grew more intensively and better orchestrated. '[F]rom 1987–88 the economic elite' began to join efforts against 'state interventionism' and to demand greater 'deregulation' of the economy, higher participation of 'foreign' investments and 'privatisation' of state-owned enterprises, ideas that 'became predominant in the media and spread out into the middle classes' (Sallum Jr 2003, p. 185–6).

> For business, support for neo-liberalism emerged as a result of the increasingly chaotic presence of the state in the economy. A range of problems—from the uncertainty produced by frequent and wild swings in policy and the inability to contain the public deficit to the increasing negative impact of chronic inflation—all contributed to a profound sense that something had to change. The business community identified the state in particular as a source of problems and, as a result, supported neo-liberalism with the emphasis on reducing the size of the state. In addition, most businesses felt that they could compete in an open economy if they had a fair chance to adjust. The size of Brazil's internal market and the sophistication of the industrial economy made that truer for Brazilian business than for any other country in the region.
>
> (Kingstone, Constitutional reform and
> macroeconomic stability: implications for
> democratic consolidation in Brazil 1999, p. 138)

The Domestic Companies

The performance of the local private sector was used as an excuse in the campaign for the reduction of the role of the state in the economy. In the end of the 1980s, part of the business community was already drawing attention to what it identified as two 'conflicting' realities in Brazil. On one side was the public sector, which was regarded as 'outdated, clientelistic and inefficient', and on the opposite side was the private sector, which was generally seen as 'modern, affluent and socially advanced' (Brazil em Exame 1989, p. 7).[12] Not surprisingly, given this negative image of the public sector, the Brazilian business community considered itself in better position to take the lead in the country's efforts to modernise the economy.[13] This task that began by reducing the role of the state in the economy should also pave the way for greater integration of the country into the world economy.

Despite the fact that Brazil did not have any truly world-class companies in the late 1980s that could match the scale of a global giant, two factors seemed to have given ground to the belief that local companies were capable enough to compete in a more open environment. First was the impressive growth, at least in local terms, that the large companies in Brazil had reached within a short period of time,[14] and second was the remarkable survival skills that these same companies had shown when put in strongly adverse economic situations. For some analysts, the economic crises that the country had gone through in the 1980s, instead of being harmful to the large Brazilian companies had, on the contrary, forced these companies to become more flexible and adaptive to external shocks. It was exactly this argument that extolled the success of the local companies in situations of adversity that was used by more liberal analysts to convince sceptical sectors of the business community that the challenges imposed by a more open economy could be also overtaken.[15]

Finally, another fact that cannot be ignored and which helped to add optimism to the image of efficiency of the local companies was the country's notable export growth towards the end of the 1980s. In the most difficult period of the economic crisis in Brazil (from 1982 to 1989), the country export indicators ignored all downward expectations and recorded a growth of nearly 60%. This growth, which was responsible for a historical trade surplus in 1988 and 1989 of, respectfully, US\$19bn and US\$16bn, also contributed to give extra confidence to the local business community, particularly by the fact that 70% of what was exported actually corresponded to manufactured products. For some analysts, this was a clear indication of the dynamism that the local industrial sector had reached in a short period of time and that the precepts of an infant and incipient industry were not applicable anymore.[16] Within the time span of one generation, Brazil's portfolio of export had shifted from being intrinsically based on primary commodities to becoming more heavily dependent on manufactured products.

Although it was expected that the opening up of the economy was likely to penalise a good part of local companies, there was a common view among more liberal sectors of the Brazilian industrial class that the final outcome would still be positive. For this group, the private sector was going to emerge stronger after this period of transition and better prepared to deal with the challenges of an increasingly globalised economy. The hardship that some companies were going to face would be compensated in the future. In other words, all the pain these companies were going to go through with the opening up of the Brazilian economy would be later turned into gains.

The Failure of the State-Led Development Policies

The vast literature that emerged in the 1980s and which brought back to the centre of discussion the benefits of a free-market economy had a particular appeal to large Latin American countries. One by one, these economies started to engage in neo-liberal reforms. As mentioned by Cardenas, Ocampo and Thorp (2000), in the introduction to their book on 'industrialisation and state in Latin America', all of a sudden in the early 1980s expressions like 'protection', 'import substitution' and 'intervention' became 'dirty words' to be avoided and banned. In the wake of a massive economic crisis that hit all these economies, a broad consensus was gaining strength. Rather than reforming the state, the real solution was in dismantling it.

For the Brazilian entrepreneurial class, this approach was particularly valid. After four decades of state-led development, the concrete achievements of the country's social and economic aspects had left considerable room for disappointment. In the social arena, Brazil not only had failed to solve its most enduring problems but, in many cases, living conditions had even worsened. Although Brazil had shown the highest annual growth among Latin American countries from 1950 to 1980, the country's social records, when compared to its neighbour economies, gave clear indications of a poor performance. In 1989, Brazil's social statistics of *infant mortality, poverty, illiteracy, child labour* and *human development* were far behind those of Argentina, Chile, Colombia, Costa Rica, Mexico and Venezuela (Camargo and Barros 1993, p. 62). Social inequality grew tremendously in this same period, which contributed to placing Brazil as one of the most uneven societies in the world. From 1960 to 1980, the income share of the top 10% richest grew from 39.6% to 50.9%, whereas the bottom 50% of the population saw their participation in the national income fall from 17.4% to 12.6%. In 1990, the bottom 40% and 20% of the population enjoyed access to only 8.5% and 2.4% of the national income. With regard to poverty alleviation, the small improvement witnessed in the 1960s (Fields 1980, p. 221) was followed by erratic behaviour in the 1970s and 1980s.[17] In those two decades, the share of the population living below the poverty line in Brazil, although falling from 48.2% to 26.4% between 1976 and 1986, witnessed a quick rise to 41.9% in 1990 (ibid.). In fact, Brazil's effort to reduce absolute poverty instead of showing a steady improvement was rather marked by the volatility that characterised its irregular economic growth in the late 1970s and 1980s.

Given the rise in income gap, the inconsistency at reducing absolute poverty and the persistent social debt, it is not difficult to conclude that the most vulnerable segment of the Brazilian population remained largely excluded from the benefits of the outstanding economic growth the country witnessed from the post-war period until 1980. In the case of Brazil, the development policies of the state failed to reach those who needed them most. In the economic area, as previously mentioned, a series of flawed measures taken by the government in the face of the two oil crises ended up jeopardising its state-owned productive sector and putting the whole economy at risk.

The state was under scrutiny not only for what it delivered but also for what it began to represent. Once seen as Brazil's main inducer of growth due to its developmental policies, as economic crises and recession struck, the state became more strongly associated with its main weaknesses (Kingstone, Crafting coalitions for reform: business preferences, political institutions, and neoliberal reform in Brazil 1999, p. 48). At the top of the list were the Brazilian government's pervasive bureaucracy, lack of transparency and clientelistic practices.[18] Although some industrial groups had themselves made constant use of the discretionary power of the state for their own benefit, the unprecedented crisis into which the country plunged called for drastic changes. In addition, the collapse of Brazil's military government in the mid-1980s led the local entrepreneurial class to re-evaluate the country's business–state relations. The result of this reassessment on the part of a growing proportion of the Brazilian business community was not a surprising one. For a variety of political, social and economic reasons, the conspicuous presence of the Brazilian state engendered a considerable amount of public distrust.

Finally, it is also worth noting that this internal crisis of the Brazilian state coincided, in the global sphere, with the strident collapse of the Soviet bloc. This was a major twist of fate in the international political and economic scenario that undeniably gave extra ammunition for growing criticism on state-led models of development.[19]

Re-Democratisation and Liberalisation

It is impossible not to establish a strong interconnection between the political and economic reforms that were carried out in Latin America after the debt crisis of the early 1980s. In the same way that the poor performance of the Latin American economies in that decade had a fundamental influence on the collapse of the region's authoritarian governments,[20] the very process of reinstating civilian governments across the region also gave a new boost to the implementation of structural reforms. In the case of Brazil, reasons for a considerable reshuffle of the economy were ample. As previously mentioned, drowned in foreign debt and being constantly hit by economic crises, the country had gone, in the 1980s, through a record decade of dismal growth in which inflation had become rampant the investment power of the state was reduced to basic operational levels and local entrepreneurial planning was constantly undermined by political uncertainties and economic instabilities. There was a widespread belief that the end of Brazil's political reform should necessarily lead into an institutional and economic reform.

Not surprisingly, the beginning of Brazil's economic liberalisation coincided with the end of the period of transition from authoritarian rule. The first comprehensive measures to open up the economy were put forward by the first elected president to come to power after more than two decades of military rule.[21] The implications of such a political change should not be ignored. The newly inaugurated government obtained the necessary support and political legitimacy to carry out long-awaited structural changes. After the poor performance of the Brazilian economy in the 1980s and the alleged exhaustion of the ISI policies that, in different ways, had dominated the priorities of Brazil's developmental state for more than four decades, attention was then drawn towards an economic model that could reflect the comprehensive institutional changes the country was both calling for and was willing to take. The end of an authoritarian regime could only be complete once the practices the regime was associated with were equally abandoned.

For the social groups that were pressing for a neo-liberal reform, the opening up of Brazil's economy was therefore a necessary step to consolidate the re-democratisation process. According to Eli Diniz (2002, p. 243) in her work on the Brazilian 'industrial class and strategies for development', Brazil's economic opening, which gained full steam at the onset of Cardoso's government, marked the beginning of a period of legal and institutional deconstruction which would pave the way for the redefinition of the state and society according to new international parameters. For a growing number of policy makers in Brazil, such change should involve the privatisation of state-owned enterprises, market liberalisation and the reduction of the direct participation of the state in the economy.

Brazil's Need to Catch Up

When compared to other Latin American economies, Brazil was definitely a latecomer in implementing market-oriented reforms. In the late 1980s, economic reforms were already well under way in Chile, were in progress in Mexico and Argentina and were fundamental in turning Bolivia into living proof, at least for those who were involved in designing the country's economic transition, that 'shock therapies' and market-oriented reforms could quickly deliver positive results.[22]

For the debt-ridden and capital-stripped Latin American countries of the 1980s, the international business and financial communities were very much eager to reward those that were ready to implement market-oriented reforms. Examples that reinforced this claim were in fact increasingly common across the continent. Until the late 1980s, Mexico was perhaps the most notable example of the rewards that comprehensive economic reforms could immediately bring. The country had successfully managed to negotiate a debt-reduction package with international lending institutions which, in conjunction with fiscal discipline measures, was fundamental in restoring the country's economic stability and growth.

In Argentina, the scale and sheer magnitude of economic reforms and their initial rewards were even more staggering. After a period of economic and political instability that reached its peak in the late 1980s, the newly elected Argentinean president Carlos Menem launched, in the early 1990s, a comprehensive programme to reduce the role of the state in the economy, lift trade barriers and reinstate fiscal discipline in the government accounts. In addition, from 1991, Argentina's reforming agenda started to adopt a 'convertibility plan', which pegged the local currency to the US dollar. The economic stability that was achieved immediately after the implementation of these structural changes in the economy not only put an end to a period of nearly two decades of dismal growth but was also fundamental, in a way that was similar to what happened in Mexico, in regaining the country's deeply shattered credibility with the international financial institutions (Kiguel and Nogués 1998).

The most remarkable example at that time in Latin America of a country that was committed to a drastic and rapid change to a more open economy was possibly that of Bolivia. In the mid-1980s, Jeffrey Sachs, while working as economic advisor to the Bolivian government, helped to design what he described, in a paper co-authored with Felipe Larraín, as 'the most comprehensive case of shock therapy that had yet been undertaken in the post-war world economy'. The Bolivian programme of deep and fast market liberalisation was regarded as such a model of success that the authors claimed that it should 'subsequently' help 'to influence similar programs in Eastern Europe and the former Soviet Union' (Larraín Bascuñain and Sachs 1998, p. 149).

The first results of Bolivia's economic reforms were indeed astonishing. Within a few months, the country had not only successfully curbed a chaotic inflation rate—which, in its worst four months of mid-1985, had reached the annualised figure of 60,000 percent—but had also managed to finally show some signs of recovery after a whole decade of dismal or negative growth (Sachs 1987).[23] The neo-liberal foundation of Bolivia's economic reform was clearly evident, and the programme went far beyond macroeconomic stabilisation measures of exchange rate unification to include a comprehensive plan of fiscal discipline, 'trade liberalisation, internal price decontrol, and the decentralisation or privatisation of public enterprises' (ibid., p. 281). Full commitment to this last item was finally reached in 1992 with the approval of a new law on privatisation. This new act allowed the divestiture of all state-owned enterprises with the sole exception of the Bolivian tin and oil companies (Larraín Bascuñain and Sachs 1998, p. 157).

The first positive results that a comprehensive programme of trade and finance liberalisation, deregulation and privatisation of state-owned enterprises brought to these countries had a tremendous impact on the Brazilian entrepreneurial class and undoubtedly put strong pressure on the country to follow the same path. Suddenly, Brazil's neighbour countries were enjoying the benefits of investments in previously depressed sectors, access to international capital and the resurgence of their idle industrial capacity. Considering the impressive magnitude of the Latin American crisis of the 1980s, these economies, due to their comprehensive neo-liberal reforms, were showing signs of a quick and astonishing recovery. Not surprisingly, any measure Brazil was planning to adopt towards long-term development would inevitably have to take into account the apparently successful path taken by its neighbour economies.

The Mainstream Literature

The lobbying for economic reforms by part of the Brazilian entrepreneurial class would not have been possible without the appropriate backing of a well-established economic theory, a task that in the late 1980s came to be largely monopolised by the supporters of market-oriented reforms.

For orthodox economists, the failure of Latin American countries to reach a higher level of sustainable development was an unequivocal example of the pitfalls of the state in controlling economic activity. As previously mentioned, the growing disillusion with Latin American governments helped to put in question not only their policies but, more importantly, the very existence of the controlling state. Governments became target of a series of criticisms which identified their very existence as the source of mismanagement.

In many cases, as in the Latin America of the 1980s, it became evident that the state had not managed to meet the goals that justified its predominance over market structures. Not rarely, as was highlighted by Anne Krueger in her critique of state-led models of development, 'colossal government failures' had 'considerably outweighed market failure' (Krueger 1990, p. 10). Therefore, the previous belief that the existence of market failures justified a case for state intervention was, according to the author, largely 'insufficient' (ibid., p. 20). In most of the cases, decision making was not restricted to development plans designed by economists and technocrats, but it invariably resulted from the pressure of political groups. The 'disproportionate' influence of pressure groups, particularly in the case of Latin America, constantly led to outcomes that were quite remote from what was economically or socially desirable. The poor performance of all Latin American economies in the 1980s conjured an indicative lesson that government policies were not always efficient at inducing growth, as was believed in the initial phase of the continent's state-led development (ibid., p. 13–14). The very assumption that governments were 'benevolent social guardians' ruled by 'selfless bureaucrats' turned out to be highly contested and sometimes, as when it came to poverty alleviation, even fallacious. Not only were bureaucrats also plagued by vested interests, but governments seemed unable to adjust the 'market imperfections' that were believed to be more largely perceived in developing markets.

In addition to the alleged intrinsic failures and contradictions of the state as a managerial body and an inducer of growth, its ubiquitous presence in all levels of the economy also became a focus of intense criticism. At the heart of the debate was the state-led model of development, which was constantly condemned by analysts for being based on 'exceptionally high-cost public sector enterprises' (ibid., p. 10) and on an allegedly outdated programme for the promotion of 'infant industries'. In both cases, critics claimed that the state's persistent intervention in the economy was the main obstacle barring the transition of its most stagnant sectors to more efficient forms of production. Moreover, these critics were equally fierce in criticising what they regarded as an overuse of interventionist mechanisms such as price controls and subsidies. There was a growing consensus that the intervention of the state in the economy was acting as a hindrance to the modernisation of their own economies, and 'the scope and height' of the protectionist barriers commonly adopted by these countries were 'usually far greater' than could be credibly 'defended on infant industry grounds' (ibid., p. 14).

In response to the poor performance of the Latin American state-led development policies, proponents of market-oriented reforms emphasised that only a reduction of tariffs, the decontrol of prices and the adoption of more competitive exchange rates could unlock the continent's debt-ridden economies and make them move back to more sustainable levels of growth. The new developmental path to be taken by these economies had necessarily to go through the restoration of a healthier and less 'distorted' market environment. Such reforms were fundamental for the region to identify its 'comparative advantages', invest in product specialisation and get more fully integrated into the world economy. Therefore, if such changes really were to be taken forward, it was necessary for the Latin American countries to considerably reduce their protectionist barriers.

The opening up of the economy as a means of combating economic stagnation and restoring growth enjoyed undeniable support from a growing proportion of the academic community. In addition to the alleged benefits of eliminating 'market distortions', of contributing to the best allocation of resources and of being a key mechanism for the decontrolling of prices, the lifting of trade barriers in tandem with the efficient specialisation of production was believed to lead to a 'virtuous circle' of trade expansion and sustainable growth. According to Jagdish Bhagwati (1989), an enthusiastic supporter of market reforms in debt-ridden developing economies, the lowering of tariffs tends to induce more trade, which results in higher growth and ultimately has a positive effect on improving the average income. Closing the full circle, rises in income would therefore enable more tariff cuts.

The Success of the Outward-Looking East Asian NICs

Finally, another issue of debate among scholars was the inevitable comparison between the meagre performance of the inward-looking Latin American economies and the relative success of the outward-looking model of East Asian newly industrialised countries (NICs). Partially claimed to be a result of robust export incentives put forward by their governments, the superior performance of these East Asian countries merits attention. While per-capita income in the 'four little tigers' managed to grow approximately six-fold from 1950 to 1985, Latin American countries like Argentina, Uruguay and Venezuela recorded, in that same period, a dismal income growth of no more than one-half[24] (Balassa 1988). This difference in performance, which is frequently linked to the exporting performance of the East Asian countries, becomes more evident when their foreign trade figures are given a more careful analysis. Bela Balassa (1988), in his study on the export growth of twelve large newly industrialised developing economies from East Asia, South East Asia and Latin America, defended the existence of a positive correlation between 'economic growth' and 'growth in exports'.[25] According to the author, the success stories of Korea and Taiwan are the two clearest examples of the correlation between foreign trade and economic growth. While the Korean share of non-fuel exports grew from 0.9% to 17.3% between 1963 and 1984 and the Taiwanese share increased from 3.6% to 18.2%, the participation of the three largest Latin American economies in this group of twelve developing countries was either stagnant or relatively lower. Argentina saw its participation in exports decline from 14.8% to 4.7%, Brazil moved from 15.3% to 16.2% and Mexico's exports witnessed a fall from 9.0% to 5.4% (ibid., p. S278).

In addition, when absolute figures were analysed, the four little tigers produced an equally astonishing result. Exports from the four East Asian NICs (Hong Kong, Korea, Singapore and Taiwan) increased nearly sixty-fold, moving from US$1.4bn in 1964 to US$83.7bn in 1984. The three largest Latin American economies (Brazil, Mexico and Argentina), however, produced a far lower growth record, with their exports having grown twelve-fold from US$3.5bn to US$43.1bn. Although starting from lower levels of exports, by 1984, the four East Asian NICs had already outperformed the three largest Latin American economies by almost 100% of their total exports (ibid.). The alleged superiority of the export-oriented model of development became even more evident with the oil-related recession of the 1970s. Although Latin America and East Asia were equally hit by the oil crisis, the latter economies managed to adjust far more quickly than the inward-looking and debt-ridden Latin American ones.

Although the East Asian NICs indisputably achieved a remarkable degree of success in their attempt to shift part of their production towards exports, very little can now be said about their real commitment to free-market policies.

Countries like Korea and Taiwan extensively adopted protectionist practices, and both governments constantly intervened in their respective economies. In reality, their infant industry programme was not different from a successive use of the usual mechanisms of price controls, subsidies, entry restrictions and special incentives. However, in a paradoxical way, these interventionist practices were rarely acknowledged or were even conveniently ignored by mainstream economists. This behaviour by some of the Western analysts was particularly evident when they were advising the adoption of market-oriented reforms by other developing economies. According to Ha-Joon Chang (1996), in his work on the case of Korea's industrial development, orthodox economists tended to provide a 'biased' account and to turn a 'blind eye to the active role of the state' when they were analysing Korea's economic activity. For this group of economists, 'it was simply unthinkable that a successful non-socialist economy such as Korea may not be a free-market economy' (ibid., p. 91). Provided that the interventionist practices of these countries were downplayed, it sounded legitimate to make use of their impressive growth rates as a model to be followed by other developing economies.

The stories of the success of the East Asian NICs as an example of the advantages of the market-oriented model of development, if not fully realistic in their content, served at least to stimulate the imagination of policy makers from other developing countries as an alleged example of success that, by the end of 1980, was already showing signs of influence in Latin America.

In the midst of this period of deep economic instability of the 1980s and the region's disillusion with the past inward-looking development policies, a report published by Bela Balassa, Gerardo Bueno, Pedro-Pablo Kuczynski and the Brazilian economist Mario Henrique Simonsen in the mid-1980s gave a clear indication that an incipient movement towards comprehensive market-oriented reforms was gaining strength among Latin American academic and technocratic groups (Balassa, Bueno, et al. 1986). This study, which consisted of a strong critique of the region's state-led model of development, claimed that the restoration of growth in the region would necessarily require shifting to an outward-looking model of development, reduction of the productive role of the state, implementation of fiscal discipline and the revitalisation of the private sector. Apparently, the foundations of broad and market-oriented reforms were showing signs of wider acceptance across the region. Years later, the confederation of industries of the state of São Paulo in Brazil released a document (the previously mentioned 'Free to grow: a proposal for a modern Brazil') that essentially followed the same principles (FIESP 1990).

THE OPENING-UP PROCESS

Given the growing interest from part of the business class in support of the implementation of economic reforms and the reasons that motivated its change of behaviour towards a less state-interventionist model of development, attention must now be shifted to the measures that were actually taken by the Brazilian government to ensure the country's transition to a more open economy. By the end of the 1980s, there was already a widespread perception among local policy makers that comprehensive reforms needed to be carried out.[26] The main concern was to find the political means that would orchestrate the dismantling of the entrepreneurial state and replace it with the necessary mechanisms to transform the country into a more market-oriented economy.

In the local sphere, the opening up of the Brazilian economy in the early 1990s was marked, as will be described later in this chapter, by an initial disastrous attempt from the government to curb inflation and by a persistent concern on the part of the executive to achieve and maintain economic stability in the country. Market-oriented reforms in Brazil first emerged during the ill-fated Collor administration and reached full steam during the double mandate of Fernando H. Cardoso, which lasted from 1995 to 2003.

In the economic sphere, Brazil's liberalisation is also a compelling case for analysis, as it was carried out in a period when the world economy was experiencing an unprecedented expansion which was strongly marked by an impressive surge of cross-border capital flows. This greater freedom of capital flows was understood by many analysts as a necessary component of the new liberal economic order. It didn't take long, however, for these economies to realise that capital liberalisation could also bring a considerable degree of risk. The high mobility of capital in the late 1990s culminated in a chain of financial crises which hit in a more severe way the developing economies whose markets were more poorly regulated. This wave of financial instability had its epicentre in East Asia (1997–98) and Russia (1998) and rippled through all the emerging markets across the world. It emitted signals of concern in Brazil and had a devastating effect in Argentina, where the country plunged into economic collapse in 2001.

Whether benefiting from a period of world economic expansion in the early 1990s or facing the sudden contraction of the emerging markets in the late 1990s, the liberalisation process in Brazil became increasingly susceptible to transformations in the global economy. Not surprisingly, the primary concern of Brazilian policy makers who were in charge of implementing market-oriented reforms was to bring back economic stability in the country. This goal was considered a sine-qua-non condition to make the economy more attractive to private (either local or foreign) investments, a task that, given the country's previous record of high inflation, unsuccessful anti-inflationary programmes and growing exposure to the high volatility of international capital, was by no means easy to achieve.

The path that led Brazil to a more open economy was designed to move the country away from its long-standing debt crisis. Under the premise of 'putting the house in order', a series of policies was implemented in Brazil which echoed similar measures that were taken by other highly indebted countries of the Latin American region. These measures, which became common to all economies across the region, were in reality in compliance with the precepts of and to a certain extent dictated by leading multilateral lending institutions (most notably the World Bank and the IMF). In essence, this Washington-backed set of measures called for ten major 'adjustments' in the economy: the adoption of 'fiscal discipline'; the re-evaluation of the 'public expenditure priorities', which were encouraged to move away from the indiscriminate use of subsidies and state-led industrial promotion programmes and to head towards more direct investments in basic infrastructure as well as in public services such as health and education; the implementation of a comprehensive 'tax reform' to reduce production costs; the pursuit of 'interest rates' that could more actively reflect the dynamics of the market; the implementation of competitive 'exchange rates'; the liberalisation of imports with the abandonment of protectionist incentives and the shift to a more outward-looking 'trade policy'; the lifting of barriers against 'foreign direct investments'; the 'privatisation' of state-owned enterprises; the 'deregulation' of the allegedly excessive state interference in the economy; and, last but not least, the keen observance to 'property rights'.[27]

Each of these measures pursued by the Washington-based multilateral lending institutions concealed a high degree of complexity and a stark rupture from the previous economic instruments of development prevailing in Latin America. The implementation of this package of policies was expected to face the hostility of deep-rooted local interests, the scrutiny of the business class, the eventual surge of popular opposition and, in many cases, even to deal with a large variety of constitutional impediments. The implementation of reforms of such magnitude would ideally require the establishment of a constant line of negotiation between the main parties involved in the process, most notably the government, the local business class and the general public opinion. As the pace of the reforms was ultimately set by the government, their implementation therefore depended on the bargaining and discretionary power of the state. This led to a paradoxical conclusion that the dismantling of the state-led model of development required a strong and efficient government, a condition that proved to be particularly true in the case of Brazil.

The opening up of the Brazilian economy in the 1990s was marked by two distinct periods. One was characterised by the problematic and short-lived Collor administration, which lasted only from 1990 to 1992, and the other was marked by the first long period of economic stability achieved under the double mandate of Fernando H. Cardoso from 1995 to 2003. A striking finding is, however, worthy of attention. Both periods, although completely distinct in their approach to carrying out the economic liberalisation agenda, shared in their own way and for different reasons a considerable lack of attention, as will be shown later in this chapter, to the demands of the local business class.

The Collor Administration

As the first elected president of Brazil after two decades of military rule, Mr Collor de Mello was responsible in the early 1990s for promoting the first major attempt to rebuild the foundations of a more market-oriented economy. Collor's economic programme, ingeniously titled 'New Brazil', was strongly based on the rhetoric of modernisation.[28] It proposed a deep rupture with the state-led economic policies of the past and promised the transition to a more dynamic, efficient and fast-growing economy which would be controlled by private initiative. For a country that was experiencing a decade-long period of stagnation, this project of structural reforms couldn't have brought a more appealing message.[29]

Among its various measures, President Collor's economic programme addressed three fundamental topics which were in tune with the more orthodox precepts that were gaining acceptance across the Latin American region: (i) the lifting of import barriers, (ii) the privatisation of state-owned enterprises and (iii) the deregulation of the economy. The first, which was part of a larger price-stabilisation programme to combat inflation, was primarily meant to bring competition to the market.[30] The cut of tariff and non-tariff barriers experienced by Brazilian industry was wide ranging and of an unprecedented scale. With the stroke of a pen, the new president in 1990 abolished a list of more than one thousand products whose import had been prohibited. Moreover, in addition to the phasing out of non-tariff barriers, an equally ambitious programme to reduce tariff barriers was also put forward. By mid-1993, import tariffs were projected to reach an average level inferior to 15%, a figure that was almost three times lower than the average import rate of 51% set by the Brazilian government in the 1980s. An interesting aspect of Brazil's trade liberalisation programme that needs to be highlighted was its sole concern with the orthodox preaching. The trade liberalisation process was chiefly designed to rectify a pervasive 'market distortion' in the economy that was believed to have its roots in the country's long history of protectionism. Therefore, the issue of policy reciprocity did not become a concern among Brazilian policy makers. This was by all means a unilateral opening.[31] The lifting of import barriers in Brazil was not followed by reciprocal measures of tariff reduction from any of Brazil's main trade partners.[32]

Another target of reforms included the divestiture of state-owned enterprises whose implementation programme was officially launched in April 1990 with the announcement of the National Privatisation Programme, Programa Nacional de Desestatização—PND.[33] One of the first measures of the programme was the creation of a Privatisation Steering Committee composed of eleven members, 'four representing the public sector and seven from the private sector' (Longo 1993, p. 50). The commission defined the companies to be divested, the calendar of privatisations and the way in which the company was going to be sold; the actual execution

of the programme was under the responsibility of the Brazilian development bank, BNDES. In terms of asset transfer, the programme introduced
an innovation that is worth mentioning. In contrast to the previous timid
and unsystematic attempts to divest public assets in Brazil,[34] the new privatisation programme authorized a larger participation of foreign capital. According to the new legislation, foreign investors were 'allowed to
acquire up to 40 per cent of voting shares and 100 per cent of non-voting
shares' (ibid.).[35]

In addition to the two immediate goals of (i) bringing new investments to
the former state enterprises and (ii) stimulating competition, the privatisation programme was fundamental to provide public evidence of the government's intention to reinforce market laws, reduce public-sector debt and
strengthen the stock market (Longo 1993; Goldstein and Schneider 2000).
The original schedule of the privatisation programme estimated the sale of
one company per month starting with the steel, mining and petrochemical
sectors. Opposition from the National Congress, SOE employees and various sectors of Brazilian civil society brought the programme to a halt for
nearly two years. The National Privatisation Programme was only resumed
in December 1991.

Finally, in a manoeuvre designed to show his commitment to the creation
of a 'minimal state' as part of the process of deregulating the economy, Collor
also put forward a drastic administrative reform. The number of ministries
shrank from thirty to a 'mere 12', and a substantial number of state agencies
were abolished (Longo 1993, p. 52). In a similar way, the government had
plans to lay off about '360.000 public sector workers' (Baer 2001, p. 180).[36]
In addition to administrative reforms, the government also tried to show commitment to a more accountable fiscal budget.[37] Consistent with the government's commitment to building a more market-friendly environment, a series
of subsidies to imports, exports and agriculture was eliminated; fiscal incentives to the less developed North and Northeast regions of Brazil were abolished; and special regimes for the development of some high-tech and strategic
sectors, as in the case of the computer industry, were simply abandoned (ibid.).

President Collor's economic plan, however, contained deep contradictions. If on one side it laid the foundations for a more market-friendly economy, on the other it brought forth the most interventionist measures the
Brazilian economy had ever experienced. The most problematic component
of the plan, which would later be responsible for its own ruin, was the stringent and ineffectual way it dealt with monetary issues. In an attempt to solve
the pressing problem of the country's hyperinflation, which had reached a
stratospheric monthly rate of 81% (ibid.), the economic plan made use of
strict interventionist methods.[38] All prices and wages were frozen for an
initial period of forty-five days, and 'all deposits in the overnight market,
transaction and savings accounts that exceeded Cr\$ 50.000 (equivalent to
US\$ 1,300 at the then prevailing exchange rate)' were confiscated by the
government for a period of eighteen months (ibid.).[39] The exchange rate

was allowed to float free, and a new special tax on financial transactions (which included withdrawals from savings accounts) was put into practice. Disciplinary measures to avoid tax evasion were also implemented.

The sudden and unexpected drain of liquidity had a massive recessive effect on the economy. Not surprisingly, the immediate reaction of all the agricultural, industrial and service sectors was a substantial contraction of their activities.[40] 'Inflationary expectations' were indeed 'abruptly reversed' (Longo 1993, p. 42), but the cost and consequences of this drastic anti-inflation plan produced an even more harmful effect. The plan made blatant use of measures of doubtful legality and caught all sectors of Brazilian society simply unprepared for the shock tactics of its measures. The worst, however, was still to come. The draconian monetary policies that were imposed on the economy were soon to prove ineffective as, three months after its implementation, inflation was back and the government had already lost control of its attempt to stabilise the economy. With the government's inability to curb inflation, it became patent that the hardship imposed on the population was in vain.

A series of rescue measures was put forward by the government in the following two years in an attempt to regain control of the economy and to remedy the flaws of the original plan. These measures, however, proved to be equally unsuccessful. In general, they did not differ from the re-use of mechanisms of price and wage freezes, arbitrary interventions in the financial market, exchange rate controls and use of high interest rates. Such policies, combined with the growing wariness and discontentedness of the local financial and productive sectors, only contributed to driving the economy into deeper stagnation and recession.[41] The picture of institutional disarray became even more evident when the entire economic team was reshuffled sixteen months after the First Collor Plan was announced. Although the new economic team rushed to assure the population they would no longer employ drastic interventionist methods, the communication channels between the executive and all the other sectors of Brazilian society were already broken. What was initially taken as economic mismanagement on the part of the executive evolved into an institutional and political crisis. In December 1992, Mr Collor de Mello was finally impeached and forced out of the executive under allegations of corruption.

For the local business class, the combination of trade liberalisation, recessive monetary measures and persistent economic instability could not have had a more harmful effect.[42] The opening up of the Brazilian economy was visibly marked by the executive's struggle to sustain its failing monetary policies and the government's complete neglect of the domestic entrepreneurial sector. As business–state relations deteriorated, local entrepreneurs became even more unable to adjust to the new scenario of increasing competition with foreign companies. To make matters worse, these same local entrepreneurs were already facing the hardship of having to cope with a situation of deep economic crisis, which was very much the consequence of the ineptitude of their own Brazilian government.

The Cardoso Administration and the *Real Plan*

In contrast to the environment of profound economic instability that marked the Collor administration, the opening up of the Brazilian economy in the second half of the 1990s was characterised by the government's success in bringing down some macroeconomic indicators, such as the rampant inflation rate, to manageable levels. However, despite suggestions that the newly gained economic stability would be key for the local companies to adjust to the challenges of a more open and competitive environment, the mechanisms taken by the Brazilian government to ensure low levels of inflation proved, as will be shown later in this section, also to contain harmful components for the local entrepreneurial class. Similar to what happened in the early 1990s, the second half of the decade was also marked by predominant attention to macroeconomic issues and constant neglect of microeconomic policies.

In December 1993, Fernando Henrique Cardoso, while Finance Minister of the government that took power after the impeachment of Collor de Mello, set forth the first economic plan after the debt crisis that successfully solved the country's pressing problem of high inflation. From the outset, Cardoso's economic programme tried to avoid the mistakes of previous administrations. Alternatively, the new government decided to establish a more fluent dialogue with different sectors of Brazilian society. In contrast to the centralised and authoritarian way in which the former administration had carried out its economic policies, the measures that were put forward by the new economic team were now sent first to be discussed and voted on in the National Congress. In addition, the shock component that constituted a key element in the launch of all previous anti-inflation campaigns, but which proved to have a negative effect in raising public expectations and in contributing to financial speculation, was straightaway repudiated by the new economic team. This decision of the executive to set its policies in a more transparent way turned out to be highly effective for the new government to gain credibility with the public, particularly in the wake of the profound political instability that Brazil had just gone through. The economic team built further confidence by giving public reassurance that they would not make use of any mechanism of price and wage freezing.

This new economic package that became known as the *Real Plan* consisted of two main parts: the adoption of a series of fiscal adjustment policies and the establishment of an indexing system that led to the creation of a new currency, in this case the *Real* (Amann and Baer 2000, p. 1806). On the fiscal front, the proposed changes consisted of an attempt of the federal government to address several of the budgetary problems that had been neglected in previous adjustment programmes. These changes, which were meant to tackle the country's long record of fiscal deficits, foresaw, among other measures, the cut of US$7bn in government spending (this measure came on top of a US$6bn cut that the government had implemented a couple of months earlier), the application of an 'across-the-board tax increase of 5%', and the tight control of debt obligations of the states to the federal government.[43] More importantly, the government also announced 'long-term plans for constitutional amendments that would transfer to state governments and municipalities responsibilities in health, education, social services, housing, basic sanitation and irrigation' (ibid.). In summary, the clear objective of the government was to convert the country's fiscal deficit into surplus and therefore reduce its inflationary pressure.

On the monetary front, the plan introduced an ingenious system of indexation that was temporarily based on a virtual currency, the URV—Unidade Real de Valor. This new index was pegged on a one-to-one basis to the US dollar and had its Cruzeiros Reais' quotation in the local currency (Cruzeiro Real) changed daily according to inflation. 'Official prices, contracts, and taxes were denominated in URV, and the government encouraged its use on a voluntary basis by private economic agents. Gradually, an increasing number of prices were set in URVs although transaction occurred in Cruzeiros Reais' (Amann and Baer 2000, p. 1806). In July 1994, nearly five months after the creation of this transition currency, the government converted all prices denominated in URV into a new currency called *Real*. The daily exchange rate between Cruzeiros Reais and URVs was predefined by the Central Bank according to a conversion table whose last entry was July 1, 1994, when 2,750.00 old Cruzeiros Reais were pre-set to correspond to 1 URV, which would equal to 1 *Real*, or 1 US dollar. This marked the end of the indexing system, and the *Real* was allowed, in principle, to float against the North American currency (ibid.).

The *Real Plan* was extremely successful from its outset, as the temporary indexing system seemed to have done the trick in curbing inflationary expectations. Price rises plummeted from a monthly rate of 50.7% in June 1994 to 0.96% in September (ibid., p. 1807), and in the following months, inflation fell steadily. In 1995, the general price index recorded an annual figure of 15% and, in 1998, inflation reached only 1.7%, without doubt a far cry from the staggering rate of 2,708% recorded in 1993 (Amann and Baer 2003, p. 1035). These positive results were warmly welcomed by the population and had a decisive impact on the political arena. In October 1994, nearly eleven months after the *Real Plan* was launched, Fernando H. Cardoso, the founding father of the economic plan, ran for president. The immediate success of the *Real* gave Cardoso the necessary popular support to be elected president in the first round of elections. With Cardoso's subsequent re-election in 1998, the country was to witness its most dynamic period of economic reforms, which lasted from 1994 to 2002.

Once inflation was brought down, the second half of the 1990s was marked by a relentless effort to keep it under control. Price stabilisation was believed to be a key element if the country wanted to join in a virtuous circle of new investments (either foreign or local), higher productivity and growth. However, the internal and external shocks Brazil was going to face in consequence of its newly implemented capital and trade liberalisation were soon to impose tremendous challenges to its economy. To make matters worse, the government encountered constant opposition to some of its most politically sensitive measures, particularly those calling for budget cuts.

The fiscal issue—Following the precepts of the World Bank and of the IMF, a central component of Cardoso's economic plan relied on the maintenance of a sound fiscal policy. 'Washington believes in fiscal discipline', as John Williamson briefly reminded us in his influential book on 'Latin American [economic] adjustment' (1990, p. 8).

The implementation of disciplinary fiscal measures, however, turned out to be far more difficult than initially expected. The economic team not only failed to curb the 'rise in expenditure at every level of government' but proved unable to pass a crucial money-saving reform of the civil service pension system. While expenditures in the public sector payroll nearly doubled between 1993 and 1998, the deficit in the social security system 'rose from 4.9% of GDP in 1994 to 6% in 1998' (Amann and Baer 2000, p. 1809). To make matters worse, the government also decided to launch a bailout programme to help the local banking sector, which was severely hit by the policy of high interest rates adopted by the government to curb inflation. This rise in interest rates spurred a significant surge in non-performing loans, which, as a consequence, produced a destabilising effect on the banking system as a whole.[44] This bailout programme, however, turned out to be particularly costly for the government, as in the first years after its launch, it had already drained an amount equivalent to 4% of the country's GDP (Cintra 2000, p. 59). Finally, there was a continuous reluctance on the part of the congress to approve any measure put forward by the government that would 'restrict the fiscal autonomy of the states and municipalities or would have adversely affected conditions of employment in the public sector' (Amann and Baer 2000, p. 1811).

The exchange rate anchor—As the fiscal measures proposed by the economic team proved too politically sensitive to be quickly and fully implemented, the Brazilian government decided to give greater emphasis to the monetary side of the economic package. The main anti-inflation mechanism that came to be adopted by the government (and which lasted for the first four years of the *Real Plan*) was based on the maintenance of an overvalued exchange rate.[45] Despite strong criticism, the use of this 'exchange rate anchor' was regarded by some policy makers at that time as a particularly efficient instrument to prevent inflationary expectations, increase competition (mainly due to the consequent inflow of imports) and ultimately exert downward pressure on the domestic price of tradable goods.[46]

Although the maintenance of an overvalued exchange rate effectively held down inflation, the costs associated with this policy were soon to show harmful side effects. The first and most obvious was the anti-export bias that the policy caused to local producers. Although a certain deterioration of the trade balance was a predictable outcome, the complete shift from surplus to deficit emitted signs of a worrying trend. While the decennium prior to the implementation of the exchange rate anchor witnessed an average annual surplus of US$12.68bn, the first four years of the *Real Plan* recorded an average trade deficit of US$5.82bn. For the local business community, this quick change of scenario marked by a drastic inflow of imports brought about a double challenge. At the same time that the domestic productive sector was still recovering from the decade-long crisis of the 1980s and the short recession period of the early 1990s triggered by the ill-fated *Collor Plan*, this domestic sector was now forced to face the consequences of an exchange rate policy that deliberately favoured imports and (due to its underlying policy of high interest rates) restrained consumption.

The policy of high interest rates that was central to keep the 'exchange rate anchor' moved to even more worrying levels when the country began to suffer the monetary pressure caused by the Asian (1997) and Russian (1998) crises. Foreign investors, fearful of the 'directions of the Brazilian economy', started to orchestrate a withdrawal of their portfolio investments in the country. This capital flight produced a critical destabilizing effect in the economy. Since the launch of the *Real Plan*, a considerable amount of the country's trade deficit had been financed by foreign capital, particularly mid- and short-term portfolio investments. In addition, the decision of the government to maintain an anti-inflation policy based on high interest rates produced a considerable deterioration of the country's fiscal account. Within only two years, Brazil's public debt jumped from 34.4% of GDP in 1997 to 49.4% of GDP in 1999. As foreign investors grew wary of the country's ability to meet its contracts (in the bond market, the risk index for Brazilian papers tripled immediately after the Asian crisis), the local currency became a target of speculative attacks. The Brazilian economy, now subordinated to the volatility of the financial market, was forced to enter a vicious circle if it wanted to keep its exchange rate anchor. '[T]o maintain the exchange rate and to finance its deficit it had to borrow at a rising interest rate, which in turn worsened the fiscal situation and, by extension further undermined investor confidence' (Amann and Baer 2000, p. 1811).

Although the exchange rate mechanism was showing clear signs of not being sustainable, the government decided not to abandon the currency-peg mechanism. There was a strong concern in the economic team that were the exchange rate anchor to be lifted, the *Real* would devaluate considerably and produce an inflationary spike. This was not a desirable prospect, particularly during the year 1998, when elections were in progress and the president himself was running for re-election.

The decision of the Brazilian government to keep the exchange rate anchor during a period in which the international capital market was under intense pressure due to the Asian and Russian crises forced the economic team to seek alternative solutions to counterbalance the continuous degradation of Brazil's current account. This problem was partially solved by the intensification of the national privatisation programme. It was exactly during this period, from 1997 to 1999, when the country was most severely hit by the Asian and Russian crises that the government carried out the bulk of its privatisation programme. In value terms, this turned out to be the largest privatisation programme ever carried out by a developing economy, and between 1997 and 1999, it accounted for almost US$63bn in proceeds. The decision of the Cardoso government to lift all barriers to the participation of foreign capital in the acquisition of state-owned enterprises was decisive to attract the attention of foreign investors. Between 1994 and 2002, almost 53% of the privatisation proceeds came from foreign investors, a figure that undeniably contributed to the impressive rise of foreign direct investments. Between 1997 and 1999 only, the amount of FDI to Brazil accounted for US$78.4bn.

Not only the public sector endured major changes with the privatisation of several of the largest Brazilian enterprises; the private sector also witnessed an equally revolutionary process. The second half of the 1990s was marked, as will be shown in the following chapter, by an impressive surge in mergers and acquisitions which in their great majority also counted on the participation of foreign capital. Across all its most dynamic industrial sectors, from auto parts to telecom equipment manufacturing, the country witnessed an increasing internationalisation of its industrial capacity. Apparently, despite the fact that the economy had finally reached stability, the government's anti-inflation macroeconomic policy had in some aspects proved harmful for the local companies. This resulted particularly from forcing these companies to adjust to a new market environment which was not only marked by growing foreign competition but was also dictated by greater freedom of capital flows, a combination of capital and trade liberalisation that tended to favour foreign investors.

THE REACTION FROM THE BUSINESS COMMUNITY

After more than a decade since the first campaign launched by FIESP and part of the business community in Brazil for the reduction of the role of the state in the economy and for the liberalisation of the local market, the initial consequences of these reforms can now be examined. The reforms carried out in Brazil in the 1990s were definitely not small in scale, and several of the demands put forward by the entrepreneurial class in Brazil were actually implemented by the government. As mentioned earlier in this chapter, the reforms were comprehensive enough to deal with every aspect of the Brazilian economy: import barriers were reduced, incentives and subsides to local production were abolished, state monopolies were broken, large state-owned enterprises were privatised, barriers against foreign investments were lifted and the country's capital market was liberalised. In summary, the state dedicated a considerable part of the 1990s working on the organisation of its withdrawal from core producing activities and on the construction of a regulatory framework to monitor the activities of the newly privatised sectors. In tune with the demands of the business community, the reforms implemented by the government in the late 1980s and early 1990s really constituted a decisive step away from the state-led and inward-looking model of development and represented a move toward the restoration of a more open market environment.

Although these changes were in accordance with the demands of an influential part of the business community, the first outcomes of Brazil's economic liberalisation revealed, however, a completely different reality to many of the local companies. Brazilian companies in the mid-1990s were forced to go through a complete restructuring process, and the country's long-established arrangement between domestic and multinational corporations was quickly dismantled. The multinational corporations, which in the years of state intervention in the economy retained practically a fixed share of the Brazilian market, witnessed with the opening up of the economy a sudden expansion of their businesses. The local companies, on the other hand, had to deal with the double challenge of having to adjust themselves to operate under strict monetary policies and of having to cope with the fierce and growing competition of their foreign counterparts.

[With regard to the Brazilian economic reforms in 1990s] a profound economic restructuring in the country was observed with the change of the fundamentals of the industrial capitalism inherited from the previous development policies. The tripod model deepened during the military government, and which was characterised by a certain equilibrium between the *state*, the *local private* and the *foreign sectors*, was drastically changed by the withdrawal of the entrepreneurial-state, by the privatisations, by the growing influence of the transnational corporations and also by the drastic reduction of the role taken by domestic firms. The denationalisation of the economy reached unprecedented levels creating a new economic order marked by the predominance of international capital. In addition, the absolute priority to reach economic stability, fiscal austerity and the equilibrium of the public accounts resulted in the poor performance of the economy. [Brazil's economic performance] oscillated between periods of stagnation and sporadic surges of growth, which were reverted every time that the external conditions became adverse. Low growth rates, reduction of industrial output, rise in unemployment and expansion of the informal sector, high interest rates and shortage of credit, and the fall of exports and rise in imports kept domestic production under particularly rigid boundaries, which resulted in a large number of bankruptcies, mergers and ownership restructuring.

(Diniz and Boschi 2004, p. 87, translated
from Portuguese by the author)

In fact, the domestic companies were so strongly hit by the reforms that the Brazilian industrial class was forced to review its initial positive projections about the opening up of the economy. Despite the fact that this discontent was never strong enough to halt or even considerably slow the opening-up process of the economy, it contributed to redefining the strategies for the Brazilian companies and to questioning the way the reforms were being conducted by the government.

In the mid-1990s, Mr Mário Amato, the president of the National Confederation of Industries (CNI), former president of FIESP and a business leader who used to be one of the most enthusiastic supporters of the opening up of the Brazilian economy, drew attention to what he considered the 'indiscriminate way' the reforms were being carried out and to the 'harmful consequences' that it could eventually bring.

> The number of import licenses has grown in geometric proportions and without proper control. This is an issue that worries the Brazilian entrepreneurs, who are not afraid of competition, but are aware that the indiscriminate inflow of foreign products can be a threat to their companies (. . .)
>
> (Mário Amato in Folha de São Paulo, 1994,
> translated from Portuguese by the author)

This change of perception among those who were at the forefront of the movement for the opening up of the economy helped to raise the first warning signs about the real chances of the local industrial sector to compete in a more open environment. It became evident to the local companies that without a conscious effort to quickly bridge the gap that separated them from their foreign counterparts, the economic reforms could have a disastrous result. One issue is, however, worthy of notice. Although this shift toward greater integration of Brazil into the world economy exposed the national industry to a degree of competition that had never been experienced before and threw these same companies into uneven conditions of competition, the failure of the local companies to compete in a more open environment was considered by the Brazilian business community a result of its own domestic limitations. Very little was blamed, for instance, on the worldwide restructuring process that the large global companies were going through at exactly the same time or on the impact that the impressive surge of cross-border mergers and acquisitions was having on the reformulation of the global value chains. For the Brazilian business community, the failure of the local companies was the result of a set of local constraints, which according to them was responsible for reducing the competitiveness of the Brazilian industrial production. This view, which became known in the mid-1990s as 'Custo Brasil', was used by some industrialists in Brazil to condemn the state for a myriad of obstacles that were not found in other countries.

'CUSTO BRASIL'—BRAZIL COST

Although it is expected that industrial production in any country will always lead into costs, what Brazilian industrialists claimed was that these operating costs tended to be higher in Brazil than in other countries. It was exactly this higher overhead allegedly paid by the Brazilian companies for having to produce and do business in Brazil that was at the core of their complaints and which characterised the so-called Custo Brasil. For the Brazilian business community, the opening up of the economy had already forced the local companies to adjust themselves and fully restructure their activities. It was up to the state, then, to do its part and tackle the structural problems that were hampering the competitiveness of the local companies.[47]

Brazilian entrepreneurs claimed that once these problems were tackled, the local companies would be able to compete on more even terms with their foreign counterparts. In short, for the local business community, the state was once again the main reason behind Brazil's lack of competitiveness. Among the main complaints were the country's outdated transport infrastructure, inadequate tax system, restrictive monetary policy and high labour costs. As the local companies remained committed to the opening up of the economy, one of the main concerns of the Brazilian business community was finding ways to reduce those costs.

Transport Infrastructure

Brazil's deficient transport infrastructure was a recurrent example given by the Brazilian entrepreneurial class about the excessive costs of doing business in Brazil. Local export-oriented companies were in a disadvantageous position not only because the transport system was predominately based on roads instead of cheaper means of transportation such as railways and waterways but also due to the fact that Brazil's transport network had long exceeded its capacity and was in poor condition. Lack of adequate investment in the sector was also a common problem. While in '1975 investments in transport infrastructure represented 1.76% of the GDP', in 1990, this figure saw a vertiginous drop to '0.19% of the GDP' (Biondi et al. 1997, p. 125).

Brazil's inefficient freight system added extra costs to a country that was already plagued by long transport distances. In the export-oriented agribusiness sector, where the country's largest farms are concentrated in a region 1.500km away from the coast, the overhead paid by Brazilian producers was even higher. Whereas in the US, Brazil's main competitor in grain production (particularly soyabeans and corn), freight costs from the plantation areas to the port were around US$12 or US$20 per ton, in Brazil this same figure had an average cost of US$70 (ibid., p. 114). The amount lost every year by Brazil due to bad conservation of the railway system and the use of roads as the predominant means of cargo transport was estimated at US$3bn according to studies done by the World Bank (Oliveira 2000, p. 149). In the mid-1990s, 74% of Brazil's grain export production was transported by trucks, 25% by train and only 1% through waterways. In the US,

Brazil's greatest competitor in the sector, these figures were, respectively, 16%, 25% and 61% (Biondi et al. 1997, p. 122). To make matters even worse, the National Department of Roads estimated that no fewer than 25.6% of all Brazilian roads were in bad or poor condition. This implied 58% more fuel used, 38% extra operational costs and delays of almost 100% of the regular travel time (ibid., p. 126).

In the Brazilian port system, the situation was equally precarious. Mahrukh Doctor (2002, p. 83) provides us with a concise and bleak picture of the sector. Her work on the attitudes and actions of the Brazilian business community during the modernisation process of the ports described that the Brazilian dock system was 'plagued by crumbling equipment and infrastructure, out-dated technology, the government's arbitrary and precarious system of taxation, entangled port bureaucracy, inefficient customs procedures, as well as an unproductive labour regime'. The negative implications of this record of neglect were evident and considered too costly by the local companies. According to a study by the National Confederation of Industries, the average cost of clearing a container in the international market was between US$160 and US$240. In Brazil, this cost was around US$300 in Porto do Recife and US$550 in Rio de Janeiro. With regard to clearing time, while in Chile, Germany and the United States they handled twenty-two, twenty-four and thirty containers per hour, in the biggest Brazilian ports, the average clearing time was around thirteen or fourteen containers per hour (Oliveira 2000, p. 150).

Tax System

For the Brazilian National Confederation of Industries (CNI), the country's allegedly heavy taxation throughout the entire production chain was the main hindrance obstructing the competitiveness of the local companies. In their view, the Brazilian tax system was responsible for three major inconsistencies: it was considered excessively high when compared to other developing export economies, it inhibited production and, in most cases, despite its alleged high value, it did not translate into expected benefits or equivalent improvements in infrastructure.[48] This confederation of industries, which counted on the support of Brazil's main industrialists, was fierce in its critique of the country's tax burden and equally severe when setting out the solution to solve what it considered one of the main reasons Brazilian companies were lagging behind in international trade.

The large quantity of overlapping taxes, the burden of indirect taxation, the complexity of the system and the taxation of exports and investments are elements of our tax system that we do not find parallel in other countries that are competing with Brazil for investments and market. The basic principles that should guide the changes of the tax system are known. They include a better distribution of the tax burden through the *elimination of excessive taxes on the industrial sector*, the *complete tax exemption of exports and investments* (. . .) and the commitment to the stability of tax legislation.

(CNI 1996, p. 3, translated from Portuguese by the author, emphasis added)

Brazil's tax burden had a substantial rise in the first half of the 1990s: it moved from a historical average of 25% of GDP to a record high of 30% in 1994.[49] This tax rise, which coincided with a period when the government seemed to have lost control of its public accounts, was fundamental in setting off alarm bells among business leaders in the country. Brazilian industrialists were particularly concerned about the state's overuse of taxes to compensate for any inefficient use or reckless spending of public money. Another target of complaints from the part of the business community was the structure of the Brazilian tax system, which according to them overcharged industrial production as opposed to charging income and assets or simply targeting end goods or services. Their main concern was the taxation of exports, which in their view, due to the cascading effect of Brazil's tax system, was responsible for considerably reducing the competitiveness of local products.

Brazil charged taxes over every step of the production process, which added considerable costs to the end value of a product. The longer the supply chain, the greater the number of accumulated taxes. An example of this chain of overlapping taxes was the incidence of PIS (Programa de Integração Social) and Cofins (Contribuição para o Financiamento da Seguridade Social), two distinct compulsory tariffs that together added an extra cost of 2.65% to each step of the production process (Folha de São Paulo 1996). In 1990, the burden of indirect taxes on Brazilian industrialised exports was an average of 11.7% according to a study by the World Bank. In more developed economies as well as in those developing countries that were competing with Brazil, this incidence of indirect taxation was, in most of the cases, just slightly over 0% (Villela and Suzigan 1996, p. 47). In the case of steel, for instance, one of Brazil's main exports, a study carried out by the Brazilian Steel Institute (IBS) revealed that the tax burden made up to 26.9% of the end value; in Japanese exports, this figure was 15% and in Korea, 10% (ibid.).

Monetary Policy

Although there was a general consensus in the business community about the success and efficiency of the *Real Plan* in bringing down inflation, the same cannot be said about the perception of this same group of the monetary policy that was adopted by the government in the years that followed the launch of the economic plan. The main complaint by business leaders was the strong reliance of the *Real Plan* on an exchange rate anchor, which, although effective in curbing inflation, also led to a number of negative implications for the local companies. The impressive surge in real interest rate in the first two years of the *Real Plan* (24.4% in 1994 and 33.1% in 1995),[50] apart from allowing the local currency to appreciate, had the devastating effect of restricting domestic consumption, inhibiting production and making credit comparatively more expensive for the local companies. The issue raised strong discontentment from the local business community and received top priority in the pro-reform manifesto sent to the federal government by the CNI in mid-1996.

> Brazilian companies, especially the smaller ones, are being harmed by the asymmetry of finance when compared to their foreign competitors. The shortage of credit and its extremely high cost put the Brazilian products at disadvantage when compared to foreign products (. . .).
>
> (CNI 1996, p. 2, translated from Portuguese by the author)

For most critics, the rigid monetary policy which followed the launch of the *Real* was in part a result of the government's failure to tackle what they considered a more politically sensitive problem: the implementation of a comprehensive set of disciplinary fiscal measures. For these critics, the government should not have made the country's macroeconomic stability so strongly dependent on monetary measures but should have focused its efforts on tackling the country's pressing problem of fiscal discipline. In their view, far more effective than controlling inflationary pressures by means of an orthodox monetary policy of high interest rates would have been cutting down on public expenditure and implementing a deep reform in both the country's tax and social security systems.

> The Real Plan is a dividing line in the country's recent history whose success in tackling inflation comes from its ingenious conception and careful implementation. The same cannot be said about the construction of its macroeconomic structure. The excessive reliance on the exchange-rate anchor has imposed high costs to the normal operation of the economy, which have turned into losses in production and employment and are threatening the survival of several companies in the productive sector. (. . .) Deeper and more definitive adjustments should be made to replace the exchange rate and the interest rate as anchors of the economic stabilisation.
>
> (CNI 1996, pp. 1–2, translated from Portuguese by the author)

The long-awaited alleviation of the monetary policy that Brazil aimed to conduct in 1996 proved to be short lived. The external shocks that came as a result of the Asian and Russian crises in 1997 and 1998 added pressure on the country's already fragile mechanisms of economic stabilisation. In the face of a strong speculative attack against the local currency, Brazil's Central Bank decided to tighten once again its monetary policy and raise the country's basic interest rates. The immediate consequence of this measure was the formation of a spiral of higher debt, greater uncertainty and growing interest rates. Brazil's annual interest rates that amounted to 15% in September 1998 jumped to 29% in December, 37% in January and 42% in March 1999.[51] In an attempt to preserve the exchange rate anchor (the alleged key pillar of the *Real* economic stabilisation plan), the government once again forced the Brazilian companies to deal with a scenario in which access to capital became even scarcer and domestic consumption more restrained.

By the end of the second half of the 1990s, it was already clear to the business community that the productive sector was paying a high price for the maintenance of a monetary policy that proved insufficient to handle not only Brazil's internal inflationary pressures but also the speculative attacks that had viciously hit the local currency in 1997 and 1998. The harmful side effect of this monetary policy can be roughly measured by the impact it had on a few selected macroeconomic variables: (a) Brazil's public debt nearly doubled from 28.5% of GDP in 1994 to 49.9% in 1999; (b) international reserves plummeted from US$60.11bn in 1997 to US$30.01bn in 2000; (c) trade deficit witnessed an accumulated record low of −24.7bn USD between 1995 and 1999; and (d) the country's current account registered an equally impressive record low of −131.1bn USD in the same period.[52] In the face of such an unprecedented deterioration of the public account figures, the two pillars of Brazil's economic stabilisation, the exchange rate anchor and its inherent high interest rates, became targets of criticism by the business community. Despite the achievements of the long-awaited economic stabilisation, local companies claimed to have their operations harmed in the late 1990s by a monetary policy that put them at a clear disadvantage to their foreign competitors.

Labour Cost

Another item that raised protests from industrialists and business leaders in Brazil was related to the alleged high cost of the local labour force. The focus of complaints was not on the workers' earnings *per se* but on what they considered the large amount of labour obligations that their companies were forced to pay on top of the basic payroll. In their view, these labour obligations added costs to production, which, although high in volume, were not accounted for properly in studies of competitiveness.

Complaints over these extra labour costs gained academic support when in the mid-1990s a study by José Pastore from the economics department of the University of São Paulo claimed that labour obligations in Brazil could in fact reach a value higher than the salary itself and make 102% of the original wage (Pastore 1994). This figure was in strong contrast with the more developed economies, where, according to the author, labour obligations added an average value of just 35 to 40% to the base wage (Pastore 1995,

p. 19).[53] By the author's calculations, Brazil's labour obligations were particularly inflated by monthly expenditures on social security (20% on top of
the original wage), on the *Fundo de Garantia por Tempo de Serviço* (*FGTS*),
which constitutes a kind of social security programme based on a guarantee
fund proportional to the time on professional duty (8%) and on additional
expenses related to holidays, week-breaks and a compulsory Christmas
bonus (formally known in Brazil as the thirteenth wage), which together
added an extra cost of 47.3% to the original wage (ibid., p. 135). By pointing out the different types of benefits and obligations that a formal worker
was entitled to receive in Brazil, the study cast doubts about the effectiveness
of these labour incentives and urged the reduction of what it considered as an
excessive burden on the productive sector. In the author's view, a reduction of
these labour obligations was decisive in making the Brazilian economy more
competitive and more in tune with what was practiced in other countries.

The alleged high cost of the Brazilian work force, at least with regard to
labour obligations, was not the only source of complaint from the Brazilian
business community. Brazil's labour legislation was also criticised for being
too interventionist. In their view, for the local companies to be able to survive
in a new scenario of fierce international competition, Brazil's labour regulations needed to become more flexible and allow greater autonomy of negotiations between employers and employees. When compared to other developing
economies, the Brazilian labour legislation was regarded as rigid, outdated
and ill prepared to meet the challenges of a more liberal and global economy.

> The more regulated are the [labour relations] in a country, the greater
> are the difficulties in generating jobs in the current days where com-
> petition requires agility and economic globalisation demands qual-
> ity. Countries that have not implemented mechanisms to make their
> labour laws more flexible ended up facing high rates of unemployment.
> In Europe, there are cases of more than 20% unemployment (Spain),
> whereas in the United States this rate is 6%; Japan, 2%; Korea, 2%;
> Taiwan, 1.5%; and Hong Kong, 1%. (. . .) In Brazil the situation is all
> or nothing. We make contracts either by paying all the labour obliga-
> tions, or without paying a single one—in the informal sector. Our leg-
> islation does not specify any form of contract with a minimum amount
> of labour obligations, even in a period where the informal market is
> booming, unemployment is growing and companies need to become
> more flexible to compete. (. . . .) The legal framework in Brazil continues
> to be highly regulated.
>
> (Pastore 1995, p. 20, translated
> from Portuguese by the author)

Under the argument that excessive legislation was responsible for bringing about illegality, informality and unemployment to the labour market,
proponents of more flexible labour regulations believed that once a less

interventionist regulatory model was implemented, labour relations would become more dynamic and better in tune with the demands of a more open and competitive economy. The reduction of the burden imposed by rigid labour regulations would make local companies more competitive and also bring positive implications to employment. In other words, what analysts argued was that a more flexible labour legislation, and its implicit cut of long-established rights, would produce positive results not only for the companies but also for the workers. In this aspect, the reduction of labour costs would be providential to cutting production costs, allowing greater investments and ultimately creating new jobs.

There was fierce opposition to those claims. Critics pointed out that the excessive emphasis on the alleged large amount of labour obligations tended to hide a reality that was frequently ignored—that is, the low wages that were still being paid to the local workers. While in Brazil, a worker earned on average US$2,70 per hour, in Japan, in the US and in Germany, a worker received, respectively, US$16, US$17 and US$24 per hour (Süssekind 1997). As a consequence, even if the claims about the high amount of labour obligations in Brazil were correct, the country's low wages more than compensated for the extra costs that labour obligations could possibly bring, a fact that was, however, conveniently omitted by those who argued against the excessive amount of labour obligations.

With regard to the pressure for the introduction of a more flexible labour legislation, opponents of this view were particularly concerned about the loss that such change could bring to social welfare in the long term. Although all the positive arguments about closer negotiations between employers and employees sounded tempting at a first glance, these critics called attention to the visible differences between the two negotiating parts. They included the low bargaining power of the workers in general, the large gap between jobs in demand and those that were in fact being created and the growing weakening of the labour unions. In the face of such disparities, it was a consensus among critics that the country's labour legislation could not be granted a secondary role. In those cases where critics agreed that reforms were needed, they made it clear that any change for more flexible labour relations could not be put forward without a complete understanding of the advantages and disadvantages of the existing labour legislation (Souto Maior 1995).

The lobby for the reduction of labour obligations was backed by the business community, which was also very successful in applying its influence over the media and even large sectors of the federal government. For most business leaders, the definition of more flexible labour legislation was a key item of the structural reforms the country had to go through. In view of the gains such changes were expected to bring for their companies, scarce attention was given to whether allegations about the high cost of the labour force were in fact legitimate. The claims behind Brazil's high labour costs were especially convenient to the business community and allowed them to bargain for more cost-effective labour relations.

Finally, in addition to all complaints that were made about Brazil's monetary policy, tax system, lack of infrastructure and outdated labour legislation, a few other issues were also often claimed by the local business community as responsible for Brazil's lack of competitiveness. Despite their apparent marginal relevance to the debate on 'Brazil cost', three of these issues at least are worthy of attention: Brazil's deficient education and health systems and the dramatic escalation of urban violence. Each of them posed a major problem to the country. Brazil's functional illiteracy in 1992 comprised 36.9% of the population over 25 years old,[54] and data related to years of schooling placed the country far behind its neighbouring Latin American economies. According to data from the United Nations, the average number of years of schooling in Brazil was only 3.9 years, which left the country at a clear disadvantage to Argentina (8.7 years), Chile (7.5), Uruguay (7.8), Venezuela (6.3), Peru (6.4), Colombia (5.7) and Bolivia (4.0) (Paes de Barros, Pinto de Mendonça and Shope 1993).[55] To make matters even worse, the negative consequences of Brazil's poor schooling records became more pronounced with the opening up of the economy. As expected, Brazil's long history of lack of investment in education hindered the introduction of new technologies, made local companies less efficient and, in most cases, restricted production to low-value-added goods. On the education front, Brazil has given signs of having a long way to go before catching up with its main competitors. An equally gloomy picture can also be drawn with regard to Brazil's long-neglected health system. For some Brazilian business leaders, the poor conditions of Brazil's public health forced their companies to pay costs that in other economies were normally absorbed by the state. With the public budget being too tight to provide adequate services for the entire population, corporate and individual users were under growing pressure to spend on complementary health plans. Finally, there is the pressing issue of urban violence, the astonishing rise of which in the 1990s forced companies and individuals in Brazil to spend massively on private security. According to data from the Brazilian Institute of Geography and Statistics, in two decades only, between 1980 and 2000, the homicide rate of the male population in Brazil jumped from 21.2 to 49.7 deaths per 100 thousand inhabitants (IBGE, 2004).

CONCLUSIONS

The Brazilian business community was a key element in the economic reforms the country went through in the 1990s. Although the decision to open up the economy was greeted with reluctance by several business leaders, the pressure for reforms gained, from the beginning of the last decade, growing and unexpected support from leading groups of the Brazilian business community. The pro-reform campaign launched by two of Brazil's largest and most powerful confederations of industries (the FIESP and the CNI) is the most remarkable example of this change of attitude by the business community in favour of a more open economy. This shift was, in fact, a milestone in the way business was carried out in Brazil, as the reforms meant the end of a long period of state intervention and the withdrawal of the state from key sectors of Brazilian industry.

The sharp deterioration of the Brazilian economy in the 1980s and the series of disastrous attempts by the government to bring back economic stability turned the business community into fierce critics of the Brazilian state and the state-led model of development. In contrast to the country's previous history of economic development, the business class began to believe that Brazilian economic growth could only be restored with the implementation of large-scale reforms. The reduction of the role of the state, the opening up of the economy and the greater integration of the country into the world economy were thus seen as key measures to modernise the economy. One aspect is worthy of note: the pressure for reforms was not only set by domestic economic issues, the reforms were also in tune with the neo-liberal wave that swept the Latin American economies in the early 1990s.

Despite this, the support of the Brazilian business community in the opening up of the economy revealed an intriguing behaviour: the decision of the local companies to abandon the protectionist economy in which they had been created to embark on a market environment ruled by global competition. Although the business community claimed to have strong justifications for seeking reforms, the implications of such changes were still unknown. There are real doubts about whether the Brazilian companies were fully aware of the challenges they were going to face or, at least, whether they were too optimistic about their chances of surviving in a more global economy.

Although the prospects of modernisation sounded promising to the local companies, very little attention was given to their lack of competitiveness. Without an appropriate programme guiding local companies to integrate themselves into the world economy in a more cautious way, the Brazilian business community was mostly left to the rules of the market. The challenges confronted by the Brazilian companies were huge. First, after decades operating in a highly protectionist environment, the local companies were very poorly prepared to compete with the large global companies. Second were the changes in the world economy in the 1990s, which witnessed a massive boom of mergers and acquisitions as well as an impressive concentration of business among leading firms and their closer ties with their first- and second-tier suppliers. The so-called big business revolution brought about the complete reshuffle of the global supply chains of practically all producing sectors and which, in the case of Brazil, severely hit local companies such as the auto-parts sector. Third came the economic crises of Mexico, Russia and East Asian countries, which led to the brink of collapse other developing economies that had, like Brazil, gone through similar processes of capital market liberalisation. Fourth was the adverse scenario of the Brazilian economy in the 1990s, primarily due to problems of political instability (impeachment of president Collor) and later due particularly to the implementation of a restrictive monetary policy based on an exchange rate anchor and on one of the world's highest interest rates. And finally came the government's lack of attention towards the development of any kind of microeconomic policies.

The years following the economic reforms were marked by tremendous changes in Brazilian big business. Several sectors of the economy went through intense restructuring processes, and a substantial number of large, traditional local companies, after adjusting their operations to the new market-oriented environment, were finally forced to close down. The number of mergers and acquisitions, particularly of those involving foreign capital, skyrocketed to an unprecedented level; vertically integrated systems across several industrial sectors were almost completely dismantled, and multinational corporations won, for the first time, the lion's share of the 'top 500 companies' in Brazil (see Part IV of this volume). Barriers against foreign capital were lifted, and Brazilian firms were abruptly exposed to a global and highly competitive market environment.

Despite all the problems confronted by local companies, the Brazilian business community remained committed to the neo-liberal agenda. The country's shift to a more open economy was never actually put in check. On the contrary, in response to the problems brought about by the economic reforms, the domestic companies decided to blame once again the state for their hardship and lack of competitiveness. The decision by the business community to concentrate its efforts on combating what they called Brazil Cost reinforced in reality their support for the economic reforms. Their belief was that once the obstacles related to the Brazil Cost were solved, Brazilian companies would finally be in position to compete. Therefore the main problem was not the reforms per se but the fact that they were incomplete. The alleged contribution of the state to the high costs of production in Brazil was taken by business leaders as an indication that the presence of the state in the economy was still harmful.

For the Brazilian business community, the country's competitive integration into the world economy was chiefly based on a few key policies: reaching economic stability, liberating the economy from the intervention of the state and ensuring competition through the reduction of trade barriers. Strangely enough, the sole concern with neo-liberal orthodoxy left little room for business leaders to focus on what should probably have been the most crucial strategy, empowering local companies to compete with their foreign counterparts.

NOTES

1. Brazil's long-standing history of trade surpluses was drastically curtailed in the second half of the 1990s as a consequence of a temporary overvaluation of the local currency that came in tandem with several measures to lift tariff and non-tariff barriers against imports. This scenario was finally reversed with the devaluation of the local currency, the *Real*, in 1999. More details concerning this issue can be found in the following sections of this chapter.

2. The claim that recent reforms in Brazil were carried out at a fast pace is not a consensus among Brazilian scholars. Armando Castelar Pinheiro, Regis Bonelli and Ben Ross Schneider in their work on the Brazilian economic reforms described the country's liberalisation process as 'gradual' and 'incomplete' (Pinheiro, Castelar, Bonelli and Schneider 2004). However, the impressive changes that several sectors of the Brazilian economy underwent in the time span of only half a decade, as will be shown in the following chapter, suggest just the opposite, particularly by the fact that the liberalisation process in Brazil was carried out in a way that did not provide the necessary conditions for the local companies to restructure themselves and compete with their foreign counterparts. Finally, if we compare the Brazilian experience of market reforms with the transition process of other economies, most notably the Chinese one, the authors' claim that Brazil adopted a 'gradual' reform programme becomes even more arguable.

3. Such a polarised scenario, which is extremely simplistic in terms of analysis as well as of policy making, permeates, however, the entire discussion in the document.

4. Needless to say, this specific emphasis on the benefits of portfolio capital is nowadays highly debatable, particularly in the light of the adverse effect that this type of highly volatile capital had in the financial crisis of Mexico (1994), Southeast Asia (1997), Russia (1998) and Argentina (2001). Motivated by the prospect of quick access to foreign capital, FIESP clearly overlooked the risks and negative implications associated with the liberalisation of capital in less developed and poorly regulated capital markets, as in the case of Brazil and many other developing economies.

5. While GDP growth from 1971 to 1973 registered an annual average of 12.41%, the same period in the 1980s registered a negative growth of −2.11%.

6. A brief comment made by Delfim Netto, a former finance minister of Brazil, illustrates very well the scenario of chaos that emerged in the economy: 'Brazil is going through a singular moment of its history: there is no government, everything is falling apart' (Veja 1988, translated from Portuguese by the author).

7. Data from IPEA—Instituto de Pesquisa Econômica Aplicada (www.ipea.gov.br) and FIPE—Fundação Instituto de Pesquisas Econômicas (www.fipe.org.br).

8. Two sound indicators of the deterioration of the investment power of the state can be taken, for instance, from the participation of the federal government in gross capital formation as well as from government savings. Both indicators show depressing figures. The participation of the federal government in gross capital formation was cut by half, with figures falling from the annual average of 4.11% of GDP between 1970 and 1973 to 1.99% between 1983 and 1985. In the same period, federal government savings dropped from 6.54% to 0.29% (FIESP 1990, p. 24).

9. As mentioned by Mauricio Font (2003, p. 129), the '[p]oor economic performance in the 1980s led the country to question dirigisme and begin to search for alternatives'. In this scenario of continuous economic instability, 'liberalising reforms' sounded the 'death knell for the old development strategy'.

10. A detailed analysis of the measures and implications of each of these five economic stabilisation plans that were launched in the second half of the 1980s can be found in Moura (1993), Franco (1993), Longo (1993) and Baer (2001).

11. 'The problem of Brazil is the government' claimed in 1989 Mr Delfim Netto, a former Planning Minister of Brazil in the early 1970s (Veja 1989, translated from Portuguese by the author). This view was shared by leading members of the Brazilian business community. Mr Antônio Ermírio de Moraes, the owner of one of Brazil's largest private industrial conglomerates, was, for instance, particularly vocal in a campaign to reduce the role of the state in the economy. 'We [the private sector] need to absorb some functions of the government,

which wants to do everything but in reality has not been able to do anything' (ibid.).

12. In mid 1980, Mário Amato, while vice president of the Federation of the Industries of the State of São Paulo, drew a strong critique about the inefficiency of the public sector and its negative implications for the Brazilian economy. According to him, '[t]he greatest mistake of authoritarianism was the creation of the entrepreneurial state with its corollary of inefficiency and clientelism of the majority of the state enterprises, of which politicians always benefited themselves to get elected or to get a new public mandate. In Brazil the entrepreneurial state took the place of the private initiative. Its growth got to the point that it represents today 70% of the national economy, providing an insufficient number of job opportunities to meet the needs of the youths who are getting into the labour market every year. For these young workers, it is the private initiative that is making an effort to open the doors of production' (Eli Diniz 1993, p. 15), translated from Portuguese by the author).

13. Not only was the public sector the target of attacks from part of the Brazilian business community, this group was equally fierce to what they considered the country's 'old entrepreneurial elite', members of the private sector known for their deep 'corporatism', 'low productivity' and strong reliance on state assistance. For this business community, this so-called old elite should be replaced by or turned into a more 'creative', 'autonomous' and dynamic entrepreneurial class (Diniz 1993, p. 36).

14. A study released in the late 1980s and carried out by Revista Exame Melhores e Maiores, an annual publication about the biggest companies in Brazil, showed that local enterprises had a higher growth rate when compared to their foreign counterparts. According to this study, the great majority of the top 200 fastest-growing companies in Brazil between 1973 and 1987 were controlled by those of Brazilian capital and amounted to a total of 152 firms. Within this group of 152 companies, only 32 were state owned; the remaining 120 companies were local private enterprises (Revista Exame 1989). The study also confirmed the high degree of diversity that the local industry had reached. Not only restricted to the production of commodities, the fastest-growing companies in that period were particularly in the consumer, durable and capital goods sectors.

15. In an interview to *Revista Veja* in the late 1980s, for instance, Mr Roberto Campos, a leading economist in Brazil, openly criticised the inefficiency of the public sector in what he blamed for the collapse of the state. The private sector, on the other hand, was the object of only positive comments by the economist. 'It is a fact that the problem of Brazil is mainly in the public sector. The private sector is relatively capitalized. It is possible to observe that these companies have reacted well to the challenges they have faced. They have shown resilience in an unfavourable environment' (Veja 1989, translated from Portuguese by the author).

16. A clear example of the belief that the local private companies were in condition to compete in a more open market environment can be found, for instance, in the editorial letter of one of the main journals of economics published in Brazil, *Conjuntura Economica*, by Fundação Getúlio Vargas. This editorial, published in early 1990, drew attention to the changes the large global companies were going through and the need of the Brazilian companies to quickly adapt themselves to this new scenario. 'It is not an easy path. But it is the only one open in this new context of globalisation where even the most industrialised nations cannot escape. Huge competitive efforts have been made by companies, previously regarded as inaccessible, and which are now seen in a

daily and a worldwide effort of modernisation. Why would Brazil, or the Brazilian companies, be protected from this competition? More specifically, why would the Brazilian people keep financing the inefficiency of certain [industrial] sectors (and their extraordinary profits) if the majority of them have the basic necessary conditions to face international competition?' (Conjuntura Econômica 1990, p. 12, translated from Portuguese by the author).

17. Data from IPEA (www.ipea.gov.br). Please note that the works of Gary Fields (1980) and IPEA made use of two different methodologies to calculate Brazil's poverty line. While the first set the benchmark according to a given amount of local currency (NCr$2,1000), the second was based on the necessary amount to acquire a food basket with the minimum intake per capita of daily calories recommended by the Food and Agriculture Organization—FAO.

18. In the early 1990s, Helio Jaguaribe, one of Brazil's most notorious social scientists, drew a fierce comment that well illustrates the image of distrust that the government became associated with. 'The Brazilian state has been showing an increasing structural and functional deterioration. This deterioration reaches the three levels of the Federation: the central government, the sub-states and the municipalities, as well as its three powers: the legislative body, the executive body and the judiciary. The problem is in general related to a loss of the rationality, transparency, functionality, efficiency and the responsibilities from the part of the public bodies. (. . .) The corrosion of the State is notable, in its most acute way, in the sub-state governments and in the municipalities of the big urban areas. It is present in the out-of-control clientelism, in the negligent decision-making and in the most blatant self-gratification of the legislative in the three levels of the federation. Finally, it is also notable in the sluggishness and venality of the judicial system. The Brazilian state has become incompetent, insolvent and corrupt' (Jaguaribe 1990, pp. 11–2, translated from Portuguese by the author).

19. The Finance Minister of Brazil in 1989, Mr Maílson da Nóbrega, in a meeting with representatives of the biggest companies in Brazil, drew attention to the need to reduce the role of the state in the economy. According to him, the private sector was in better condition to take the lead in a transition to a more open and modern economy. 'The [development] model based on the strong intervention of the state has aged and it is outdated. (. . .) The [state] intervention that was needed [in the beginning of Brazil's industrialisation] is now in several sectors a hindrance to growth and to a faster solution to the [country's economic] crisis' (Revista Exame 1989, translated from Portuguese by the author).

20. As Celso Martone (2003, p. 139) mentioned in his assessment of the interrelation between the country's political and economic reforms, '[d]evelopments in Brazil have mirrored the general pattern of Latin America, although the country has been a latecomer in some important aspects. Democracy was re-established in 1985, in a situation of no access to foreign lending, high inflation, serious fiscal problems and, perhaps more significantly, pressing demands on the new government'.

21. The first direct presidential election in Brazil after two decades of military rule was held at the end of 1989, with public opinion polarised between two main candidates, Mr Luiz Inácio Lula da Silva from the Worker's Party—PT (Partido dos Trabalhadores) and Mr Fernando Collor de Mello from a small and newly created Party for National Reconstruction—PRN (Partido da Reconstrução Nacional). With regard to issues related to economic policies, both candidates were clearly identified by their distinct agendas. Whereas Lula 'offered a more statist solution', Collor was an enthusiastic preacher of the modernisation of the economy through strong reduction of the role of the state. Although the

final victory was given to Collor de Mello, such an endorsement from the voting ballots may not be directly interpreted as an indicator of a comprehensive popular support for neo-liberal reforms. As pointed out by Peter Kingstone in his work on 'Constitutional Reform and Macroeconomic Stability: Implications for Democratic Consolidation in Brazil', the election of Collor could have been the result of the conjunction of different factors. While 'business supporters' did opt for Collor 'as the only alternative to the leftist Lula da Silva', the low-income part of the population, 'who made the bulk of Collor's electorate', was in fact attracted by 'his right wing populism', which consisted of blatant 'attacks on corruption and privileges' (Kingstone, Constitutional reform and macroeconomic stability: implications for democratic consolidation in Brazil 1999, p. 138).

22. Reforms aiming to reduce the participation of the state in the Chilean economy were first implemented in 1973, immediately after the overthrow of Salvador Allende's socialist government. The response of Chilean private institutions to the two oil crises in the early and late seventies proved, however, to be remarkably similar to those given by the state-led Latin American economies. Equally overwhelmed by debt in the early eighties, the Chilean economy was also forced to go through major economic adjustments. For more on the privatisation of the Chilean productive sector in the 1970s and the country's economic crisis of the 1980s, see Wells (1986) and Yotopoulos (1989).

23. The highest inflation in Latin American history and 'one of the highest in the world history', (Sachs 1987, p. 279).

24. When compared to the other Latin American countries, only Brazil 'achieved a tripling of per-capita incomes between 1950 and 1985' (Balassa 1988, p. S274).

25. The twelve developing economies analysed by Bela Balassa in his work on 'The Lessons of East Asian Development' consisted of India; the four Eastern NICs of Hong Kong, Korea, Singapore and Taiwan; the Southeast Asian countries of Indonesia, Malaysia, Philippines and Thailand; and finally the Latin American countries of Argentina, Brazil and Mexico.

26. As described by Edmund Amann (2003, p. 110) in his work on the economic reforms in Brazil after the reinstatement of a civilian government, '[b]y the end of President Sarney's term in 1989, a consensus of opinion had emerged within the political and business elite that the policies that had been associated with import substitution industrialisation were no longer sustainable. In common with other Latin American economies—especially Chile, Mexico and Argentina—a strategic decision was taken to break with the inward-oriented legacy of the past and to pursue a much more open, liberal and foreign investor friendly strategy which had as its core the insertion of Brazil into the global economy'.

27. For a more detailed analysis of the implementation of this group of measures in Latin America, see Williamson (1990). This set of measures, termed by John Williamson the Washington Consensus, was later addressed as the first-generation reforms. In the mid-1990s, another set of ten measures was put forward to complement some of the gaps and adjust some of the flaws existent in the original list of reforms. This second generation of reforms had a broader concern of building and developing long-term obligations and can be briefly described as consisting of a 'legal/political reform', creation of 'regulatory institutions', adoption of 'anti-corruption measures', flexibilisation of the 'labour market', observance of the 'WTO agreements', adherence to international 'financial codes and standards', '"prudent" capital account opening', 'non-intermediate exchange rate regimes', creation of 'social safety nets' and, finally, reduction of poverty (Armendariz 2003).

28. 'I want to show the face of a new Brazil that we are going to build. A modern and efficient Brazil which is competitively integrated into the world economy' (Collor de Mello quoted in Revista Exame 1990, translated from Portuguese by the author).

29. For a more detailed account of the objectives and rationale of the Collor administration's economic plan, see Baer (2001), Brum (1999) and Longo (1993).

30. 'I am totally against any form of market reserve. (. . .) I can not realize a capitalist system where there is no competition, respect [to property rights] and efficiency' (Collor de Mello, quoted in Revista Exame 1990, translated from Portuguese by the author).

31. With the single exception of the other Mercosur countries (Argentina, Paraguay and Uruguay), which at that time were going through the negotiation rounds of the common tariffs for the commercial bloc.

32. The fast opening up of the Brazilian economy in the first year of the Collor administration, when drastic cuts of tariff and non-tariff barriers were implemented by the government, was in stark contrast with the ineffectual participation of Brazil in the GATT meeting that was held in that same year. Although Brazil had done its part to attend to the demands of the more developed economies with regard to trade, patents and investment rules, Brazil left this last meeting of the Uruguay Round without securing an adequate solution to some of its main problems, namely the high level of agricultural subsidies in Europe and the continuous taxation of tariffs from the more developed economies to Brazil's main exports. For a country that was making its way to a larger integration into the world economy, Brazil made one of the major mistakes on foreign trade, the one of making drastic concessions without first getting anything in return (Revista Exame 1990). This critique of the unilateral way that was adopted by Brazil to open up the economy was not, however, a consensus amount leading Brazilian economists. Maílson da Nóbrega, a former finance minister, was, for instance, a strong supporter of this unilateral opening of the economy to what he considered the most reasonable path the Brazilian government could have taken at that time (Nóbrega 2000).

33. After four decades of ISI and state intervention in the economy, the public sector had become impressively large in Brazil. '[I]n 1990 the largest SOEs accounted for 37.2% of the gross revenues, 63.6% of the net worth and 75.5% of the net fixed assets of a list of the 500 largest Brazilian nonfinancial companies'. In the mining sector, federal SOEs accounted for '88.6% of gross revenues, 85.7% of net worth and 83.3% of net fixed assets'. In the metallurgy sector, the state was responsible for 'half the revenues, two-thirds of the net worth and four-fifths of the sector's net fixed assets'. In chemicals, 'the 11 largest federal SOEs in the sector accounted for about one-fourth of revenues, two-fifths of the net worth and a third of the net fixed assets'. Finally, in the public utilities sector (power, water and sanitation), the state equally enjoyed a widespread presence. Twenty-five SOEs accounted for 'almost all sales, net worth and net fixed assets'. This configuration was equally similar in the telecommunications sector (Pinheiro and Giambiagi 1994, pp. 738–9).

34. In the late 1970s, a National De-bureaucratisation Programme for the privatisation of deeply indebted SOE was put into practice. By the end of 1989, the programme had only privatised thirty-eight companies and raised US$824 million in proceeds (Longo 1993).

35. This greater participation of foreign capital as a key part of the government plans to bring back economic growth in Brazil was defended by Collor even before he took office. As Collor made clear in a press conference weeks before

his inauguration as chief of the executive, the opening of the economy to foreign investment was not an issue of choice but of necessity: 'we can not rely anymore on empty words by saying that Brazil will find in its own local economy the necessary resources and capital that will give the basis for its growth' (Veja 1990, translated from Portuguese by the author).

36. Due to legal constraints, after four months of the Collor Plan, only 30.000 civil servants, less than 10% of the initial prediction, were actually laid off (Baer 2001, p. 196).

37. Despite its alleged commitment to introducing fiscal austerity, the Collor administration failed, however, to implement real cuts in public expenditure. The budget cut of only 0.5% of the GDP had a minor impact on reducing the overspending capacity of the state and helped to keep the fiscal deficit almost intact (Revista Exame 1990). The budgetary looseness of the state, which was one of main the reasons behind the country's impressive rise of inflation, was never, from its very beginning, properly tackled by the Collor Plan.

38. The recovery of economic stability was the top priority of the Collor Plan. It was a common belief in the government that once the inflation problem was solved, the path would be opened for further adjustments in the economy—most notably, the rise of private investments (both foreign and local) in the productive sector. For more details on the first Collor attempt to curb inflation and to bring back economic growth in Brazil, please see the interviews given at the launch of the Collor Plan by its three main architects, Mrs Zélia Cardoso de Mello (Veja 1990), Mr Antônio Kandir (Revista Exame 1990) and Mr Ibrahim Eris (Veja 1990).

39. The amount confiscated was to be returned in twelve different instalments adjusted by the prevailing inflation rate and added by an extra bonus of 6% a year.

40. GDP growth in the first two quarters of 1990 recorded a respective contraction of −2.5% and −8.2%. In 1990, Brazil witnessed a negative growth of −4.4% (Baer 2001, p. 182).

41. By the end of the Collor administration, the economy had accumulated a GDP growth of −3.15% (Baer 2001, p. 182), a clear indication of the harm and ineffectiveness of its policies.

42. Total sales of the top 100 companies in Brazil (including state, private and foreign ones) recorded during the three years of the Collor administration show, for instance, a drop of respectively 23.3%, 20.6% and 14.3% when compared to the corresponding figure from 1989, the year before the implementation of the Collor Plan (*Revista Exame Melhores e Maiores*, various issues).

43. In 1993, the states carried a total debt of nearly US$36bn with the federal government (Amann and Baer 2000, p. 1806).

44. Non-performing loans rose from 7% of total loans 'in December 1993 to almost 21% in December 1995' (Amann and Baer 2000, p. 1816).

45. The initial objective of allowing the *Real* to freely float against the US dollar was therefore abandoned.

46. However, the series of economic crises that hit Asia (1997), Russia (1998) and Argentina (2001) cast doubts to the real effectiveness of the use of exchange rate mechanisms as a mean to reach economic stability. This scepticism proved particularly valid for those economies that had carried out capital and trade liberalisation without implementing safeguard structures.

47. As pointed out by Wagner Mancuso (Mancuso 2004) in his work on the industrial lobby of Brazil's National Congress, the reduction of the 'Custo Brasil' had become since the mid-1990s 'the main demand of the industrial community to the public sector'. By cutting these costs, the business community

believed it was promoting above all 'the economic growth of the country' and in particular the 'strengthening of the industry'.

48. As also noted by Dennison de Oliveira (2000, p. 147), '[w]hen compared to other countries, the Brazilian tax burden was too high and without any equivalent compensation in the form of goods and services provided by the state. Therefore, this cost for the productive sector was one of the main, if not *the* main, cause of the *"Custo Brasil"*' (translated from Portuguese by the author).

49. In early 2000, Brazil's tax burden expanded again and reached 36% of the GPD.

50. Data from Edmund Amann and Werner Baer (2003, p. 1038).

51. Data from Eduardo Refinetti Guardia (2004, p. 119).

52. Data from Edmund Amann and Werner Baer (2003).

53. Pastore calculated that labour obligations represented on average an extra cost of 60% of the base wage in Germany, 45.5% in Belgium, 11.6% in Denmark, 79.7% in France, 58.8% in England, 56.0% in Ireland, 51.3% in Italy and 41.7% in Luxemburg and less than 20% in countries like Korea, Taiwan, Singapore, Indonesia and Malasia (Pastore, Flexibilização dos mercados de trabalho e contratação coletiva 1994, p. 142) and (Pastore, Flexibilização dos mercados de trabalho, a resposta moderna para o aumento da competição 1994, p. 405).

54. Data from the Brazilian Institute of Geography and Statistics, www.ibge. gov.br.

55. More recent data about the average number of years of schooling in Brazil still places the country at a disadvantage to its main competing economies. While Brazilians usually spend on average 4.56 years at school, this figure is much higher in Argentina (8.49 years), Chile (7.89), Mexico (6.73), China (5.74), Russia (10.49) and India (4.77) (Guimarães 2005).

REFERENCES

Amann, Edmund. "Economic policy and performance in Brazil since 1985." In *Brazil since 1985: economy, polity and society*, by Maria D'Alva Gil Kinzo and James Dunkerley, 107–37. London: Institute of Latin American Studies, 2003.

Amann, Edmund, and Werner Baer. "The illusion of stability: the Brazilian economy under Cardoso." *World Development*. Vol. 28 (2000): 1805–19.

Amann, Edmund, and Werner Baer. "Anchors away: the cost and benefits of Brazil's devaluation." *World Development*. Vol. 31 (2003): 1033–46.

Armendariz, Edna. "Capital market liberalisation and financial crises: the case of Mexico, 1988–1994." *PhD Thesis*. Cambridge: Judge Business School. University of Cambridge, 2003.

Baer, Werner. *The Brazilian economy: growth and development*. 5th edition. Westport: Praeger Publishers, 2001.

Balassa, Bela. "Lessons of East Asian development: an overview." *Journal of Economic Development and Cultural Change*. Vol. 36 (1988): S273–90.

Balassa, Bela, Gerardo Bueno, Pedro-Pablo Kuczynski, and Mário Henrique Simonsen. *Uma nova fase de crescimento para a América Latina*. Washington, DC: Institute for International Economics, 1986.

Bhagwati, Jagdish. *Protectionism*. Cambridge: MIT Press, 1989.

Biondi, Aloysio, Frederico Bussinger, Odacir Klein, and Wilson Quintella Filho. "Custo do transporte e da infra-estrutura." In *Custo Brasil: mitos e realidade*, by Luiz Inácio Lula da Silva, Guido Mantega and Paulo Vanuchi, 107–55. Petrópolis: Editora Vozes, 1997.

Brazil em Exame. "O Brasil dos anos 90 tem muita pressa." São Paulo: Editora Abril, 1989.

Brum, Argemiro J. *Desenvolvimento econômico Brasileiro*. Ijuí: Editora Vozes in co-edition with Editora Unijuí, 1999.

Camargo, José Márcio, and Ricardo Paes de Barros. "Poverty in Brazil: a challenge for the future." In *Brazil: the challenges of the 1990s*, by Maria D'Alva Gil Kinzo, 60–77. London: Institute of Latin American Studies and British Academic Press, 1993.

Cardenas, Enrique, Jose Antonio Ocampo, and Rosemary Thorp. *An economic history of twentieth-century Latin America. Volume 3. Industrialisation and the state in Latin America: the postwar years*. Oxford: Palgrave, 2000.

Chang, Ha-Joon. *The political economy of industrial policy*. London: Macmillan Press, 1996.

Cintra, Marcos Antonio Macedo. "Brazilian structural adjustment in the nineties: dependence without development." *Vierteljahrsheffe zur Wirtschaftsforschung*, Vol. 69 (2000): 53–68.

CNI. "Brasil industrial: competitividade para crescer." In *Mimeograph*. Rio de Janeiro, Brazilian National Confederation of Industries, 1996.

Conjuntura Econômica. "A abertura e a política industrial." Rio de Janeiro: Fundação Getúlio Vargas, 31 March 1990.

Diniz, Eli. "Neoliberalismo e corporativismo: as duas faces do capitalismo industrial no Brasil." In *Empresários e modernização econômica: Brasil nos anos 90*, by Eli Diniz, 14–42. Florianópolis: Editora da UFSC, 1993.

———. "Empresariado e estratégias de desenvolvimento: dilemas do capitalismo brasileiro." *Lua Nova. Revista de Cultura e Política*. (2002): 241–62.

Diniz, Eli, and Renato Boschi. *Empresários, interesses e mercado: dilemas do desenvolvimento no Brasil*. Belo Horizonte: Editora UFMG, 2004.

Doctor, Mahrukh. "Business and delays in port reform in Brazil." *Brazilian Journal of Political Economy*. Vol. 22 (2002): 79–101.

Fields, Gary S. *Poverty, inequality and development*. Cambridge: Cambridge University Press, 1980.

FIESP. *Livre para crescer: proposta para um Brasil moderno*. Edited by Maria Helena Zockun. São Paulo: Cultura Editores Associados, 1990.

Folha de São Paulo. "Abertura do mercado." São Paulo, 04 August 1994.

———. "Chega de impostos!" São Paulo, 21 January 1996.

Font, Mauricio A. *Transforming Brazil: a reform era in perspective*. Oxford: Rowman & Littlefield Publishers, 2003.

Franco, Gustavo. "Brazilian hyperinflation: the political economy of the fiscal crisis." In *Brazil: the challenges of the 1990s*, by Maria D'Alva Gil Kinzo, 24–35. London: Institute of Latin American Studies and British Academic Press, 1993.

Goldstein, Andrea, and Ben Ross Schneider. *Big business in Brazil: states and markets in the corporate reorganisation of the 1990s*. Paper presented at Workshop on Brazil and South Korea, Institute of Latin American Studies, University of London, 7–8 December, 2000.

Guardia, Eduardo Refinetti. "As razões do ajuste fiscal." In *Reformas no Brasil: balanço e agenda*, by Fabio Giambiagi, José Guilherme Reis and André Urani, 105–26. Rio de Janeiro: Editora Nova Fronteira, 2004.

Guimarães, Carlos. "O Brasil competitivo: desafios à frente." *Press Release*. Washington, DC: Inter-American Development Bank, 04 August 2005.

IBGE. "Síntese dos indicadores sociais 2003." Rio de Janeiro: Coordenação de População e Indicadores Sociais, 2004.

Jaguaribe, Hélio. *Alternativas do Brasil*. 3rd edition. Rio de Janeiro: José Olympio Editora, 1990.

Kiguel, Miguel A., and Julio J. Nogués. "Restoring growth and price stability in Argentina: do policies make miracles?" In *Economic reform in Latin America*, by

Harry Costin and Hector Vanolli, 125–44. Orlando: The Dryden Press. Harcourt Brace College Publishers, 1998.

Kingstone, Peter R. "Constitutional reform and macroeconomic stability: implications for democratic consolidation in Brazil." In *Markets and democracy in Latin America: conflicts or convergence?* by Philip Oxhorn and Pamela K. Starr, 133–59. London: Lynne Rienner Publishers, 1999.

———. *Crafting coalitions for reform: business preferences, political institutions, and neoliberal reform in Brazil.* University Park: The Pennsylvania University Press, 1999.

Krueger, Anne O. "Government failures in development." *Journal of Economic Perspectives.* Vol. 4 (1990): 9–23.

Larraín Bascuñáin, Felipe, and Jeffrey Sachs. "Bolivia 1985–1992: reforms, results and challenges." In *Economic reform in Latin America*, by Harry Costin and Hector Vanolli, 145–68. Orlando: Dryden Press. Harcourt Brace College Publishers, 1998.

Longo, Carlos Alberto. "The state and the liberalisation of the Brazilian economy." In *Brazil: the challenges of the 1990s*, by Maria D'Alva Gil Kinzo, 36–59. London: Institute of Latin American Studies and British Academic Press, 1993.

Mancuso, Wagner. "O lobby das indústria no Congresso Nacional." *Revista Dados.* Vol. 47 (2004): 505–47.

Martone, Celso L. "The external constraints on economic policy and performance in Brazil." In *Brazil since 1985: economy, polity and society*, by Maria D'Alva Gil Kinzo and James Dunkerley, 138–59. London: Institute of Latin American Studies, 2003.

Moura, Alkimar A. "Stabilisation policy as a game of mutual distrust: the Brazilian experience in post-1985." In *Brazil: the challenges of the 1990s*, by Maria D'Alva Gil Kinzo, 5–23. London: Institute of Latin American Studies and British Academic Press, 1993.

Nóbrega, Maílson da. *O Brasil em Transformação.* São Paulo: Editora Infinito, 2000.

Nolan, Peter. *China and the global business revolution.* Basingstoke: Palgrave, 2001.

Oliveira, Dennison de. "A cultura dos assuntos públicos: o caso do 'Custo Brasil.'" *Revista de Sociologia Política.* N. 14 (2000): 139–61.

Paes de Barros, Ricardo, Rosane Silva Pinto de Mendonça, and James Alan Shope. "Regional disparities in education within Brazil: the role of quality of education." *Texto para Discussão 311.* Rio de Janeiro: Instituto de Pesquisa Econômica Aplicada, IPEA, 1993.

Pastore, José. *Flexibilização dos mercados de trabalho e contratação coletiva.* São Paulo: Editora LTr, 1994.

———. "Flexibilização dos mercados de trabalho, a resposta moderna para o aumento da competição." *Revista LTr.* Vol. 58 (1994): 402–5.

———. "Relações do trabalho numa economia que se abre." *Revista LTr.* Vol. 59 (1995): 19–20.

Pinheiro, Armando Castelar, and Fabio Giambiagi. "Brazilian Privatisation in the 1990s." *World Development.* Vol. 22 (1994): 737–53.

Pinheiro, Armando Castelar, and Fabio Giambiagi. "The macroeconomic background and institutional framework of Brazilian privatisation." *Ensaios BNDES 10.* Rio de Janeiro: Banco Nacional de Desenvolvimento Econômico e Social, BNDES, 1999.

Pinheiro, Armando Castelar, Regis Bonelli, and Ben Ross Schneider. "Pragmatic policy in Brazil: the political economy of incomplete market reform." *Texto para Discussão 1035.* Rio de Janeiro: Instituto de Pesquisa Econômica Aplicada, IPEA, 2004.

Revista Exame. "Collor busca um ponto de apoio." São Paulo: Editora Abril, 07 February 1990. 18–22.

———. "Entrevista: Antônio Kandir. Este plano não tem como dar errado." São Paulo: Editora Abril, 04 April 1990. 44–7.

———. "Não almoçou e pagou a conta." São Paulo: Editora Abril, 12 December 1990. p. 7.

———. "O creme do creme entre as empresas do país." São Paulo: Editora Abril, 14 June 1989. 74–80.

———. "O estado quebra a harmonia." São Paulo: Editora Abril, 20 September 1989. 56–8.

———. "O jeito é de recessão, mas a economia volta a funcionar." São Paulo: Editora Abril, 04 April 1990. 16–19.

Sachs, Jeffrey. "The Bolivian hyperinflation and stabilisation." *The American Economic Review.* Vol. 77 (1987): 279–83.

Sallum Jr, Brasilio. "The changing role of the state: new patterns of state–society relations in Brazil at the end of the twentieth century." In *Brazil since 1985: economy, polity and society*, by Maria D'Alva Gil Kinzo and James Dunkerley, 179–99. London: Institute of Latin American Studies, University of London, 2003.

Schneider, Ben Ross. "Business politics in democratic Brazil." In *Reforming the state: business, unions and regions in Brazil*, by Maria D'Alva Gil Kinzo, 3–23. London: Institute of Latin American Studies, University of London, 1997.

Souto Maior, Jorge Luiz. "A justiça do trabalho no Brasil moderno." *Revista LTr.* Vol. 59 (1995): 1627–34.

Süssekind, Arnaldo. "A globalização da economia e o direito do trabalho." *Revista LTr.* Vol. 61 (1997): 40–4.

Veja. "No olho do furacão." São Paulo: Editora Abril, 26 October 1988.

———. "Entrevista: Roberto Campos. Um país fora de moda." São Paulo: Editora Abril, 21 June 1989.

———. "O país que parou no tempo." São Paulo: Editora Abril, August 02 1989.

———. "Entrevista: Ibrahim Eris. Quero sucesso logo." São Paulo: Editora Abril, 28 March 1990. 5–8.

———. "Perfil de presidente." São Paulo: Editora Abril, 31 January 1990. 30–7.

———. "Entrevista: Zélia Cardoso de Mello." São Paulo: Editora Abril, 25 April 1990. 5–7.

Vernengo, Matias. "What's next for Brazil after neo-liberalism?" *Challenge.* Vol. 46 (2003): 59–75.

Villela, Annibal, and Wilson Suzigan. "Elementos para discussão de uma política industrial para o Brasil." *Texto para Discussão 421.* Brasilia: Instituto de Pesquisa Econômica Aplicada, IPEA, May 1996.

Wells, John. "Latin America: can't pay . . . won't pay." *Marxism Today.* August (1986): 16–22.

Williamson, John. *Latin American adjustment: how much has happened?* Washington, DC: Institute for International Economics, 1990.

Yotopoulos, Pan A. "The (rip)tide of privatisation: lessons from Chile." *World Development.* Vol. 17 (1989): 683–702.

Part IV
Market-Oriented Reforms and Brazil's Largest Companies

I am aware that the government's role is to guarantee the security of all investors.

—Former President of Brazil Luiz Inácio Lula da Silva (2003–2011) quoted in the *Financial Times*, August 19, 2003

INTRODUCTION

The 'integration of Brazil into the world economy' cannot be understood without an initial analysis of the sudden surge of foreign investments in the second half of the 1990s. This rise in the inflow of foreign capital reveals a radical change of attitude of international institutions towards investments in Brazil and seems to come as a reaction to (a) the atmosphere of economic stability reached by the Brazilian economy in the mid-1990s; (b) the privatisation of its largest enterprises; (c) the lift of capital controls; (d) the deregulation of several sectors that used to enjoy strong intervention of the state; and (e) the creation of the Mercosur trade bloc, which helped to expand trade opportunities for any company operating or willing to operate in Brazil.

The **amount of FDI** to Brazil in the 1990s is in sharp contrast to the sum of investments it had attracted in the previous decade. Whereas in the 1980s, total investments in Brazil did not exceed US$662m, in the following years of the 1990s, Brazil witnessed an impressive increase of FDI, which peaked with the inflow of US$32.7bn in 2000. A more detailed analysis will also reveal that investments became more significant towards the end of the 1990s. Whereas in the first half of the decade (from 1990 to 1996), the annual average of FDI to Brazil had only reached US$3.2bn, it climbed to soaring figures in the following years of 1997 (US$18,9bn), 1998 (US$28,8bn), 1999 (US$28,5bn) and 2000 (US$32,7bn). As can be observed in Table 4.1, the participation of Brazil in the global share of foreign investment doubled in the same period, from an average rate that was lower than 1.3% in 1990 through 1996 to 2.7% in 2001. With regard to Latin America and the Caribbean, Brazil saw

Table 4.1 Foreign direct investments to Brazil, 1990–2013 (in US$ millions)

Region/economy	1990–1996	1997	1998	1999	2000	2001	2002	2003	2004	2005	2006	2007	2008	2009	2010	2011	2012	2013
Brazil	3.2	18.9	28.8	28.5	32.7	22.4	16.5	10.1	18.1	15.0	18.8	34.5	45.0	25.9	48.5	66.6	65.2	64.0
South America	13.6	49.3	52.6	69.6	57.0	37.8	27.9	22.6	36.8	44.0	43.4	71.6	93.3	56.7	92.1	129.4	144.4	133.3
Latin America and the Caribbean	22.3	73.3	85.5	104.5	98.0	80.7	58.4	47.9	96.2	78.0	98.2	171.9	210.6	150.1	189.8	249.4	243.8	292.0
Developing economies	82.0	192.4	189.0	231.0	264.5	224.0	169.2	193.7	280.2	334.5	432.1	589.4	668.4	530.2	637.0	735.2	702.8	778.3
World	248.7	488.1	705.9	1,091.4	1,413.1	836.0	626.0	601.2	734.1	989.6	1,480.5	2,002.6	1,816.3	1,216.4	1,408.5	1,651.5	1,350.9	1,451.0
Share of Brazil (%)																		
South America	23.9	38.5	54.8	41.0	57.5	59.3	59.3	44.7	49.2	34.2	43.3	48.3	48.3	45.7	52.6	51.5	45.2	48.0
Latin America and the Caribbean	14.6	25.9	33.7	27.3	33.4	27.8	28.4	21.1	18.9	19.3	19.1	20.1	21.4	17.3	25.5	26.7	26.8	21.9
Developing economies	4.0	9.9	15.3	12.4	12.4	10.0	9.8	5.2	6.5	4.5	4.4	5.9	6.7	4.9	7.6	9.1	9.3	8.2
World	1.3	3.9	4.1	2.6	2.3	2.7	2.6	1.7	2.5	1.5	1.3	1.7	2.5	2.1	3.4	4.0	4.8	4.4

Source: Revista Valor: Grandes Grupos, 2002; (UNCTAD) World Investment Report, various issues.

its share of foreign investments in the continent jump from 14.6% in 1990 through 1996 to 33.4% in 2000. In addition, foreign direct investments to Brazil were not dramatically curbed by the Asian Crisis in 1997 and the Russian Crisis in 1998 and, even more spectacularly, from 1998 to 2001, Brazil remained (along with the US, China and the UK) among the top four countries with the highest rate of FDI Confidence Index (ATKearney 2002). Foreign investments to Brazil only showed signs of dropping in 2001 when the bulk of its privatisation programme was already over. Besides, there were clear indications at the end of that year that the world economy would suffer a temporary downturn. This downward trend of foreign investments to Brazil was only broken in 2004 with the inflow of US$18.1bn. In 2011, foreign investments to Brazil broke again a new all-time record when they reached US$66.7bn.

When the question is posed about the **origin of capital**, North America and the European countries have taken the lead as main investors in Brazil, with only three countries (the US, the Netherlands and Spain) accounting for 44.5% of the accumulated inflow of capital between 1996 and 2009 (Table 4.2). This period also witnessed considerable growth in the inflow of capital from countries like Spain, Portugal, France and the Netherlands, a tendency that came as a result of the strong participation of these countries in the privatisation of public utilities and the acquisition of local financial institutions. When a more detailed analysis is made of the origin of capital in recent years, two intriguing findings are worth noticing: (a) the low amount of investments from the Mercosur countries, which represented no more than 1.1% of the accumulated inflow of capital to Brazil between 1996 and 2009 and (b) the large amount of investments from tax havens like the Cayman, Bermudas, Virgin Islands and Luxembourg, which suggests the repatriation of Brazilian capital that was kept offshore.

Finally, with regard to the **destination of FDI**, the last decade, as shown on Table 4.3, was also marked by a radical shift in the stock of foreign investments in Brazil. In the time span of just five years, the bulk of foreign investments migrated from the Brazilian traditional manufacturing sector to the then booming service sector, while the share of manufacturing in the inflow of foreign investments between 2001 and 2009 shrank to 36.9% and the inflow of foreign capital into services jumped to 49.4%.

Telecommunications and energy services accounted together for the most impressive change on the inflow of foreign capital, with their figures moving from negligible values in 1995 to account for nearly 25% of the stock of foreign investments in 2000. Other services that succeeded in grabbing the attention of foreign investors were related to banking, retailing and wholesale sectors. In the turn of the new millennium, these three sectors accounted for more than 20% of the total stock of foreign investments. On the manufacturing front, the largest stocks of foreign investments were in chemicals, food and beverages, automotive vehicles and basic metallurgy. An important aspect that is worthy of note is the low stock of foreign investments in

Table 4.2 Main investors in Brazil, 1996–2009 (in US$ millions)

Countries	Stock		Inflow												Total
	1995	1996–99	2000	2001	2002	2003	2004	2005	2006	2007	2008	2009			
United States	10,852.18	19,137.79	5,398.71	4,464.93	2,614.58	2,382.75	3,977.83	4,644.16	4,433.68	6,039.19	6,917.95	4,878.32			64,889.89
Netherlands	1,545.80	7,422.10	2,228.04	1,891.85	3,372.46	1,444.88	7,704.85	3,207.92	3,494.94	8,116.13	4,623.68	5,721.78			49,228.63
Spain	251.01	11,954.85	9,592.86	2,766.58	586.9	710.47	1,054.93	1,220.43	1,513.74	2,163.52	3,787.47	3,415.19			38,766.94
Cayman Is.	891.68	7,960.23	2,034.50	1,755.07	1,554.46	1,909.58	1,521.80	1,078.17	1,974.39	1,604.47	1,554.67	1,091.97			24,039.31
France	2,031.46	5,992.71	1,909.71	1,912.82	1,814.97	825.23	485.86	1,458.41	744.59	1,214.40	2,856.13	2,136.48			21,351.31
Germany	5,828.04	1301.57	374.56	1,047.46	628.29	507.61	794.73	1,269.32	848.27	1,756.78	1,036.57	2,459.22			12,024.38
Portugal	106.61	5,048.21	2,514.80	1,692.26	1,018.76	201.2	570.2	334.62	300.31	468.08	1,025.91	376.97			13,551.32
Japan	2,658.52	1086.34	384.74	826.6	504.48	1,368.35	243.17	779.08	647.52	464.63	4,098.78	1,672.57			12,076.26
Canada	1,818.98	908.72	192.82	441.1	989.35	116.78	592.54	1,435.32	1,285.51	818.35	1,438.02	1,371.41			9,589.92
Luxembourg	408.05	752.65	1,027.20	284.66	1,012.78	238.69	746.94	139.1	745.09	2,855.30	5,937.32	536.77			14,276.50
Switzerland	2,815.30	811.54	306.84	181.78	347.36	335.58	364.58	341.54	1,631.01	858.58	772.86	369.07			6,320.74
UK	1,862.61	1,670.71	393.74	416.23	474.36	254.22	275.36	153.26	395.18	1,003.54	641	1,025.17			6,702.77
Bermudas	853.07	571.05	315.35	606.86	1,468.78	623.49	210.94	38.92	514.68	1,497.57	1,038.06	359.94			7,245.64
Italy	1,258.56	1124.81	488.02	281.27	472.5	390.44	429.21	345.68	200.73	258.98	326.27	214.69			4,532.60
Virgin Is.	901.22	880.2	231.34	911.91	500.45	548.73	245.39	254.53	280.24	371.52	1,046.64	403.16			4,627.47
Panama	677.41	1821.33	21.38	132.99	146.41	147.47	150.52	165.56	139.25	143.9	96.04	132.2			3,097.05
Belgium	558.23	1259.65	384.49	113.08	45.25	18.26	8.1	685.58	271.53	83.13	72.58	91.73			2,960.80
Bahamas	509.69	666.8	80.69	264.18	204.85	35.62	98.35	87.83	63.01	602.66	1,098.47	52.34			3,254.80
Uruguay	874.15	258.91	199.5	180.62	237.46	154.69	160.59	169.21	229.48	212.52	421.98	194.98			2,419.94

Sweden	567.16	949.15	628.6	54.26	204.92	43.11	89.88	32.91	19.31	57.92	52.52	213.48	2,346.06
Argentina	393.58	418.06	112.71	56.77	88.47	76.16	80.5	112.23	124.96	71.07	125.62	80.09	1,346.64
South Korea	3.81	255.74	25	0	0	0	0	168.01	109.53	265.13	631.01	131.88	1,586.30
Paraguay	3.16	0	0	1.23	3.63	1.08	0.69	1.4	0.66	1.91	3.73	7.86	22.19
Other countries	4,028.53	12,850.86	4,385.40	757.39	486.96	586.02	458.38	3,398.38	2,263.69	2,775.30	5,402.24	3,506.70	36,871.32
Total	41,695.62	85,104.00	33,331.00	21,041.90	18,778.43	12,920.41	20,265.34	21,521.57	22,231.31	33,704.58	43,886.30	30,443.97	343,228.81

Source: Brazilian Central Bank, www.bacen.gov.br.

Table 4.3 Destination of foreign direct investments to Brazil, 2001–2009 (in US$ millions)

Economic Activity	Stock				Inflow						Total Inflow	
	1995	%	2000	%	2001-04	2005	2006	2007	2008	2009	2001–2009	%
Agriculture, livestock and mining	924.99	2.22	2,401.08	2.33	4,691.24	2,194.37	1,363.12	4,982.07	12,995.57	4,474.27	30,700.64	13.65
Oil extraction	72.01	0.17	1,022.48	0.99	2,517.95	896.9	734.05	650.37	1,338.97	2,533.23	8,671.47	3.85
Iron ore mining	566.71	1.36	611.19	0.59	1,518.20	995.69	392.86	3,223.02	10,644.69	1,303.24	18,077.70	8.0
Agriculture and cattle ranching	207.23	0.5	288.13	0.28	419.58	210.18	176.11	316.91	498.11	255.02	1,875.91	0.83
Others	79.04	0.19	479.27	0.47	235.5	91.61	60.09	791.75	513.80	382.78	2,075.53	0.92
Manufacturing	27,907.09	66.93	34,725.62	33.71	29,770.12	6,402.81	8,743.78	12,166.08	14,012.97	11,924.74	83,020.50	36.93
Chemical products	5,331.12	12.79	6,042.71	5.87	5,397.89	763.66	1,133.88	587.62	789.33	753.34	9,425.72	4.19
Food and beverages	2,827.52	6.78	4,618.65	4.48	8,190.28	2,074.83	739.33	1,816.75	2,238.24	542.32	15,601.75	6.94
Automotive vehicles	4,837.70	11.6	6,351.39	6.17	5,122.77	924.86	287.6	871.71	964.13	2,163.46	10,334.53	4.59
Basic metallurgy	3,004.90	7.21	2,513.35	2.44	1,736.54	310.3	1,712.52	4,699.75	4,984.26	3,768.64	17,212.01	7.65
Machines and equipment	2,345.29	5.62	3,324.35	3.23	1,304.09	254.97	429.73	431.31	506.05	390.42	3,316.57	1.47
Electronic and tele-com equipment	785.42	1.88	2,169.23	2.11	2,301.97	395.98	325.11	159.05	145.17	326.67	3,653.95	1.62
Pulp and paper	1,633.66	3.92	1,572.73	1.53	686.40	158.62	1,797.38	262.52	204.85	771.85	3,881.62	1.72
Others	7,141.48	17.13	8,133.20	7.9	5,030.19	1,519.60	2,318.24	3,337.37	4,180.94	3,208.04	19,594.38	8.71
Services	12,863.54	30.85	65,887.81	63.96	38,526.39	12,924.38	12,124.40	16,556.44	16,877.75	14,044.96	111,054.32	49.40
Post and telecommunications	398.74	0.96	18,761.54	18.21	14,100.38	1,899.66	1,215.53	307.99	446.70	309.91	18,280.17	8.13

Services rented to companies	4,952.70	11.88	11,018.53	10.7	3,202.55	2,978.10	1,067.01	300.63	372.76	254.82	8,175.87	3.63
Financial services	1,638.38	3.93	10,671.26	10.36	4,380.11	888.61	2,647.35	5,828.19	3,802.57	2,503.18	20,050.01	8.92
Electricity and gas	0.29	0	7,116.35	6.91	4,804.80	1,570.89	2,331.81	618.22	909.18	970.07	11,204.97	4.98
Wholesale	2,132.20	5.11	5,918.09	5.74	2,178.04	680.75	914.4	666.36	1,640.38	1,474.93	7,554.86	3.36
Retailing	669.11	1.6	3,892.99	3.78	2,706.55	2,099.62	546.77	2,099.45	923.26	1,292.67	9,668.32	4.30
Real estate services	1,109.24	2.66	798	0.77	718.81	296.95	1,405.01	721.85	1,721.40	596.12	5,460.14	2.42
Data processing	115.11	0.28	2,542.91	2.47	1,184.86	144.29	192.32	187.96	389.57	857.7	2,956.70	1.31
Others	1,847.77	4.43	5,168.13	5.02	5,250.29	2,365.50	1,804.20	5,825.79	6,671.93	5,785.56	27,703.27	12.32
Total	41,695.62	100	103,014.51	100	72,987.75	21,521.57	22,231.30	33,704.58	43,886.30	30,443.97	224,775.47	100

Source: Brazilian Central Bank, www.bacen.gov.br.

the primary sector in 1995 and in the year 2000. The accumulated inflow of investments from 2001 to 2009 shows, however, that greater participation of foreign capital in the primary sector (particularly oil extraction and iron ore mining) is in course.

The sudden surge of foreign direct investment to Brazil in the second half of the 1990s also coincides with the most dynamic period of its privatisation programme. According to Lacerda (2004), from 1996 to 1998, nearly 25% of FDI to Brazil were destined for the acquisition of state-owned enterprises.

Mixed consortia between foreign and domestic investors—It is also worth noticing that this rise of FDI engendered a form of mixed consortia between foreign and domestic investors. In many respects, this surge in mergers and acquisitions (M&As) very much resembled the first boom of MNCs in Latin America in the 1960s and early 1970s. In a similar way, 'foreign investors [we]re expected to bring in technology and capital assets, plus international connections', whereas 'local investors' contributions' were more a matter of providing 'knowledge and understanding of framework conditions such as competitive environment, legal and social norms, and also cultural features of the country' (Mendes de Paula, Ferraz and Iootty 2002, p. 483). Ferraz and Hamaguchi (2002, p. 391), in their assessment of this process in the 1990s, concluded, however, that 'these mixed consortia tended to be inherently unstable because of conflicting business motivations and profit-making time horizons among investors'. Some investors had a 'long-term growth strategy', and others were mainly characterised as 'financially motivated asset-seekers'. This incompatibility of goals between local and foreign investors was commonly seen in the Brazilian cases of M&As in the 1990s, and they usually ended up with the full incorporation of the local company by foreign investors. In addition, as it is also shown by De Paula and colleagues (2002, p. 482), mixed consortium was an 'ownership mode' more 'extensively' used in privatisations than 'in private M&A operations'. Whereas mixed consortia were present in 53% of the privatisations carried out in Brazil in the 1990s, in the private cross-border M&As, the foreign participation had a dominant position and accounted for 98% of the capital. In other words, cross-border transactions are better regarded as acquisitions than as mergers. The greater interest of foreign investors in the formation of mixed consortia for the privatisations can be partially explained by the high level of bureaucracy and the legal and deadline constraints that most of these operations usually inflicted, features that are more flexible in private M&A transactions. In this latter case, negotiations can be directly and independently conducted by the interested parties.

OPENING UP THE MARKET

As mentioned before, the first significant measures to lift tariff and non-tariff barriers in Brazil were taken during the short-lived Collor administration.

These measures, which were part of a broad price stabilisation programme to combat inflation, were mainly meant to bring competition to the local market. With the stroke of a pen, Brazil abolished in 1990 a list of more than one thousand products whose import was prohibited. In addition, an ambitious programme to reduce tariff barriers was put in place; by mid-1993, tariffs on imports reached average levels inferior to 15%, a figure almost three times lower than the average import rate of 51% implemented by the Brazilian government in the late 1980s.[1]

This lifting of tariffs in the early 1990s taken in tandem with the over-valuation of the local currency during the first four years of the *Real Plan* had an immediate effect in destabilising Brazilian accounts. 'Imports, which had remained practically stagnant between 1990 and 1992, expanded approximately 25% in 1993, 31% in 1994 and 51% in 1995' (Cysne 2002, p. 44). Trade surpluses, which had been continually more than US$10bn for more than a decade in the years prior to 1994, saw their figures plummet to negative values in the following years. Brazil's trade balance reached its low-est level in 1998, when it registered a deficit of US$8.3bn, an outcome that called for immediate intervention by the government. At the beginning of 1999, the *Real* started a process of free flotation and, by the end of the year, it had already lost 40% of its value against the US dollar. The devaluation of the local currency along with a comprehensive export promotion policy succeeded in bringing Brazil's trade balance back to positive and growing figures. This trend was, nevertheless, considerably dragged upwards due to Brazil's highly competitive commodities sector.[2]

Labour Market

The decade of the 1990s was also marked by profound changes in the Brazilian labour market. A survey on labour activity of the six largest metropolitan areas in Brazil (São Paulo, Rio de Janeiro, Belo Horizonte, Porto Alegre, Recife and Salvador) carried out by the Research Institute of Applied Economics (IPEA) at the tenth anniversary of the Brazilian economic reforms sheds some light on the immediate consequences of the liberalisation of the Brazilian economy in the sector. Although the study only deals with Brazil's largest industrial areas, its findings are fairly representative, as these regions correspond to 25% of the Brazilian workforce (Ramos and Britto 2004). In addition, these six areas are also the only ones where the Brazilian Institute of Geography and Statistics (IBGE) has kept a detailed monthly-based record of labour activity. A brief analysis of employment data from 1991 to 2003 is sufficient to give us a picture of the changes in the Brazilian labour market and the pressure faced by its workforce. In this first decade of economic reforms, the Brazilian labour market witnessed (i) a *near three-fold growth of unemployment*, (ii) a *steady rise in informal jobs* and (iii) a *substantial drop of average income*.

With regard to the first point, after a brief period following the launch of the anti-inflation *Real Plan* in 1994, when the unemployment rate had dropped to the low figure of 3.4%, the level of unemployment started to rise again and almost reached 8% in 1999. In the year 2001, however, new changes were introduced to the calculation of labour activity as the Brazilian Institute of Geography and Statistics decided to update its survey methodology to match recommendations from the International Labour Organization (ILO). This new methodology, which is more sensitive to real changes, showed even higher unemployment rates for the years 2002 and 2003, when figures reached their highest levels, 11.7% and 12.3%, respectively. In addition to growth of unemployment, another figure that gave room for concern was the continuous rise of the informal sector in the years immediately after Brazil's economic liberalisation. Between 1991 and 2003, the share of informal jobs moved from 40% to reach 55% of the workforce.

Finally, when it comes to real income, this figure also dropped in the first decade of the reforms. In 2003, average real wages in Brazil of R$792 were 18.7% lower than the peak of R$975 in 1996. Although real wage had risen since 2003, its value in 2006 was still 8.9% lower than in 1996.[3] In addition, according to a report from the Brazilian Institute for Industrial Development (IEDI), in these same metropolitan areas in the period from 1999 to 2003, the total mass of wage had shown an accumulated fall of nearly 14%. Bearing in mind that this total mass of income formed the basis of the domestic market, the consequences for local consumption and production were enormous. The industrial sectors that were most immediately hit by this loss of the consumer market were the ones that were related to intermediary goods (apparel, textiles, shoes and food), which were also the ones that were more labour intensive (IEDI 2004).

The second decade after the reforms, however, showed a significant recovery. In December 2013, unemployment had already dropped to 4.3%, when it reached its lowest annual level since the implementation of a new methodology in 2001. In that same month, formal jobs corresponded to 55.1% of the total workforce in the six largest metropolitan areas, and average real wages for the whole mass of workers had jumped to R$2,045.50.[4]

Productivity—Many of the post-reform gains in labour productivity in the first decade of the reforms came as a direct result of drops in employment. According to a study that was also carried out by IEDI (2004) on labour productivity in the whole Brazilian industrial sector from 1990 to 2002, annual productivity for this period had grown by 2.6%, and employment had an annual retraction of –0.6%. In total, the opening of Brazil's industrial economy was marked by an accumulated productivity growth of 35.3%. The sectors that witnessed the most impressive growth rates were actually the ones that during the 1990s had gone through major restructuring processes. According to the IEDI report, these sectors were the automotive industry, steel making, oil refining and petrochemicals and electrical equipment manufacturing. These four industrial sectors presented accumulated productivity growth that was higher than 100%, which, respectively, corresponded to 102.5%, 137.5%, 156.2% and 163.1%. Not surprisingly, those were also the sectors that presented higher drops in employment levels, which, respectively, corresponded to –30.6%, –40.6%, –47.3% and –44.2%.

Among the industries that registered low productivity with accumulated growth lower than the average of 35.3%, there are three sectors that are worth mentioning: apparel, shoes and leather products and textiles. These three sectors not only showed low or negative accumulated growth in productivity (–23.4%, –0.2%, 28.1%), but they also presented a small growth or even a reduction in employment levels (respectively, 3.4%, –8.3% and –40.3%). The consequences for the local market were enormous, as these were all labour-intense sectors that represented together 27.9% of the Brazilian industrial workforce. Productivity growth in the first decade of the reforms was notably high in the more capital-intensive industrial sectors, where the opening of the economy was also followed (as will be shown later in this chapter) by strong participation of local private and foreign investments. However, it is important to remind ourselves that for some sectors, this rise in productivity was not reached without considerable drops in employment.[5]

From 2002 onwards, records show steady growth in industrial productivity that coincided with an expansive cycle of employment and average income. This virtuous cycle lasted from 2004 to 2008. Side effects of the world economic crisis were felt in 2009, with falls in productivity, employment and average income. Signs of recovery of all these indicators were only seen in 2010.

Changes in Ownership Structure

Economic liberalisation in Brazil was also characterised by a dynamic choreography of mergers and acquisitions, which accounted for more than nine thousand transactions in the twenty years that followed the launch of the *Real Plan* in 1994. Once again, the participation of foreign investors was decisive in shaping the ownership structure of Brazil's largest enterprises.

Apart from four distinct years, the number of cross-border M&As largely outnumbered the ones that involved only domestic companies (see Figure 4.1). In total, foreign capital took part in 54.7% of the mergers and acquisitions carried out in the period. The number of cross-border transactions grew steadily from 1994 onwards and, after reaching its peak in the year 2000, when it accounted for 230 mergers and acquisitions, it suffered a dramatic fall in 2002. This drop of cross-border M&As was, however, short-lived. In 2004, cross-border transactions were already twice the number of domestic-only M&As; and three years later, the amount of cross-border transactions reached again a new record high. This temporary drop of cross-border mergers and acquisitions seems to have been the outcome of a series of factors: the scepticism of foreign investors over the Latin American economies after the Argentine crisis, the risk-averse attitude of the international community in the aftermath of the slowdown of the North American economy immediately after the events of September 2001, and finally the strong concern of foreign investors about the prospect of a victory of the left-wing candidate in Brazil's presidential elections in 2002.[6]

The rise of mergers and acquisitions in Brazil was only interrupted again by the world economic crisis in 2008. The number of transactions in 2009 was 35% lower than in 2007. Similarly to what had happened in the previous economic crisis of 2001, there was a temporary withdrawal of foreign capital. In the years 2002 and 2008, the domestic transactions were notably higher than the cross-border ones. In 2010, mergers and acquisitions gained steam again. In 2011, a new record was set with a total of 817 transactions. The figures for the following year were roughly the same.

In the universe of cross-border mergers and acquisitions, the vast majority of transactions corresponded to the acquisition of Brazilian-based assets by foreign companies. Between 2006 and 2013, for instance, 51.8% of these cross-border transactions were of foreign companies that acquired Brazilian enterprises and a further 24.7% of the transactions were of

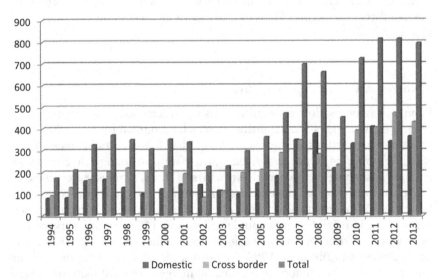

Figure 4.1 Mergers and acquisitions in Brazil, 1994–2013 (in units)
Source: Revista Valor: Grande Grupos (2002) and KPMG (2014).

foreign companies acquiring Brazilian-based subsidiaries of other foreign companies.[7]

THE TOP 500 COMPANIES

A quick analysis of the sales revenues of the top 500 state-owned, domestic and foreign non-financial enterprises in Brazil in the last decade is enough to reveal the strong impact that the opening up of Brazil's economy had on the ownership structure of its largest companies. While the share of private domestic companies and state-owned enterprises between 1991 and 2013 dropped by 8% and 21%, respectively, the percentage of foreign companies rose by 29%, adding up to 40% of the top 500 companies in 2013 (Figure 4.2).[8]

Not surprisingly, although both numbers of private national enterprises (PNEs) and state-owned enterprises (SOEs) have shown a continuous fall, the number of companies controlled by foreign capital has witnessed steady growth. Attention must be drawn to the intersection of the curves in relation to the number of PNE and multinational corporations in 1998. This year marks the middle of President Cardoso's double-term mandate and celebrates the fourth anniversary of his anti-inflation programme, the *Real Plan*. As previously mentioned, the *Real Plan*, launched in 1994, was decisive in stabilising the economy, and it empowered the government with the necessary political support to promote the reforms that deregulated the role of the state in the economy, lifted the barriers against capital control and conducted the privatisation of the largest SOEs. Although the *Real Plan* was successful in bringing economic stability to the economy, little or no

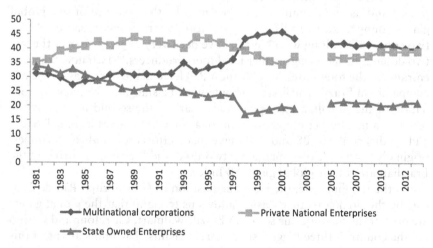

Figure 4.2   The top 500 companies in Brazil by sales revenues, 1981–2013 (in %)
Source: Revista Exame Melhores e Maiores, various issues.

attention was given to safeguarding the local private companies as they started to face competition from their foreign counterparts. The result can be easily observed in the diminishing participation of domestic enterprises, either state owned or private, among Brazil's largest companies.

THE TOP TWENTY-FIVE COMPANIES

When the focus of analysis is narrowed down to the top twenty-five companies, the dominance of foreign global companies in the Brazilian economy is equally evident. Whereas 60% of the companies on the list are multinational corporations, the share of domestic private and state-owned enterprises is, respectively, 28% and 12%. With regard to total sales revenues, the state-owned enterprises still count with the lion's share of the top twenty-five companies. Their leading position is kept, however, due to one single company, Brazil's oil giant Petrobras.

The list reveals that the different sectors of the top twenty-five companies (Table 4.4) are also the ones that undertook the most intensive restructuring processes in the 1990s, most notably oil, mining, steel, telecom, automotive and consumer goods (food and beverages) companies. These sectors, which account for 64% of the top twenty-five companies, went through comprehensive programmes of market liberalisation and, in some cases, privatisation. Not surprisingly, 24% of the top twenty-five companies are actually composed (or are spin-offs) of former state-owned enterprises. In this regard, telecoms stand out, with three companies on the list. Virtually all the big telecom players operating in Brazil are on the list.[9]

The recent concentration process of the Brazilian food sector, on the other hand, is in a certain way represented by the presence of two global giants (Bunge and Cargill) among the top twenty-five companies. These two companies, along with Nestlé, have been very aggressive over the last two decades in acquiring smaller local food producers.[10] Two new domestic entrants in the food industry (JBS and BRF) have made their way to the top companies in Brazil. The first is the outcome of a staggeringly quick consolidation of the Brazilian meat-processing market; the second is actually the result of a merger between two traditional food companies in Brazil, Sadia and Perdigão. Both JBS and BRF have made efforts to go abroad. Ambev, originally the result of a merger of two domestic brewers, is currently the Brazilian arm of the global giant AB InBev.

On the retailing side, the recent acquisition of GPA (Grupo Pão de Açucar) by the French retailer Casino allows us to claim that the global giants are now at the heart of this sector in Brazil. Walmart, Carrefour and Casino are the country's three biggest supermarket chains. The implications of this dominance on the supply chain of consumer goods are definitely worthy of further investigations. Finally, the list of twenty-five companies shows a

Table 4.4 The top 25 companies in Brazil by sales revenues (in US$ millions)

2013	2012	Company	Sector	Sales	Exports as % of sales	Ownership control
1	1	Petrobras	Oil and petrochemical	104,250.8	13.4	State owned
2	2	BR Distribuidora	Oil wholesale	38,021.8	2.3	State owned
3	3	Vale	Mining	27,986.0	89.0	Brazilian
4	4	Ipiranga Produtos	Oil wholesale	23,416.5	0.1[†]	Brazilian
5	9	Raízen	Ethanol wholesale	17,891.5	3.9	Anglo-Dutch
6	17	BRF	Consumer goods	12,471.7	39.8	Brazilian
7	10	Bunge	Consumer goods	11,589.8	62.5	Dutch
8	5	Volkswagen	Automobiles	11,037.4	15.5	German
9	6	Cargill	Consumer goods	10,775.0	71.4	North American
10	11	Braskem	Chemicals	10,338.1	28.9	Brazilian
11	7	Fiat	Automobiles	10,331.9	13.5	Italian
12	23	Telefônica	Telecom	10,183.0	—	Spanish
13	90	Via Varejo	Retailer	9,547.8	—	Brazilian
14	12	GPA (Casino)	Retailer	9,476.1	—	French
15	14	JBS	Consumer goods	9,211.1	36.1	Brazilian
16	13	TIM	Telecom	8,538.2	NA	Italian
17	33	Samsung	IT	6,798.0	2.0	South Korean
18	19	E.C.T.	Postal services	6,496.1	—	State owned

(Continued)

Table 4.4 (Continued)

2013	2012	Company	Sector	Sales	Exports as % of sales	Ownership control
19	18	Walmart Brasil	Retailer	6,382.7	NA	North American
20	24	ArcelorMittal	Steel	6,251.5	13.3	Anglo-Indian
21	20	Carrefour	Retailer	6,225.9	NA	French
22	—	Ambev	Consumer goods	6,191.7	0.1[†]	Belgian
23	36	CSN	Steel	6,116.8	25.4	Brazilian
24	16	General Motors	Automobiles	6,044.8	NA	North American
25	27	Claro (Telmex)	Telecom	5,900.1	NA	Mexican

Note: NA—Not Available. †—Data from 2012.
Source: Revista Exame Melhores e Maiores (2014).

complete absence of South American enterprises. Apart from Samsung, all multinational corporations are from either North America or Europe. The list also illustrates the export bias of the large commodity enterprises in Brazil. The top three exporters are the mining giant Vale and the agribusiness multinationals Bunge and Cargill.

IMPACT ON TECHNOLOGY INNOVATION

A certain dismantling of the systems of innovation that were built in Brazil during the period of state intervention was a recurrent finding by authors that analysed the consequences of trade and market liberalisation in the second half of the 1990s in Brazil (Gonçalves 1999; Moreira 2000; Amann 2002). For most of these studies, the prevalence of measures towards macroeconomic adjustments to the detriment of implementing microeconomic policies paved the way for foreign companies to expand their participation in the Brazilian economy at the same time that the local companies became more vulnerable to the entry of global players. The fast pace of trade and market reforms reduced the chances of the local companies to adjust to the demands of a more open economy. In the early years of market liberalisation, Brazilian companies had to struggle under an adverse economic environment which included, among other issues, high interest rates, an overvalued exchange rate from 1994 to 1999 and low growth.

Costa and Queiroz (2002, p. 1432), in their work on foreign direct investment and technological capabilities in Brazil, made an intriguing remark when they suggested that 'since the import substitution period, FDI has been one of the main mechanisms for gaining access to industrial technology'. If such a claim is correct, the reforms of the 1990s in Brazil represented in their initial stage a temporary move from *state-led* to *foreign capital–led* industrialisation. When considering this new environment, where foreign capital had become dominant, if not to all but at least to most of the key sectors of the economy, some issues related to technology dependency are worthy of analysis.

Some of the first implications of the increasing foreign participation in privatisation and M&A transactions can be observed in the immediate growth of imports, with special emphasis on 'technologically sophisticated capital goods, substituting in many cases for the domestically produced alternatives' (Amann 2002, p. 885). With regard to the many domestic companies which had their shares taken over by foreign capital in the years following the opening up of the Brazilian economy, a work by João Furtado (2000, p. 39) pointed out that these companies 'under new controllers' were able to reach 'wider and more globalised structures', although in a more 'subordinate' and 'tied' manner. To the same extent that the ability of those companies 'to act in the global arena was strengthen[ed]', their 'capability to define strategies linked with the local space' had considerably 'deteriorated'.

Another issue of concern lay in the fact that most of the decision making regarding technological strategies was no longer kept within national borders, under local development policies, but moved to where the new foreign controllers had their headquarters. These measures may prove harmful for the innovative capacity of the local subsidiaries, as their R&D decisions are constantly downplayed by the controlling companies, where the most dynamic and technology-intensive activities tended to be kept. This tendency illustrates a paradox identified by Costa and Queiroz (Costa and Reis de Queiroz 2002, p. 1432) concerning the 'technological role played by foreign firms in the Brazilian industry'; at the same time that foreign capital and companies were hailed as modernizers of the Brazilian industrial sector, they were equally active in 'downsizing their local technological efforts' in an attempt to monopolise the more dynamic and rewarding processes. Although the greater participation of the MNCs in Brazilian productive activity made an undeniable contribution to updating local means of production, it had not produced the same effect in consolidating a self-contained environment of knowledge and technology generation. In many cases, the so-called 'transference of technology' was lower than anticipated.

THE AUTOMOTIVE AND AEROSPACE INDUSTRIES IN BRAZIL

Among the several industrial sectors in Brazil, it is probably the automotive industry that best illustrates the growing participation of foreign companies in Brazil as an immediate consequence of the liberalisation of the economy in the 1990s. This sector, which started in Brazil in a tightly closed market environment, was for a long period restricted to a small number of foreign assembly companies and a myriad of multinational and domestic suppliers. Over the years, the domestic auto part companies focused their efforts on attempting to move upstream in the vertical integration of the auto supply chain, a task that was achieved to some extent by a few large local companies. When barriers that guaranteed market protection were lifted in the 1990s and liberalisation brought competition to the sector, the domestic companies quickly lost their presence in the local market.

In contrast, not far from the industrial area where for many decades Brazil had its main automotive centre, a domestic and high-technology industry managed to go through the liberalisation process and gain enough strength to become a world reference in its market segment. The aerospace industry in Brazil is a rare example of a high-technology company from a developing country which has succeeded in the current scenario of global trade and production.

The distinct trajectory of these two industrial sectors is worthy of analysis, and it poses questions as to the reasons that have allowed a developing country like Brazil to build a successful company in such a technology-intensive and highly oligopolistic sector as the aerospace industry but, on the other hand, have prevented it from building a global player in the auto assembly and auto parts sectors. Possible answers could lie in the importance of finding specific niche markets, government support in the initial years of the company, different kinds of incentives and attempts to build indigenous technological capabilities.

The Automotive Industry

Brazil, which had the largest industrial park of auto part companies in Latin America in the early 1990s, saw its indigenous automotive capacity collapse, although vehicle production in Brazil registered record highs in the same decade. This discrepancy, which at first glance looks striking, came as a result of structural changes that Brazil carried out in its automotive industry in an effort to modernise the sector and to make it more integrated with international standards. The whole automotive sector was restructured as new assembly plants were opened in the late 1990s (it more than doubled the number of assemblers that were operating in Brazil), and the relation between assemblers and suppliers was changed in order to incorporate new international practices. Attracted by (a) the newly gained stability of the economy, (b) Mercosur's regional trade bloc and (c) a large number of fiscal incentives, global giants quickly started to pour in. This was the first wave of the foreign investments that came about with the opening up of the automotive sector in the 1990s. A second one took place in the early 2010s with the creation of a new automotive regime.

After four decades in which the number of auto assemblers was restricted to Volkswagen, Ford and General Motors, all of them located in the industrial area of São Paulo, and Fiat, which in 1976 built a plant in the neighbouring state of Minas Gerais, the automotive industry in Brazil was dramatically expanded to include several global players. Chrysler,[11] Honda, Hyundai, Peugeot/Citroen, Renault and Volkswagen/Audi were among the largest investors who opened new assembly plants in Brazil in the second half of the 1990s. This rearrangement confirmed Brazil's position as of one of the largest vehicle producers among the developing countries and brought about considerable changes to the local automotive infrastructure. Automotive production in Brazil was completely redesigned as all the new entrants established their plants in areas away from the São Paulo/Minas Gerais automotive centres.

This first increase of auto assemblers in Brazil in the mid 1990s was, above all, the result of local efforts to bring in new greenfield investments.[12] Stripped of any comprehensive programme that would prioritize or preserve existing capabilities in terms of auto components, the concession of assembly plant locations was carried out in a very unstructured way, which in turn led to several problems. The most evident example was the grant of outstanding amounts of fiscal and non-fiscal incentives from regional government authorities to potential car manufacturers. Attracted by the prospects of job creation, 'technology transfer' and greater industrial dynamism, the provision of incentives engendered the emergence of 'bidding wars' among several Brazilian states in order to attract top global players to build plants within their own constituencies (Arbix and Rodriguez-Pose 2001). As competition among states became more intense, the incentives given by local governments became even more generous to include, in its most effusive moments, no less than 'donation of land'; construction of all 'necessary infrastructure for the preparation of the site' including road, rail and port connections; 'tax breaks' for a period no shorter than ten years; 'provision of loans by the state at fixed rates well below those of the Brazilian credit market'; and several other benefits, which would 'range from providing public transport for workers and nurseries for workers' children to various environmental measures' (ibid., p. 13).

There was, therefore, a certain incoherence on the part of local governments in providing large amounts of financial incentives at the same time that the Brazilian central government was actually 'retreating from industrial investment' (ibid., p. 14). The inability of local governments to reach agreements that could secure more tangible returns in terms of employment, technology transfer, capability building or any other form of sustainable development also became evident. Not rarely, after the plants were opened, their benefits to the concession areas were revealed to be lower than expected. Job creation remained low given the technology-intensive nature of the assembly activity, and spill-over effects in terms of promoting a diversified network of contractors and subcontractors were hardly achieved, as tax break clauses present in most of the concession contracts granted free entry for an unprecedented influx of auto-part imports. If Brazil's initial attempt to bring in new players, with the opening up of the automotive sector, had shown signs of deficient planning, a subsequent question is worth posing: What were the consequences for the domestic auto parts industry?

Looking back at its early years, the Brazilian automotive industry started in the 1950s as a clear example of an attempt on the part of the state to build domestic capabilities in the sector. Like other efforts in different industrial sectors that lacked development, the automotive industry in Brazil was initially structured on the synergy of three different entities: (a) multinational corporations, (b) state enterprises and (c) local private companies.[13] The first ones were mainly composed of a few large foreign vehicle assemblers; the second provided the required infrastructure in terms of loans, roads, ports, electricity and inputs, as in the case of steel. Finally, there were the local private companies that were responsible for the auto parts segment. Although Brazil never actually built a successful indigenous assembler company, it managed to develop a large auto parts sector, which supplied the local market and even built, over the years, a diversified portfolio of exports. Companies like Cofap, Metal Leve and Freios Varga (not famous brands in the international business community but constantly referred to in Brazil as sources of national pride due to their entrepreneurial drive) used to export to more than sixty countries. Considering the scale, contribution to the industrial GDP, strategic relevance and vast chain of contractors and sub-contractors, the automotive industry was commonly referred to by several authors as one of Brazil's most important engines of growth.

Despite the fact that the local auto parts sector had achieved considerable levels of efficiency, most of the domestic companies had not followed the transformations of the automotive industry on a broader scale. Outside the protected boundaries of the Brazilian market, the international automotive industry was undergoing a process of deep renovation as new production concepts were introduced and the integration between assembly companies and their suppliers was tightened, a feature that helped the auto parts market to become more highly concentrated. In this new environment, where suppliers became more involved in the design and development of the final automotive product, local auto part companies were excluded from the supply chain, as top assembly plants would give preference to their own global suppliers. Such an arrangement, which became evident in Brazil with the entry of new assemblers, had a perverse effect on the domestic companies and opened the door for the major global auto part companies. As a consequence, towards the end of the 1990s, all the largest domestic auto part companies in Brazil had their production lines taken over one by one by their global counterparts.

The costs of modernising the Brazilian automotive industry in this first wave of investments of the 1990s cannot be ignored. Although the liberalisation of the sector was positive in terms of 'output', 'quality' and 'productivity', it also produced serious setbacks with regard to 'potential loss of local technological development capability' and 'declining scale and quality of employment being generated' (Posthuma 2001, pp. 53–4).

The growth of the Brazilian middle class in the first decade of the twenty-first century and easier access to credit gave a new boost to the automotive market. This higher demand for cars in Brazil coincided with the downturn of the traditional European and North American markets after the 2008 economic crisis. Brazil became once again a recipient of investments from large foreign companies in search of more dynamic markets. This second wave of investments was marked by the entry of relatively new Asian companies, particularly from South Korea and China. In 2012, the Chinese companies Chery and JAC Motors laid the foundation stones of their new assemblers in Jacareí (state of São Paulo) and in Camaçari (Bahia), and the South Korean car maker Hyundai opened a new factory in Piracicaba (São Paulo). In that same year, the Chinese truck manufacturers Sinotruk and Shacman announced greenfield investments in Lages (Santa Catarina) and in Caruaru (Pernambuco). These investments came in tandem with announcements from other more traditional global players. The German luxury car maker

BMW is scheduled to open its first factory in Brazil in the southern city of Araquari (Santa Catarina), Mercedes-Benz in Iracemápolis (São Paulo), Audi in São José dos Pinhais (Paraná), Jaguar Land Rover in Itatiaia (Rio de Janeiro), Fiat in Goiania (Pernambuco) and the Japanese Nissan and Toyota in the respective cities of Resende (Rio de Janeiro) and Sorocaba (São Paulo). Other companies that announced the expansion of their existing facilities were Volkswagen, GM, Ford, Renault, Peugeot Citroën and Mitsubishi.

In the midst of this new wave of investments, a new automotive regime called *Inovar-Auto* was launched. Since October 2012, assembly companies in Brazil have been granted fiscal incentives as long as they commit themselves to make investments in innovation, meet targets of fuel efficiency and ensure a given level of local content. The plan is clearly aimed at making this sector in Brazil less dependent on imports and at stimulating global players to invest in production facilities. The originality of this new regime, in comparison with the first boom of investment back in the 1990s, is its attempt to combine fiscal incentives with concrete targets in terms of investments.

In 2010, the automotive industry accounted for 19.5% of Brazil's industrial GDP and 5% of its nominal GDP (BNDES 2012). In that same year, Brazil became the world's fourth-largest car market, behind only the US, China and Japan. Moreover, the annual output of 3.7 million vehicles in 2013 placed Brazil as the world's seventh-largest car manufacturer only behind China, the US, Japan, Germany, South Korea and India.[14] Despite all that, Brazil doesn't have a renowned global player, either as a system integrator or as a first- or second-tier supplier. That contrasts with other developing economies that have gone through similar stages of development, like South Korea (the land of Hyundai, KIA Motors), China (Chery, JAC Motors, Liffan, Sinotruk) and India (Tata Motors). Only a handful of Brazilian assembly companies have succeeded in the domestic market and have gone abroad. The bus manufacturer Marcopolo and the heavy construction truck maker Randon are perhaps the two most successful examples. Although these companies are competitive in their market segments, they are relatively small when compared to their foreign counterparts. Marcopolo might count with twelve manufacturing units worldwide and may have commemorated a turnover of approximately US$1.5bn in 2013,[15] but the company on the market side faces direct competition from world giants like Irisbus (Iveco), Volvo, Scania and Mercedes-Benz. In a similar fashion, the truck maker Randon, which has five production facilities and global sales of around US$1.8bn in 2013,[16] can be considered a Brazilian multinational. The gap with the world leader, Caterpillar, which in that same year recorded global sales of the order of US$55.7bn, is striking.[17]

All the other large Brazilian automotive companies are restricted to the auto parts sector. They are mostly family-owned business that have been in the Brazilian market for decades and that have survived the opening up of the sector in the early 1990s. These companies tend to have manufacturing units abroad and are active exporters. Despite evidence of their competitive capacity, in 2013, only one Brazilian company, the chassis maker Iochpe-Maxion, was listed in the top 100 global original equipment manufacturer (OEM) parts suppliers ranked by the *Automotive News* magazine. In 2012, the Brazilian battery maker Baterias Moura had net revenues of US$299m,[18] the forged metal parts maker Sifco recorded global sales of US$500m[19] and the sealing system producer Sabó of about US$375m.[20] All these figures are much lower than those shown by their global counterparts such as Bosch, Dana Holding Corp and Federal-Mogul, which in that same year had global sales of, respectively, US$36.7bn, US$7.6bn and US$4.5bn.[21]

The Aerospace Industry

The growth of the aerospace industry in Brazil, chiefly led by Embraer, is in stark contrast to the quick collapse of the domestic auto part companies in the years following the opening up of the economy. Against all the odds of establishing a high-tech industry in a developing country, Embraer has recently grabbed the attention of many scholars and investors due to the company's ability to enter a sector that is notoriously characterised by the dominance of a few global giants. Embraer is currently one of the top four commercial aircraft manufacturers in the world, behind only Boeing (US) and Airbus (European consortium) and alongside Bombardier (Canada). Issues related to technology gap and scale of production that distinguish the two leading aircraft companies need, however, to be emphasized. Boeing and Airbus are the sole competitors making large-size commercial aircraft that can carry up to 450 passengers.

Embraer's civil aircraft production is mainly focused on the regional jet market, and the company disputes with Bombardier the leading position in this segment.[22] Although Bombardier's presence in the regional jet market has preceded that of Embraer by at least three years, the Brazilian aircraft manufacturer has already provided solid evidence of being a strong competitor. By December 2013, Embraer had already delivered 998 units of its E-Series aircraft, and it counted another 429 firm orders. Embraer's firm orders of its 70- to 130-passenger jets were nearly 70% higher than the orders of equivalent aircraft produced by Bombardier. At that same time, Bombardier's CRJ- and CS-Series had together 293 firm orders.[23] Embraer is a rare example of a Brazilian high-tech 'national champion' and one of the very few from a developing economy.

Embraer was launched in 1969 as an effort on the part of the government to develop local technology in the defence and aerospace sectors in Brazil. According to the perception of the ruling military government, such investments were needed due to (i) issues of national security, (ii) the natural relevance of this industry for a country of continental dimensions and (iii) the spill-over effects that this high-tech industry could bring to other industrial sectors.[24] Embraer was actually conceived as part of a technology apparatus that had begun to be built in Brazil, years before, with the creation of the CTA (Centro Técnico de Aeronáutica) in 1945. This aeronautical research centre was based on the standards of MIT (Massachusetts Institute of Technology) and had the ambition to become 'probably the most advanced research [institution] among industrialising countries' (Dahlman and Frischtak 1993, quoted in Goldstein (2001, p. 4). Years after its creation, the CTA led to the foundation of ITA (Instituto Tecnológico de Aeronáutica), one of Brazil's most renowned engineering schools, and the IPD (Instituto de Pesquisas e Desenvolvimento), a division of the centre that pioneered the design and development of Brazil's first commercial aircraft. Embraer was intrinsically a project of the Brazilian government, which made use of technology developed in state research centres and relied on the state apparatus, by means of 'fiscal incentives and government procurement', to guarantee the financial viability of its initial years (Bernardes 2003, p. 6). Embraer's control was subordinated to the federal government and linked to the Ministry of Aeronautics.

Embraer's first attempts to build in technological capabilities were marked by a combination of policies which relied (i) on licensing agreements and cooperation partnerships as part of the company's strategy to have quick access to other sources of technology and (ii) on the company's and local research centres' own investments in R&D. Embraer's first trainer jet was assembled under a licensing agreement with the Italian firm Aermachi, and the company's first subsonic military aircraft AM-X was a joint venture with Aeritalia and Aermacchi. Embraer also benefited from the immediate success of its nineteen-seat turboprob passenger aircraft Bandeirantes, a commercial aircraft whose initial project was designed by the IPD. Bandeirantes quickly reached a relevant presence in the North American commuter turboprop market and helped Embraer expand to foreign markets (Ghemawat, Herrero and Monteiro 2000). This was also a crucial period for the company to identify its core competence and to start acting as a system integrator. 'For the most part, Embraer shied away from manufacturing high-value, high-technology components and concentrated instead on designing the aircraft, producing fuselages, and assembling the final product: already in the 1970s Embraer concluded long-term purchase agreements with its major suppliers' (Goldstein 2001, p. 5). Embraer was also quick in identifying niche markets for its military and civil aircraft, an endeavour in which the company managed to succeed in both segments. Among its best-selling aircraft were the two-seat turbo-prop military trainer Tucano and the above mentioned nineteen-seat twin-engine turbo-prop commercial aircraft Bandeirates.

The exponential growth that marked Embraer's first wave of expansion was interrupted by the debt crisis that hit the Brazilian economy in the 1980s. The company was overnight seriously stripped of capital and saw investments in R&D shrink and generous expenditures in procurement from the state drastically drop. As some of the vulnerabilities of the company were exposed, Embraer was forced to face its main weaknesses, such as lack of attention to 'cost control and marketing', strong reliance on state funding and its own 'inability to diversify its risks and hedge against them' (ibid., p. 2). The economic performance of the company started to slide.

In the beginning of the 1990s, Embraer was included in the comprehensive privatisation programme that was carried out by the Brazilian government. After twenty-five years running as a state enterprise, in 1994, Embraer had 45% of its controlling shares sold to a group of domestic investors and pension funds for the modest amount of US$89m. The period after privatisation definitely brought about a new era for Embraer, and new investments allowed the company to rebound. In the immediate years after privatisation, the company went through a massive internal restructuring, cut 40% of its work force, concentrated efforts on launching a new family of regional jets and, most importantly, restructured its partnerships with its main suppliers. At the same time as Embraer promoted a reduction of the number of suppliers, the company started to demand a closer integration and higher participation in sharing risks. The outcome of this measure was evident, whereas the ERJ-145 project had a total cost of US$350m and accounted for around 400 suppliers, its new family of larger-size aircraft demanded around US$850m and accounted for only 40 main suppliers.

During this period, and more specifically five years after its privatisation, Embraer again went through changes in its ownership structure. In mid-1999, 20% of Embraer's common stocks (around US$209m) were sold to a French consortium led by Aerospatiale Matra (5.67%), Dassault Aviation (5.67%), Thompson-CSF (5.67%) and Snecma (2.99%).[25] Although the initiative to internationalise the capital of the company had faced opposition from part of the military sector in Brazil, the alleged motivation of finding new sources of finance for the company ended up prevailing in the final decision to divest part of the company's capital. With regard to R&D, however, the French participation in the company raised for several years important issues about the much-acclaimed technological capacity of Embraer and the argument of having a high-tech global player truly based in a developing country. These four partners were among the top 600 European companies by value added and were also major investors in R&D. According to a report from the British Department of Trade and Industry, in 2003, Dassault Aviation and Snecma accounted for investments of US$182m and US$784m in R&D, and Aerospaciale Matra and Thompson-CSF, now combined into EADS and Thales, registered investments in R&D of, respectively, US$2,638m and US$545m[26] (DTI 2004). All of them had investments in R&D that were higher than and in some cases went far beyond the US$173m invested by Embraer (Embraer, 2004). In March 2006, Embraer, however, went through another major capital-restructuring programme, which marked the withdrawal of the French consortium from the ownership structure of the company. Embraer became the 'first large Brazilian company with a dispersed equity base', with 57.3% of its shares traded at the São Paulo Stock Exchange and 42.7% traded as ADRs at the New York Stock Exchange.[27] All eleven members of the company's board of directors as well as all its eight directors are Brazilian professionals.[28]

Despite all that Embraer has achieved in recent years, the future of the company still faces tremendous obstacles. First is the cost of having its industrial operations in Brazil, which makes the company constantly vulnerable to economic instabilities and the fluctuations of the local currency. Second is the still-excessive reliance on imports, as it is estimated that '[a]round 95% of the physical volume of inputs, raw material and components, turbines, aeronautic equipment, aeronautical aluminium and cabling used in Embraer's production process come from the international market' (Bernardes 2003, p. 15). Third is the fact that its new family of 98- to 130-passenger aircraft (E190-E2 series) compete with the lower end of the two giants Boeing and Airbus. This latter condition creates a kind of market ceiling for Embraer and produces a strong impediment that prevents the company from expanding to larger-size aircraft. Fourth is the emergence of three new entrants in the regional jet market that might challenge the leading position of Embraer and Bombardier. These new projects correspond to China's ARJ21, Russia's Sukhoi Regional Jet and Japan's MRJ. All of them can count on the direct support of their respective governments and are poised to leave a long-lasting impression on the regional jet market. The Chinese ARJ21 programme, which stands for 'Advanced Regional Jet for the 21st Century', is perhaps the most ambitious. It is part of a government project to 'manufacture internationally competitive large aircrafts' and is seen by the Chinese authorities as 'an integral step for developing the research, development, manufacturing and marketing capacity to sell Chinese large jets to the world' (*Financial Times* 2008). In addition to the 'strong support from the highest levels of government', the project also benefits from high procurement of state-owned airline companies and 'import tax of more than 20 per cent on regional jets' (ibid.). Analysts believe that with the creation of a Chinese jet manufacturer, the country's huge demand for regional jets will be largely supplied by locally made aircraft, which will considerably reduce what has long been considered by the current giants one of the most prospective markets in the world (ibid.). Following the same steps as China, Russia has the aspiration of also building its own family of regional jets. Sukhoi's SuperJet project equally gets the strong support of the government and is well provided for by public funding. It is part of Russia's venture to create 'national champions' in strategic industries and of the Kremilin's ambition to place the country among the top three aircraft manufactures in the world by 2025 (*Financial Times* 2008).[29] The company's target is to sell 800 aircraft by the year 2024 under the prediction of a global demand of about 5,400 regional jets.[30] Finally, Mitsubishi is the last of the three new players to reach the market, with its first aircraft expected to be delivered in 2015 (Mitsubishi Aircraft News 2012). The Mitsubishi Regional Jet counts on highly sophisticated technology as its main competitive advantage. As a member of the 787 Dreamliner project, Mitsubishi will be allowed to use some of its composite materials, which will allow the company to build an aircraft that is 20% more fuel efficient than its equivalent counterparts. If these three new players manage to succeed, they will certainly add even more pressure to a market environment where profit margins are already very slim.

Finally but no less important, in the long term, the regional jet industry might also face the competition of high-speed trains. Although this is an industry that is still in its relatively early stages, growth prospects are particularly high, not only in Western countries but also in the large developing economies. Normally used for connecting highly busy traffic hubs whose distances average between 300 and 700 km, the niche market of high-speed trains largely overlaps with that of the regional jet industry. At the moment, there are seventy projects for high-speed railways under construction, and these investments cover areas as broad as expansions of the original TGV service in France to completely new developments in China, South Korea, Turkey, Morocco, Portugal and Argentina.[31] Even Brazil has recently shown interest in constructing a high-speed railway to connect its two main hubs, the cities of São Paulo and Rio de Janeiro. Although this has been a recurrent claim from the Brazilian government, the pressure for an alternative solution was intensified by a general strike of air traffic controllers, which left the main Brazilian airports at a standstill for several weeks in 2007. At the height of the air traffic crisis, the Ministry of Transport took the first steps in launching a bidding process that could lead to the construction of Brazil's first high-speed rail system. The train service would cover a distance of 511 km and connect the cities of Campinas, São Paulo and Rio de Janeiro (Valor Econômico 2012).

The decision of a country with no recent railway tradition like Brazil to invest in high-speed trains is an emblematic example of the shift of behaviour of policy makers towards efficient terrestrial transportation. The popularisation of high-speed trains, on the other hand, while putting pressure on regional jet manufacturers such as Embraer, in fact benefits other companies like Bombardier and Mitsubishi. Embraer's main regional jet competitor Bombardier is, along with Alstom and Siemens, one of the world's three largest railway equipment suppliers.

In its search for new markets, Embraer has recently made important inroads into the defence industry. The company's new military transport aircraft KC-390 had its maiden flight in February 2015. In December 2013, it already had letters of intent for sixty aircraft.[32] Embraer KC-390 will compete with the North American Lockheed Martin C-130 Hercules.

Brazil's decision to acquire thirty-six Gripen fighter jets from the Swedish company SAAB in December 2013 opened new ground for Embraer. The company will be in charge of the assembly and delivery of all Gripen fighters for the Brazilian Air Force. SAAB and Embraer also plan a strategic partnership for the development of the next generation of Gripen fighter jets to the world market.

OTHER KEY INDUSTRIES IN BRAZIL

A quick analysis of the top twenty-five companies in Brazil (Table 4.4) is enough to identify a few sectors that have gained importance in the Brazilian economy. These sectors, which are basically related to food and beverages, steel, oil, petrochemicals and bio-fuels, telecom and telecom equipment industries, are also the ones that have been most strongly associated with the impressive wave of mergers and acquisitions of the last two decades. In all these sectors, the opening up of Brazil's economy was immediately followed by growing participation of foreign investors.

The food sector is a striking example. The consolidation of the food industry in Brazil started to take shape in the 1980s and intensified in the 1990s. In 2013, five food and beverages companies were in the top twenty-five companies in Brazil: two multinationals (Bunge and Cargill), two Brazilian companies (BRF and JBS) and one mixed capital (Ambev). All these five companies have shown impressive growth over the last decade. Cargill, which in 1990 was ranked 76 in the list of top 500 companies in Brazil, moved to the top 10 in 2013 (Table 4.4). With regard to Bunge Food, the acquisition in the late 1990s of two Brazilian family-owned companies, Moinhos Santista and Ceval, was fundamental in giving the company a stronghold position in the local market of corn- and soya-based products. In 2013, Bunge Food was Brazil's seventh-largest company. The Brazilian food company BRF (the sixth-largest company in Brazil in 2013) was created from the merger of the two biggest domestic poultry companies. The meat-processing company JBS (Brazil's fifteenth-largest company) grew from the acquisition of several slaughterhouses and other food companies in Brazil and abroad. Ambev is the Brazilian arm of the brewer giant AB InBev and it was originally created in 1999 from the merger of Brazil's two biggest brewers.

Another example of the increasing internationalisation of the Brazilian economy in recent years can be found in the telecom sector. The intense reshuffle of telecom equipment manufacturers came about as an immediate consequence of the privatisation of Telebras, the Brazilian Telecommunications System, in 1998. The privatisation, which accounted for more than US$19bn in proceeds and represented the highest amount ever paid for a Brazilian company, put an end to the state control of the twenty-five-year-old nationwide telecommunications system. Although the privatisation programme had only directly affected the national holding of state carriers of telecom services, the measure resulted in a complete restructuring of the local supply chain of telecom equipment. In the time span of only five years, most of the indigenous industrial parks that were built during the period of

Telebras were completely dismantled. Unable to compete with their foreign counterparts and unassisted by any comprehensive safeguard regulation, the local companies quickly saw their assets being acquired by the leading global enterprises. In 2013, three of the top twenty-five companies in Brazil were telecom carriers: Telefônica Brasil (Spanish Telecom), TIM (Telecom Italia Mobile) and Claro (Telmex).

Brazil's top five companies are either energy or mining enterprises.

The Food Industry

In 2002, the Swiss food group Nestlé was named Best Company of the Year for the food sector in Brazil. The award came from one of the most influential business publications in Brazil and is emblematic in the sense that it illustrates the high degree of internationalisation of the food industry in Brazil. Also in that year, Nestlé was Brazil's second-largest food producer and the country's twenty-first-biggest company.

The year 2002 was crucial for Nestlé in Brazil. Earlier that year, the company had finally acquired Garoto, Brazil's largest and most traditional chocolate company. This move assured Nestlé's dominance in that specific market and stressed the company's ambition to keep a leading position in all food segments where Nestlé operated. Garoto, the acquired company, was a domestic seventy-year-old, family-owned enterprise. The company had a solid brand in Brazil and exported to nearly forty countries (*Financial Times* 2001). This acquisition of a traditional food company in Brazil by its larger global counterpart was not, by any means, an isolated event. In reality, it only served to make more evident a tendency that had started to take shape after Brazil's market liberalisation.

In February 2004, the acquisition of Garoto by Nestlé had a complete turnaround. After a process that lasted for nearly two years, the Brazilian antitrust authority CADE (Conselho Administrativo de Defesa Econômica) decided to block the merge.[33] That was a bitter verdict for Nestlé. The antitrust authority understood that the acquiring company would have dominant participation—up to 76% in some segments of the chocolate market in Brazil. Under a resolution from the antitrust authority, Nestlé was obliged to sell the chocolate company and was given '20 days to name an accounting firm to look for buyers and oversee the transfer of assets' (*Financial Times* 2004). Although Nestlé could not appeal the decision directly to the Brazilian antitrust authority, the company was allowed to challenge the resolution in court. This is a measure that Nestlé has since then fiercely taken. In 2004, Brazil was already the world's fifth-largest producer of chocolate, and the divestiture of Garoto would allow the company to be acquired by the North American company Mars or the British Cadbury (Exame on line 2004). More than ten years after the first attempt at a merger, Garoto is still under control of Nestlé, and the case remains under judicial dispute.

The decision of the Brazilian antitrust authority to bar the Nestlé–Garoto merger is an intriguing one. In a similar dispute in 1999, CADE had allowed the merger of the two largest Brazilian brewers, Brahma and Antarctica, in their bid to create Ambev (Americas Beverage Company). The fact that the resulting company would take 71% of the beer market in Brazil seemed not to be an impediment for the antitrust authority to approve the merger.[34] Ambev became the world's sixth-largest brewer, and the approval of the merger sent a clear signal that the creation of a 'national champion' must have weighed in the final decision of the Brazilian antitrust authority. Ambev, on the other hand, did not disappoint in its bid of going abroad. Four years after the merger, the company had already invested US$776 million in a campaign to internationalise its activities and acquired production facilities in Argentina, Uruguay, Paraguay, Chile, Bolivia, Peru, Ecuador, Venezuela and the Dominican Republic (Exame on line 2004). The merger of Ambev with the Belgian company Interbrew in March 2004 led to the creation of InBev, the world's largest brewing company by volume.[35] According to the terms of the contract, the Ambev division of the new company gained control of 100% of the Canadian Brewer Labatt, 30% of Femsa Cerveza and 70% of Labatt USA (InBev 2004). The deal allowed Ambev to expand its presence for the first time to the entire Americas market. InBev's acquisition of Anheuser-Busch in November 2008 for nearly US$52bn helped to consolidate even further its position as the world largest brewer.

Such concern in trying to protect local food and beverages companies is not without reason. In the second half of the last decade, food had already become one of the most dynamic sectors in terms of mergers and acquisitions in Brazil, with a number of transactions even superior to other highly dynamic sectors such as auto parts, steel, chemicals and petrochemicals and electronic components. Not surprisingly, most of the transactions counted on strong participation of foreign capital. According to Jank and colleagues (2001, p. 367), among the most aggressive investors there were world leaders such 'as Nestlé, Parmalat, ADM, Cargill, Unilever, Bunge, Dreyfus, Carrefour, Ahold, Danone and Sara Lee'. Among the acquired companies, there were some of Brazil's most traditional brands in nearly all food segments, with special emphasis on soybeans, coffee, orange juice, dairy, chocolate and bakery products.

The immediate consequence of the growing concentration of the Brazilian agribusiness sector in the 1990s, as stressed by Jank and colleagues (2001, pp. 367–8), can be seen in the way the largest companies started to restructure themselves in the face of fiercer competition. Some of these strategies were highlighted by the authors and included, among other measures, (a) the adoption of new technologies to increase 'labour, land and capital' productivity, (b) the shift of focus to give more emphasis to the their core activities, (c) investments 'in logistics efficiency' to reduce distribution costs and finally (d) the search for better standards of 'food safety, traceability, quality and origin certification' in order to match diet and consumption patterns adopted by more developed economies. Although market liberalisation in Brazil has introduced more dynamic and efficient production practices in the food sector, it has also reduced, with the occurrence of a few exceptions, the participation of the local companies. Foreign investments in this sector have been rampant in exactly two segments, which are also the most profitable ones: large-scale agribusiness production for export and value-added food production for domestic mass consumption. The main exceptions are in the beef and poultry sectors, where three companies—Brasil Foods (poultry), JBS-Friboi (processed meat) and Marfrig (processed meat)—have consolidated a leading position in the Brazilian market and have been relatively successful in the attempt to internationalise their operations.

Brasil Foods, globally branded as BRF, was created in 2009 from the merger of Brazil's two biggest poultry companies, Sadia and Perdigão. The merger had the approval of the antitrust body and counted on the backing of the Brazilian Development Bank, BNDES. On several occasions during the merging process, the bank's president, Mr Luciano Coutinho, expressed to the business media his intention of giving support to the creation of a 'national champion' in the sector. In 2012, the Brazilian development approved a credit line of R$2.52bn (approximately US$1.26bn) to be used in the organic growth of the company. The company is partially owned by the pension funds of two of Brazil's biggest state-owned companies, namely Petrobras and Banco do Brasil. In December 2013, these two pension funds (respectively, Petros and Previ) were the two biggest single shareholders of the company, and they accounted together for 24.39% of its capital.[36]

Marfrig is a relatively new company. It was founded in 1986 and operated initially in the distribution of beef, pork and poultry cuts. The company had its first cattle slaughtering unit in the year 2000. Since then, the food company has embarked on an impressive expansion. An avid acquirer, the company also had support from the Brazilian development bank for its project to expand abroad. In 2008, Marfrig acquired the traditional Irish food company Moy Park. With the financial help of BNDESPAR, the equity arm of BNDES, in 2010 the company raised funds to buy the total stake of Keystone Foods. The former North American company is one of the global suppliers of processed meat to food chains such as McDonald's and Subway. In June 2014, up to 19.63% of Marfrig's capital belonged to BNDES, making the bank its second-largest stakeholder. The company also benefited from the decision of the Brazilian antitrust authority that some brands of 'Brasil Foods' had to be divested. These acquisitions helped Marfrig consolidate its position in the Brazilian market and, as a consequence, its expansion abroad. In 2013, the company recorded net revenues of US$7.7bn[37] and it counted seventy-eight manufacturing, commercial and distribution facilities in sixteen countries.[38]

Like the previous two companies, JBS-Friboi is another Brazilian food company that has gone abroad over the last few years. Its growth has been impressive. 'JBS-Friboi, which started life as a tiny slaughterhouse, has grown to become the world's biggest processor of animal protein, with operations on all five continents' (*Financial Times* 2010). The company began its internationalisation process in 2005 with the acquisition of Argentina's branch of Swift Armour. Since then, the company has been an aggressive acquirer, with two significant takeovers, Swift and Co. in 2007 for US$1.4bn and Pilgrim's Pride in 2009 for US$2.8bn. JBS-Friboi is currently the world biggest producer of processed meat. In 2013, the company was ranked 275 in Fortune's global 500 with total revenues of US$38.7bn.[39] Another interesting aspect of this company is that it is partially owned by the state. BNDESPAR and the Brazilian state-owned bank Caixa Econômica Federal account for 34.66% of JBS-Friboi.

State participation in each of these three companies follows the present understanding from BNDES in supporting the processed meat industry, where Brazil enjoys a natural comparative advantage and can be most competitive. This policy of picking a specific sector to nurture its development into a 'national champion' was introduced again into the Brazilian policy agenda during President Lula's administration. Needless to say, this is in stark contrast with the first stages of Brazil's market liberalisation in the 1990s.

Telecoms and the Telecom Equipment Industry

No other sector in Brazil went through a more wide-ranging restructuring process than telecoms in the second half of the 1990s. In a single day, on the 28th of July 1998, the Brazilian government divested the totality of its controlling shares of one of its most valuable assets: the nationwide telecommunications system. The auction raised at that time more than US$19bn in proceeds and accounted for the highest amount ever paid for a Brazilian company.

The privatisation of Telebras the Brazilian Telecommunications System, did not pose any barrier against participation of foreign investors and came in tandem with an extensive agenda to liberalise the sector. The auction of the telecommunications system was one of the first attempts to foster the inflow of foreign investments, and successful privatisation of the sector was fundamental in overcoming political opposition against the selling of public assets and in paving the way for the divestiture of other sectors as banking and the electricity sector.

The Brazilian Telecommunications System was created in 1972, but it was only in the late 1970s that the state-owned telecom company Telebras recorded its highest growth.[40] Under a national policy of inward-looking development, its operations were highly subsidised by the state, and its goals were mainly driven towards the consolidation of technological sufficiency and the achievement of a more even distribution of telecommunications services. Although measures related to productivity, teledensity and quality of service never reached the standards of more developed economies, during the period of state intervention, Telebras managed to build an indigenous telecommunications industry. Local engineers and technicians were encouraged to design, develop and produce hardware equipment and solutions for network management.

Telebras was a typical example of import-substitution industrialisation where emphasis was given to the development of technological capabilities and the protection of national equipment manufacturers. This strategy soon started to produce its first positive results, as

> throughout the 1970s Telebras had gradually reduced dependence on international suppliers in a context of rapidly growing demand, the emergence of new services, and a technological discontinuity in production (from electromechanical to digital). By the end of the period, the Brazilian telecom system had attained a level of service sophistication and quality without par among developing countries.
>
> (Noam 1998, p. 234)

The creation of CPqD (Centro de Pesquisas e Desenvolvimento) in 1976, Telebras's Research and Development Centre, was decisive in fostering a domestic telecommunications industry. The centre carried out very active scientific production and usually enjoyed the strong partnership of academic research groups and private companies. Within two decades of its foundation, CPqD was already regarded as one of the most advanced research centres in telecommunications outside the industrialised world and the only one of its kind in Latin America (Molano 1997, p. 28). CPqD was at the very core of a vertically integrated system of innovation for telecom equipment production in Brazil. The role of CPqD as a state-funded research centre was of developing technology innovations that would later feed a chain of domestic suppliers. The transference of technology to local firms along with the government's strategy to nationalise production was responsible for the creation of an industrial park of equipment suppliers that by the mid-1980s accounted for more than 1,200 small domestic companies (ibid.). In addition, backed up by the solutions developed by CPqD, Telebras was finally able to deal with the complexity of integrating several smaller independent networks[41] that were spread all over the country and succeeded in building a uniform and standardised nationwide telecommunications system. Among its main products there were the development of a digital switch (the first of its kind produced by a developing country), the mastering of the production process for optical fibres and the patenting of the induction-loop phone card. Thanks to the innovative capacity of CPqD and its commitment to providing technology to local companies, by 1988, nearly twelve years after its creation, almost 77% of telecom equipment revenues in Brazil came from domestic suppliers.

Hit by the debt crisis of 1982, Telebras's operational performance started to decline, and in the late 1980s when the company was succumbing to mounting debts, the path towards structural reforms was taken as inevitable. In 1995, the reforms started to take shape as the Brazilian congress approved an amendment to the national constitution allowing the privatisation of the telecommunications system. This measure was followed by the setting up of a legal framework for the deregulation of the sector and the creation in 1997 of a regulatory body for the telecommunications sector, ANATEL (Agência Nacional de Telecomunicações). The privatisation of Telebras was carried out in the following year.

The privatisation of Telebras marked the beginning of a new phase of investments and the entry of new players. Mainly attracted by the pent-up demand for telecom services, several companies, in their majority from Europe and North America, decided to invest in the Brazilian telecom market. Both segments of fixed-phone lines and mobile communications saw a rapid expansion of their respective sectors as the market was gradually opened, initially through a period of legal duopoly and then towards full liberalisation. The privatisation of Telebras also coincided with a period of fast expansion of the telecoms industry in the global market as well as the consolidation of European telecom companies in Latin America, facts that certainly contributed to the large participation of foreign investors in the opening of the Brazilian telecommunications sector.

More than ten years after the privatisation of Telebras it is probably the impressive expansion of telecom services that has been its most visible result. Between 1998 and 2013, the number of installed fixed-phone lines doubled from 20.2m to 44.7m, and the number of mobile phone subscribers skyrocketed from 5.6m to 271m.[42] It is necessary to draw attention, however, to the initial goal of the privatisation process, which deals with the creation of a competitive environment in which a more critical analysis of the privatisation and liberalisation processes can then be conducted. In the years following the opening up of the Brazilian telecommunications market, Oi (formerly Telemar), the only company totally controlled by domestic capital, had a dominant position in the northern part of Brazil, Telefonica (Spanish Telecom) dominated the region of São Paulo and Brasil Telecom dominated the Southern region of Brazil and was controlled by a consortium formed by Brazilian pension funds and Citigroup Venture Capital International.

One decade after the privatisation of the national telecommunication system, the Brazilian government reconsidered the importance of having a nationwide domestic player. In April 2008, the federal government decided to ignore existing legislation and openly supported the merger of two regional-size networks. The deal paved the way for the creation of a 'national champion' and created a company that was allegedly able to compete with Telmex and Telefonica for the Brazilian (and eventually the Latin American) market. This new company, formed by the acquisition of

Brasil Telecom by Oi (formerly Telemar), accounted at that time for 57% of the landline phones and 18.5% of the mobile phones in Brazil (*Financial Times* 2008). Although the deal was outlawed by the legislation, the Brazilian government did not find any impediment to carrying out the necessary changes in the local regulatory framework of the telecommunication services. Moreover, the state-owned development bank also agreed to fund, by means of low-interest-rate loans, nearly half of the US$3.5bn required for the transaction (ibid.). The deal faced strong criticism from sector analysts, who claimed that a significant change in the regulatory framework for the specific purpose of creating a large domestic company could harm the confidence of private investors in the Brazilian telecom market.

Despite substantial state investment, the original intention of creating a genuine domestic telecom company was short lived. In 2010, part of the company's capital was sold to Portugal Telecom. The Portuguese carrier became Oi's main shareholder, accounting for 23.3% of its total capital. Two years later, a reshuffle of Oi's ownership structure reduced the participation of Portugal Telecom. In December 2013, the Portuguese carrier had 12.1% of Telemar Participações (TmarPart), which is Oi's controlling company. The Brazilian Development Bank and the pension funds of three state-owned companies, namely Banco do Brasil (Previ), Caixa Econômica Federal (Funcef) and Petrobras (Petros), are together TmarPart's major shareholders, accounting for 37.8% of its capital.

Although in the first years after privatisation, the Brazilian telecommunications service counted on the presence of North American and European companies like Bell South, MCI and Telia, most of the global players such as Deutsche Telekom, France Telecom and Vodafone never showed interest in the Brazilian telecommunication market. The absence of global giants left the path open for the emergence of two regional powerhouses, Spain's Telefonica and Mexico's América Móvil. Both companies climbed their way to leading positions in the Brazilian market through the acquisition of smaller networks and the taking over of joint ownerships. In 1998, Telefonica entered the Brazilian market by acquiring Telesp, which was the fixed-phone network of the rich state of São Paulo. In the following years, the company benefited from the merging of several mobile phone networks in the north, northeast, middle and southeast of Brazil. Among Telefonica's latest acquisitions are two small mobile companies, Telemig and Amazônia Celular, and the Brazilian branch of Telecom Italia Moviles. América Móvil's largest acquisitions in Brazil include the local branch of the former MCI/Worldcom and NTT Mobile Communications. In December 2013, these two companies (Telefonica and América Móvil) accounted for nearly 53.8% of mobile phones and 47.1% of the fixed phone lines operating in Brazil.[43]

With regard to the local park of equipment manufacturers, the liberalisation of the telecommunication market was equally effective in bringing about a whole reshuffle of the sector. Despite the impressive rise in the supply of telecom services in Brazil in the years that followed the privatization of Telebras in 1998, the gains of such growth were hardly shared by the domestically owned companies. The privatisation of Telebras was at first a tremendous setback to CPqD, which saw its central role in the design, development and production of telecom equipment in Brazil being considerably downgraded. In the year prior to the privatisation of the Brazilian Telecommunication System, CPqD lost its status as a publicly funded research institution and became a private foundation. As a consequence, CPqD lost not only its main source of funding but also its strategic position as a key agent of technology innovation in the Brazilian telecom equipment industry. This change had a ripple effect on the local companies, which became suddenly deprived of one of their main sources of technology. As a private foundation, CPqD had to move away from risk-sharing, long-term ventures to focus its business on more short-term, market-based projects.

In addition to the demise of the innovation system led by CPqD, the second factor that contributed to the collapse of the Brazilian telecom industry was the end of the procurement scheme that allowed local companies to benefit from the purchase power of the state. Local telecom equipment manufacturers were forced to quickly adapt to a new environment in which they would be supplying to a number of newly created private operators. Most of these private carriers (in their majority foreign telecom companies), on the other hand, were integrated into wider global supply chains and already had their own first- and second-tier suppliers. Telecom equipment manufacturers like Nortel and Alcatel are plain examples that help to illustrate the connection between the liberalisation of telecom services and the entry of new equipment suppliers. While Nortel benefited from the entry of North American carriers, Alcatel had Spanish telecom as its main client. These suppliers and carriers did not operate in the Brazilian market before the mid-1990s, and their quick expansion into the Brazilian market was only made possible due to the liberalisation of the sector in 1998.[44] This strategic connection between telecom operators and giant telecom equipment suppliers considerably reduced the market power of the local companies and contributed to forcing them down to the lower end of the value chain.

And last but not least, the third negative impact on the Brazilian telecom equipment industry was the impressive rise in imports that came in tandem with the liberalization of the market. Although the new telecommunication law previewed contractual clauses that obliged the winners of a telecom concession to give preference to locally produced equipment, these clauses were easily bypassed by the new private telecom operators. Uncommitted to previous efforts of industrialisation, the new carriers found the path opened to use imports. Not surprisingly, the years that immediately followed the opening up of the telecom sector were marked by a sharp decline in trade balance. The trade deficit of telecom equipment in the second half of the 1990s of nearly US$9.6bn was more than five times higher than the one recorded in the first half of the decade.[45]

The demise of the CPqD-led innovation system, along with the end of procurement policy of the state and the free entry of imports, took a decisive toll on the Brazilian telecommunication industry. As has been pointed out by Marina Szapiro (2007), the market share of Brazilian telecom equipment manufacturers plummeted from a peak of 77% in 1988 to a dismal 4.3% in 2003. Unable to compete with their foreign counterparts and unassisted by any comprehensive safeguard regulation, the local equipment manufacturers quickly saw their assets being acquired by the leading global companies. The Brazilian telecom market soon became concentrated among global companies such as Siemens, Samsung, Ericsson, Motorola, Huawei, ZTE, Nortel and Alcatel. In 2012, the telecom parts industry recorded a total deficit of US$5.4bn. Brazil's imports of telecom components of US$5.6bn were strikingly more than twenty times higher than its exports of just US$231m (Abinee 2013).

Steel

When Brazil launched its privatisation programme in the early 1990s, the steel companies were right at the top of the list of state-owned enterprises to be sold. After several years of poor administration and political misuse of their assets, the state-owned steel companies were on the brink of insolvency, with most of them struggling with mounting debts, lack of competitiveness, obsolete technology and a chronic state of over-employment. In addition, and equally important, the divestiture of this sector did not face any legal or constitutional impediment. This was crucial for a rapid selling of the companies and would, as a consequence, help to imprint momentum for the divestiture of several other state-owned enterprises that the government had included in the privatisation programme.

Once the decision to privatise the whole set of steel companies was taken, the following step demanded the creation of an appropriate environment for their sale. In order to make the companies more attractive for private investors, in the years leading to the privatisations, the Brazilian government made several interventions with the objective of cutting jobs and injecting investments to reduce debts and update production lines in most of the steel companies.[46] The results were fruitful. From 1991 to 1993, Brazil privatised its largest steel companies, which represented nearly 70% of the country's overall production. Attracted by the government's funding facilities and protected by a legislation that, at that time, restricted the participation of foreign capital in the privatisation programme, investors were in their totality domestic groups. These groups were mainly composed of (a) existing domestic private steel companies, (b) local investment banks, (c) pension funds and (d) the companies' own consortium of employees. Under new control and administration, all companies went through comprehensive restructuring processes, which included the reshuffle of their board of directors, re-evaluation of contracts with suppliers and clients and cuts on workforce.

Although labour productivity has dramatically increased in the period after the privatisation and liberalisation of the steel sector in Brazil, this industry still lags behind the more competitive economies, as in the case of Japan and South Korea. However, as pointed out by Amann and Nixson (1999, p. 84), 'Brazil's relatively low labour productivity is offset—at least in part—by low labour, iron ore and electricity costs'. In addition, the open-cast condition of many important mines has also strongly contributed to make Brazil's steel production some of the cheapest in the world, a feature that has recently attracted the attention of many foreign investors.

Two decades after the last Brazilian steel company had moved from state to private hands and the sector had gone through a major market liberalisation programme, a few observations can now be drawn. First is the withdrawal of the local investment banks from the ownership of all major former state-owned steel enterprises; second is the ownership concentration of companies within the same industrial sector; third is the complete failure of employees' ownership consortia as a way of providing the workers larger participation in the companies' decision making. Constantly overtaken by unilateral decisions from the major stakeholders, the participation of the employees was, in most of the cases, timid or nonexistent. Finally is the entry of the top global players in a market that used to be traditionally dominated by local Brazilian companies. Probably the most significant example is ArcelorMittal, whose aggressive investments in Brazil in recent years have granted the company full control over CST (Companhia Siderúrgica de Tubarão)[47] and Acesita and Nippon Steel, which in December 2013 had 29.4% of Usiminas's capital. All of them (CST, Acesita and Usiminas) are major players in the Brazilian steel market.

The attempt of the Brazilian steel sector to expand abroad is mainly led by two domestic private companies, Gerdau and CSN (Companhia Siderúrgica Nacional). Gerdau, which is still a family-owned company, was the first, back in the early 1980s, to internationalise its operations. After the acquisition of several mid-size companies in Uruguay, Chile, Argentina and Canada, Gerdau expanded its operations to the North American market with the acquisition of Ameristeel in 1999 (*Financial Times* 2006). Over the last decade, Gerdau has been an aggressive acquirer of foreign assets. It has expanded its operations to Central America, Europe and Asia. In 2007, Gerdau took another important step towards its international expansion, the acquisition of its US rival Chaparral Steel for US$4.2bn (*Financial Times* 2007). In 2013, the company had an installed capacity of 25 million tons of steel, and it recorded net revenues of approximately US$17bn.[48] The bulk of its steel production came from abroad.

CSN was the first steel producer in Brazil. Founded in 1941, this former state-owned company was privatised in 1993, and after several changes in its ownership structure, the company is currently controlled by the Brazilian conglomerate Vicunha. CSN began its internationalisation process in 2001 with the acquisition of the North American company Heartland Steel. Two years later, the Brazilian company acquired the Portuguese steelmaker Lusosider. In January 2012, it acquired the German steelmaker Stahlwerk Thüringen GmbH (SWT). This acquisition allowed CSN to enter the long steel segment. Not all of its attempts to move abroad were successful, however. In 2007, for instance, CSN lost to the Indian group Tata the dispute over the control of the Dutch steel company Corus.

Despite all the efforts of the Brazilian companies to internationalise their industrial capacity, they still lag far behind their global counterparts. According to the World Steel Association, Gerdau was the only Brazilian capital company among the world's top fifty steel producers in 2013. The company was ranked in the sixteenth position (WSA 2014)).

Oil and Petrochemicals

For nearly fifty years, the oil industry in Brazil was under the legal monopoly of a single company. Petrobras the Brazilian Petroleum company created in 1953, had accumulated, until very recently, full control of exploration, production, refining and distribution of oil in Brazil. In addition, Petrobras also enjoyed the monopoly of imports and exports of crude and petroleum products and was responsible for setting the prices in all downstream activities. Following the policy of import substitution industrialisation, Petrobras built technological capabilities in a variety of segments from up-to downstream, with special emphasis on crude oil refining and off-shore exploration. Strongly concerned with technology innovation, Petrobras is one of the Brazilian companies with the largest investments in R&D. Petrobras is also the largest company in Brazil, with net revenues of US$104.2bn in 2013.[49]

As the history of Petrobras is closely connected with the history of Brazil's industrialisation and macroeconomic performance, it is not a surprise that when Brazil moved towards the liberalisation of its economy, the oil sector was included in the reform agenda. The rationale behind the liberalisation of the oil sector in Brazil, although with a variety of motivations, can be broadly explained by the intention of promoting economic efficiency in the sector through the entry of new players and the expected inflow of investments.

The first measures towards the liberalisation of the oil sector in Brazil started in 1995 with the approval of a constitutional amendment that brought an end to the state monopoly in the sector. This measure was also followed by the creation of a regulatory agency for the oil industry, which from the second half of the 1990s has been responsible for setting the rules that allowed the entry of new players. Price controls in downstream products were eliminated, and since 2002, the retail price of oil has floated according to market rules. The Brazilian government also carried out a complete reshuffle in the sector, which resulted in the construction of a legal framework for the total liberalisation of the Brazilian oil market from up- to downstream activities.

The quick entry of global companies like BP, Shell, Texaco, ESSO and Repsol YPF in all oil activities in Brazil has posed new and considerable challenges for Petrobras. In terms of domestic production of oil, this has been an intensive period, with production growing two-fold in the second half of the 1990s and figures related to proved oil reserves reaching record highs, particularly after 2007 with the pre-salt deepwater exploration. This has also been a period of intense transition for the company in which the definition of new targets was set. A symbol company of the developmental model of the 1960s and 1970s, Petrobras is now set to represent the new role of the state in a more liberalised economy (Scaletsky 2001, p. 138).

Although the oil market has been totally liberalised, Petrobras still holds a monopoly position in all segments and benefits from its unique competitive advantage as the only long-running player in the Brazilian market. The future of the company is still very uncertain as competition starts to gain shape and bigger players begin to consolidate their positions. The interest of the international community is evident.

In the petrochemical sector, domestic production gained steam in the early 1970s when Petroquisa (Petrobras's petrochemical subsidiary) laid down a development project in the northeast region of Brazil. The company named Copene (Petroquímica do Nordeste S.A.) opened a new era for the petrochemical industry in the country, which very much epitomized the interventionist rationale of the Brazilian state at that time. The pro-development aim of the project was clear, as it had the intention of moving the bulk of petrochemical production to one of the most underdeveloped regions in Brazil, which was located hundreds of miles away from the industrial area of São Paulo. Although it was intended to be a tripartite alliance among *state*, *foreign* and *local* capitals, the government was expected to have a controlling role. This state control over Copene was gradually reduced during the economic reforms of the 1990s until it was finally taken over in 2001 by the domestic private consortium Odebrecht/Mariani. In the following year, the merger of Copene with five other companies from the Odebrecht and Mariani conglomerates led to the creation of the fully integrated petrochemical company Braskem.

In January 2010, the merger of Braskem with the plastic resin producer Quattor (which was partially owned by Petrobras) allowed the state to raise its stake again in the domestic petrochemical industry. With the merger, 46.2% of Braskem's voting capital was handed over to Petrobras and 53.8% to Odebrecht. With net revenues of US$10.3bn in 2013, Braskem is now the biggest petrochemical company in Latin America, the second largest in the

Americas (only behind the North American company Dow Chemical), and it is believed to be among the top ten petrochemicals companies in the world.

The Brazilian Bio-Fuel and Ethanol Industry

The first years of the twenty-first century in Brazil were marked by the revival of the domestic ethanol industry. This recovery was chiefly motivated by high prices of oil in the international market and the launch of the flex-fuel technology by the Brazilian automotive industry. In 2003, Brazil's main car assemblers (Ford, VW, Fiat, Honda, Peugeot, Renault and General Motors) began the production of vehicles that could run on any blend of pure ethanol and gasoline. The flex-fuel technology was an immediate success. In 2004, bio-fuel vehicles already represented 30% of car sales in Brazil. In the following year, this figure jumped to 53%, and in early 2006, flex-fuel vehicles accounted for nearly 70% of sales. As all gasoline sold in Brazil can contain up to 26% ethanol, it is believed that by mid-2006, sugarcane-based fuel was already responsible for around 40% of Brazil's driving fuel. It is not only the local market that has recently fuelled the Brazilian ethanol industry. The success of ethanol moved beyond the domestic borders and even drew the attention of developed economies in search of an alternative and renewable source of energy. In Japan, a pro–Kyoto Treaty measure was signed for the 'substitution of up to 3% of gasoline with ethanol' (ibid.); in the EU, talks were carried out to increase the proportion of ethanol in gasoline from 5% to 10%; and in the US, an agreement was reached for the reduction of its consumption of gasoline by 20% over the next ten years (*Financial Times* 2007). The prospects of these economies becoming potential markets for Brazilian-produced renewable fuels made a tremendous impact in the sector. The rush for flex-fuel vehicles and the possible use of ethanol as a renewable source of energy in the international market are now at the centre of a complete restructuring of the bio-fuel industry in Brazil. Several new sugarcane mills were built, and the sector became the focus of interest from large foreign and domestic investors.

The Brazilian bio-fuels programme is among the most advanced in the world (*Financial Times* 2006). It was first launched in 1975 and resulted from a decision by the Brazilian government to reduce the country's dependence on imported oil. Brazil was severely hit by the first oil crisis of 1973, and the need for an alternative source of energy was made paramount, particularly by the fact that oil imports accounted for nearly 90% of its fuel consumption. The Brazilian National Alcohol Programme began with the production of ethanol to be blended with gasoline (approximately 20% of total volume) and shifted in the following years to the production of ethanol for 100% ethanol-fuelled vehicles. First experiments on ethanol-based engines were carried out by the Brazilian Centre of Aeronautic Technology (CTA) (Moreira and Goldemberg 1999), a military- and state-funded research centre, which was also responsible for developing the prototypes of the first set of Embraer aircraft. When the first models were ready to move to the assembly lines, large-scale production of 100% ethanol vehicles gained the support of the major automotive companies in Brazil: Fiat, VW, GM and Ford.

The ethanol programme was a typical example of a state-led development programme that marked the 1970s ISI in Brazil. The government offered economic incentives, mostly by means of subsidies and low-interest loans, to local private enterprises for the construction of sugarcane refineries, and the state-owned oil company, Petrobras was in charge of purchasing and distributing a given amount of ethanol. A small fiscal incentive was also created to encourage consumers to migrate to ethanol vehicles. Finally, a rigid price control was set to keep ethanol cars attractive to new users. In the first years of the Brazilian Alcohol Programme, the cost of ethanol to consumers accounted on average for 64.5% of the price of gasoline. The government was particularly efficient in selling the bio-fuel programme, and in 1986, pure-ethanol cars already corresponded to 96% of the new vehicles sold in the domestic market (ibid.).

In the early 1990s, however, the Brazilian ethanol programme faced a serious setback, which led, in the following years, virtually to the end of the project. The series of economic reforms implemented in that period to curb Brazil's soaring inflation brutally reduced the capacity of the state to invest and, as a consequence, affected the programme of incentives originally designed for the ethanol industry. Special loans for the construction of sugarcane refineries were abolished; fiscal incentives that had backed the sales of ethanol cars were eliminated; and the price of ethanol, which was initially set to be one third lower than the price of gasoline, had its price difference reduced to only 20%. This last measure had a serious impact on the viability of the ethanol programme. As petrol-fuelled vehicles are in general 30% more efficient than ethanol-based engines, the reduction of this price difference meant that the cost advantage of having a bio-fuel car was simply eliminated. Finally, a spike in sugar prices in the international market in the early 1990s caused sugarcane mills to shift to sugar production to the detriment of ethanol. These series of setbacks led to severe shortages of ethanol and ruined the confidence of consumers in its supply. Sales of ethanol cars dropped to almost zero in 1996, and the ethanol programme was only able to survive due to a decision by the government that demanded the addition of 22% ethanol in all gasoline sold in Brazil.

Towards the end of the 2000s, the ethanol industry in Brazil gained new momentum. Driven by high oil prices and the world demand for more environment friendly sources of energy, ethanol emerged for the first time as a feasible alternative for the global market. Brazil is currently the world's largest producer of sugarcane and the most efficient producer of ethanol. Although ethanol production in the US is higher than in Brazil (the

North American market is responsible for 37% of the world production whereas Brazil accounts for 35%), ethanol produced in the US is mostly based on corn, which is a far less cost-efficient crop for the production of bio-fuels. Whereas maize-based ethanol requires 28,000kcal of energy to produce one gallon of fuel, this figure is drastically reduced to 6,500kcal in the case of sugarcane. In addition, ethanol production in Brazil is also benefited from the fact that its mills make use of *bagasse*, the very by-product of sugarcane, to power their plants, which confers them self-sufficiency in terms of energy supply.

Ethanol production in Brazil was mostly dominated by local companies and spread among several family-owned groups. This predominance of the local companies in the ethanol industry stood unchallenged when their output was destined only to meet domestic demand, but as ethanol emerges as an alternative source of energy in the global market, the chances are of a complete restructuring in the sector. It is expected that the Brazilian ethanol industry will go through heavy consolidation and an intense period of mergers and acquisitions. The first major investment was made by British Petroleum, the first large foreign oil company to enter the Brazilian bio-fuel industry. In April 2008, the company confirmed investments worth US$560m in a joint venture with Santelisa Vale, Brazil's second-largest ethanol producer (*Financial Times* 2008). In 2010, the Anglo-Dutch oil giant Shell merged with Brazil's biggest ethanol producer Cosan. Raízen, the resulting company, combined Cosan's vast ethanol production facilities with Shell's nationwide distribution network. In 2013, Raízen had revenues of US$17.8bn and was already ranked fifth in the list of top 500 companies in Brazil. A sign of the interest of foreign investors in the Brazilian ethanol market is the growth of cross-border venture capital; investors range from the Hungarian mega-investor George Soros and Sun Microsystems's Indian founder Vinod Khosla to the North American investment banks Merrill Lynch and Goldman Sachs.

The above analysis of the impact of the economic reforms on a few selected sectors reveals successful cases in which domestic companies were able to adjust to the new challenges and compete in an open market environment. Some of these companies not only have become fully integrated into the world economy but have emerged as potential national champions. These new 'champions' came from a wide range of sectors and were not restricted to the traditionally competitive mining (Vale) and oil (Petrobras) industries. In aircraft manufacturing, the former state company Embraer became the world leader in the regional jet segment. In the processed food sector, the Brazilian market witnessed the quick rise of three world leaders in their respective segments, poultry (Brasil Foods) and processed meat (JBS-Friboi and Marfrig). In beverages, the domestic brewer Ambev adopted an aggressive internationalisation strategy to become, along with the Belgian company Interbrew, the world leader in their segment. Other successful companies from the set of industries here analysed are the steelmakers Gerdau and CSN, the petrochemical company Braskem and the ethanol producer Cosan.

For many of these companies, it is impossible to ignore the role that ISI played in their early years. Companies like Petrobras (oil), Vale (mining), Braskem (petrochemicals) and Embraer (aerospace) are clear examples of the long-term planning of the state-led development policies implemented in the 1960s and 1970s. Even for the sugar producer Cosan, which since its creation in 1936 has always been a private enterprise, the state was fundamental in the 1970s in giving the company a new competitive advantage through the implementation of its ethanol programme. It must be mentioned, however, that although Brazil moved towards a more market-oriented economy in the 1990s, some mechanisms of state support were not fully abolished. The Brazilian state-owned Development Bank (BNDES) is perhaps the most notable example, as it has remained an active agent of industrial policy by providing financial support for small, medium and large-sized enterprises. Disbursements over the last five years (from 2009 to 2013) amounted to R$791.9bn and, in 2013 alone, they reached the record figure of R$190.4bn (approx. US$86.5bn).[50] In the 1990s, for instance, the bank was an important source of finance for the newly privatised aircraft manufacturer Embraer.[51] More recently, BNDES has played a crucial role in the creation of large domestic conglomerates. Among several other cases, the Brazilian development bank sponsored the mergers that led to the creation of the two food giants Brasil Foods and JBS-Friboi. In the telecom sector, BNDES's financial support for the merger of two Brazilian carriers, Telemar and Brasil Telecom, paved the way for the creation in 2008 of a nationwide domestic operator. The new company was intended to match foreign competition and eventually to expand to other Latin American countries.

The Brazilian Development Bank has also taken the role of providing direct investment to some of the largest domestic private companies. The bank owns, respectively, 13% and 14.6% of the food giants JBS-Friboi and Marfrig, it is the main shareholder (31.3% of the capital) of the nationwide telecom operator Telemar and it owns 20% of the Brazilian pulp and paper giant Klabin.[52] If investments carried out by pension funds controlled by state-owned enterprises like the Banco do Brasil's powerful Previ or Petrobras's Petros are taken into account, the scale of state intervention in the Brazilian economy reaches an even greater scope. The presence of the state has then spread into sectors that are currently regarded as icons of private entrepreneurship. For instance, 12% of the voting capital of the mining company Vale,[53] 13.19% of the aircraft manufacturer Embraer[54] and 24.39% of the newly created food producer Brasil Foods[55] are under the indirect influence of the state. Finally, another sign of state intervention in the economy is given by the recent expansion strategy carried out by some of the remaining state-owned enterprises. A clear example is the merger which was carried out in January 2010 by the petrochemical giant Braskem.

This transaction was partially sponsored (48% of the total capital) by the state-owned oil producer Petrobras. The resulting petrochemical company, which is regarded as the world's eighth largest by sales revenues, is partially owned by the Brazilian state.

On the antitrust front, the Brazilian government has also shown awareness of the importance of building global giants. Since the opening up of the economy, the Brazilian antitrust authority (CADE) has often allowed the creation of large domestic conglomerates, even if this decision leads to a near-monopoly position in certain market segments. Ambev and Brasil Foods are two remarkable examples. The mergers between the two biggest domestic brewers (Antarctica and Brahma) in 1999 and the two largest Brazilian poultry companies (Sadia and Perdigão) in 2009 granted them 73.4% and 81.2% of their respective markets. In both cases, it is possible to observe the predominance of a strategy towards long-term international expansion over measures to protect domestic consumers.

The position of the Brazilian Development Bank and, to a lesser extent, the antitrust authority in the years following the reforms reveals crucial aspects of the Brazilian economy that usually pass unnoticed by the international business media. While the government was implementing an orthodox macroeconomic policy, it kept making use (particularly under the administrations of President Lula and President Rousseff) of state-led mechanisms at the microeconomic level. These initiatives from BNDES and CADE were welcomed by the Brazilian business community, despite the fact that in the early 1990s, this same group had lobbied for market-oriented reforms and lower intervention of the state in the economy.

CONCLUSIONS

An important feature that it is possible to observe in these early years of market liberalisation in Brazil is that the opening up of the Brazilian economy was marked by the rapid denationalisation of local industry. This process, which equally reached all sectors of Brazil's economy, helps to expose gaps in competitiveness that exist between domestic and foreign companies, the inability of the local groups to compete with their foreign counterparts and, more importantly, the failure of the Brazilian government to engender a restructuring programme that would be less harmful for local companies.

A finding worthy of note is that of the 'national champions' that emerged after the economic reforms, a substantial number was of those companies that were created during the state-led development period of the Brazilian economy. Although in most cases privatisation was fundamental to bringing new capital to their operations, it is impossible to deny that they benefitted in their early years from state support and market protection. It was under a long regime of state intervention, special incentives and trade barriers that some of the biggest companies in Brazil were able to lay their foundations. Recent events, however (particularly under the administrations of President Lula and President Rousseff), have shown that the state hasn't entirely abandoned its role as an inducer of growth. Although in a much more discreet fashion, the state can still be seen in a variety of ways: (i) as a major provider of credit through its development bank (covering virtually all sectors from agribusiness to aircraft manufacturing), (ii) through the strategic growth of some of its remaining state-owned enterprises (for instance, the expansion of Petrobras's petrochemical arm) and (iii) in its consent to the formation of domestic monopolies with the purpose of creating 'national champions' (Brasil Foods, JBS-Friboi and Marfrig). These are recent developments which reveal a key characteristic of the Brazilian post-reform economy: that of adopting orthodox practices at the macro level but being willing to engage in state support policies at the micro level.

This increase of the role of the state in the economy that was witnessed during Lula and Rousseff's administrations, however, bears several differences from the state-led development years of the post-war period. First and foremost, there is a full understanding on the part of the business and bureaucratic elites that the current stage of the world economy does not encourage inward-looking strategies. Instead of investing in the production of goods to replace imports, as in the ISI period, the current strategy is more focused on helping companies to operate integrated into the world economy. This view is grounded on Brazil's commitment to an orthodox macroeconomic policy whose main objective is to maintain economic stability and to provide a friendly environment for private investments. The monetary policy of using high interest rates to control inflation contributed to keeping the *Real* overvalued and created a trade environment that was actually biased towards imports. Brazil has been able to maintain a positive trade balance due in part to a growing global demand for commodities (as shown in Part I) and a strong effort from the Brazilian foreign trade ministry to expand its portfolio of trade partners.

Second, there is the expansion of the Brazilian financial market. Although the recent rise in state funding has prompted analysts to suggest there has been a move back to previous state-led policies, it is worthy of note that this revival of the Development Bank as a strategic source of funding has happened in tandem with the growth of the Brazilian financial market. In contrast to previous decades of state-led development, a growing number of domestic companies are also turning to financial markets (either in Brazil or abroad) as a viable form of raising capital. From 2002 to 2013, the trade volume of the São Paulo Stock Exchange (Bovespa) rose more than ten-fold, from R$168bn to R$1.83trn. The launching of 'Mercado Novo' in 2001 by Bovespa gave emerging Brazilian enterprises the opportunity to join on a voluntary basis in a new group of listed companies where the rules for corporative governance were more strict and therefore in greater accordance with international standards.

To a certain extent, the recent revival of state-led policies by President Lula and President Rousseff bears some similarities with policies adopted by South Korea in the 1960s and 1970s. This is particularly evident when it comes to giving direct support to large enterprises that have a strong outward-driven profile. Food giants like Brasil Foods, JBS-Friboi and Marfrig as well as the petrochemical company Braskem fit perfectly into this strategy of nurturing 'national champions' to compete abroad. It must be noted that despite the growing role of the state as a source of funding to private enterprises, Brazil has remained committed to orthodox macroeconomic policies.

Finally, it has also become evident that the losses of Brazil's technology capabilities in the course of its recent market liberalisation were decisive in re-dimensioning Brazil's position in the global supply chain. This condition, which became evident with the impressive growth of technology-intensive imports after the liberalisation of the Brazilian market, is now an issue of constant concern for the current policy makers. The reasons are fairly apparent. Brazil's diversified industrial production has not so far ensured a sustainable contribution in terms of technology innovation. This fact, which indubitably sheds some light on the role that the multinational corporations are willing to play in Brazil, also helps to expose with a few exceptions (as in aircraft manufacturing, petrochemicals, processed food and oil drilling) the failure of the Brazilian companies to grant themselves a leading position in the recent structural changes of global business.

NOTES

1. The perverse effect that across-the-board tariff cuts had on the industrial sector forced the government to review, on a limited basis, part of its tariff policies. The automotive sector, for instance, after having the import tariffs on cars reduced to 20%, saw its tariffs gradually rise again to 70% in 1995.
2. For more information on Brazil's foreign trade in the years following its economic opening, see Chapter 2.
3. Data from the Brazilian Institute of Geography and Statistics, www.ibge.gov.br.
4. Data from the Brazilian Institute of Geography and Statistics, www.ibge.gov.br.
5. Despite recent records of substantial job cuts in several sectors of the Brazilian economy, a study carried out by Regis Bonelli on labour productivity in Brazil in the 1990s contested the view that the last decade's rise in productivity growth was detrimental to employment levels. Alternatively, the study claimed that what was observed in the period was actually a shift of jobs from high-productive sectors (where MNCs' presence became more intensive throughout the decade) to the low-productive ones (Bonelli 2002). A similar change in the employment structure in Brazil was also observed by Matías Vernengo (2004), in this case by what the author identified as a move from high- to low-skilled jobs, a shift that was also followed by a widening wage gap between the two groups. However, in contrast to Bonelli's analysis, Vernengo acknowledged that Brazil's recent liberalisation process had indeed forced the country to accommodate higher rates of unemployment.

6. Probably the most notorious case of a cross-border M&A that had its operations cancelled due to the uncertainties of the new economic scenario after the victory of a left-wing candidate in Brazil's presidential elections was the one that involved the Anglo-Dutch steelmaker Corus and Brazil's largest steelmaker CSN—Companhia Siderúrgica Nacional. This US$4.3bn merger that would create the world's fifth-largest steelmaker was called off just after two weeks of the second round of Brazil's presidential elections in October 2002. This event was much commented on by the business media at that time. 'But the proposal—which would have made Corus the world's fifth largest steel producer—also carried risks. There were concerns about the direction of the Brazilian economy, particularly in the context of a new, left-wing president, Luiz Inácio "Lula" da Silva, who takes office in January' (*Financial Times* 2002).

7. Data from KPMG (various issues).

8. Although *Revista Exame Melhores e Maiores'* annual reports do not provide aggregate data on ownership structure of the top 500 companies for the years 2003 and 2004, calculations carried out by the author suggest that in 2003, the share of private national enterprises may have been higher than that of the multinational corporations, respectively 42.2% and 38.9%. This is an unexpected result which doesn't fit the existing trend and therefore requires further investigation.

9. Telemar, a Brazilian telecom company, was ranked in the 26th position in the top 500 companies in 2013.

10. The Swiss company Nestlé was ranked in the 101st position among the top 500 companies in 2013.

11. In 1998, the North American company Chrysler was acquired by the German car maker Daimler-Benz. The new group was called DaimlerChrysler AG. In August 2007, however, the Chrysler division of DaimlerChrysler AG was sold to the North American investment firm Cerberos Capital Management.

12. The ambiguous concern of the Brazilian government with regard to long-standing microeconomic policies for the sector can be observed, for instance, in the poor attention the government paid to the Automotive Sectoral Chambers. These sectoral chambers were created (or better, revitalized) at the beginning of the liberalisation of the economy in the early 1990s as a way to break with 'traditional corporatist relations' (dominant during the period of state intervention) and set the conditions for new and more representative ways of carrying out negotiations among 'business, labour and state actors' (Doctor 2003). This closer dialogue among these three entities would ultimately shed light on the weaknesses of the sector in this period of transition and, as a consequence, help to establish measures that were more in tune with their mutual needs. However, this proved to be a short-lived initiative, as these 'tripartite' chambers of negotiation ended up being suppressed by constant pressures from the state towards unilateral decisions which would, for instance, invariably deal with more immediate macroeconomic problems (ibid.).

13. An in-depth analysis of the tripartite form of alliance among the 'multinational, state and local capital' and the way it shaped industrial production in Brazil in the post-war period can be found in Peter Evans's seminal work 'Dependent Development in Brazil' (1979).

14. Data from the International Organisation of Motor Vehicle Manufacturers, www.oica.net/category/production-statistics/.

15. Total sales of R$3.6bn according to the company's 2013 annual report.

16. Total sales of R$4.2bn according to the company's 2013 annual report.

17. Data from the company's 2013 annual report.

18. Data comes from Revista Exame Melhores e Maiores (2013) and corresponds to domestic sales only.

19. Total sales of R$1bn according to the company's 2012 annual report, www. sifco.com.br/demonstracoes_financeiras_sifco_2013_pt-br.pdf.
20. Data from www.sabo.com.br/imprensa/informacoes-para-jornalistas/285.
21. Data from *Automotive News* (2013).
22. This is a market that is mostly composed of forty to ninety passenger aircraft that mainly serves regional airlines, which are known as commuters. These regional jets are commonly used to feed hubs of larger aircraft networks.
23. Data from the companies' 2013 annual reports.
24. The São José dos Campos region, where the aerospace facilities were built, was not far from the other industrial clusters dedicated to automotive and telecom equipment production.
25. The controlling stock remained with the Brazilian groups Bozano Simonsen (20%), pension funds Previ (20%) and Sistel (20%), the Brazilian government (3.2%) and other companies (16.7%).
26. Although all the figures of the publication are originally in British pounds, these values in US dollars were converted according to the exchange rate adopted by the publication: 1 GBP = 1.79 USD.
27. In December 2013, the ownership structure of Embraer was as follows: Oppenheimer Fund 10.38%, Thornburg Investment 5.34%, Baillie Gifford 5.49%, Previ (Banco do Brasil pension fund) 7.82%, BNDESPAR 5.37% and others 65.60%. The Brazilian government holds a Golden Share.
28. Data from the company's 2013 annual report.
29. 'Our first task is to become the best in terms of regional jet manufacture, and we consider our competition the likes of Bombardier and Embraer', Mikhail Pogosyan, the general director of Sukhoi, quoted in (*Financial Times* 2008).
30. Data from www.sukhoi.superjet100.com.
31. Data from www.railway-technology.com/projects/category/high-speed-rail ways/.
32. Data from the company's 2013 annual report.
33. 'Nestlé and Garoto had agreed with CADE in 2002 not to merge their operations in an "irreversible fashion"' (*Financial Times* 2004).
34. In reality, the Brazilian antitrust authority CADE approved the merger under one major condition: Ambev had to divest one of its established premium beers, 'Bavaria', that, at that time, had 7% of the market.
35. Another term of the merger contract stated that both parties would share 'equal board seats on board of InterBrewAmBev' as well as 'equal voting arrangements on a combined core shareholding structure' (InBev 2004).
36. Data from the company's 2013 annual report.
37. Total sales of R$18.5bn according to the company's 2013 annual report.
38. Data from the company's 2013 annual report.
39. Data from www.fortune.com/global500/2013.
40. According to (Noam 1998, p. 233), 'the number of lines in service more than doubled from 1973 to 1977, and it more than tripled by 1980, when it reached 4.7 million. During the five years 1976–80, over 500.000 lines a year were being placed in service'.
41. These networks were built by the several private domestic and foreign telecom companies that used to operate in Brazil before the state intervention in the sector. The fragmentation of the market created by these companies along with the high diversity of operators and the lack of integration between their networks were responsible for the generation of constant operational problems. The poor performance of the market in providing the required telecommunications services was claimed as one of the factors that motivated the state to plan its intervention in the sector in the 1960s.
42. Data from the Brazilian Telecom Regulatory Agency, www.anatel.gov.br.

43. Data from www.teleco.com.br.
44. Further comments can also be made on (i) the dismantling of the national system of innovation that was built during the Telebras period with the loss of much of the technological capacity that was accumulated in the 1970s and 1980s (Szapiro 2000) and on (ii) the unprecedented growth in the amount of imports in this sector, which resulted in a worrying trade deficit of US$3.1bn in 2001. These outcomes are equally associated with the liberalisation of the telecoms sector in Brazil.
45. Data from the Brazilian Development Bank, www.bndes.gov.br.
46. Probably one of the most dramatic examples of job cuts implemented by a single company is the one involving Açominas, a steel producer from Southeastern Brazil. From April 1990 to September 1993, the date of its privatisation, the company saw its board of employees reduced by nearly 50%, from 11,500 to 6,500. Under private control, the number of employees fell even further to nearly 3,000 in the year 2001 (Greco and Coutinho 2002).
47. In June 2006, the Indian company Mittal Steel acquired Arcelor to form the global giant ArcelorMittal group. The *CST* (Companhia Siderúrgica de Tubarão) company, which was fully owned by Arcelor, had its name changed to ArcelorMittal Tubarão.
48. Data from the company's 2013 annual report.
49. Petrobras was also ranked 45th in the FT list of the world's largest 500 companies in 2013.
50. Data from the Brazilian Development Bank, www.bndes.gov.br.
51. This credit facility called Proex was the focus of a heated commercial dispute between Embraer and its main competitor Bombardier. This trade dispute ended in 2001 with a ruling by the WTO for the phasing out of illegal credit facilities from both sides.
52. Data from Revista Exame Melhores e Maiores 2009 (2009).
53. Vale's voting capital in December 2013: 41% free float, 6.3% BNDESPAR, 52.7% ValePar (49% Litel Participações S.A., 21.21% Bradespar, 18.24% Mitsui, 11.51% BNDESPAR and 0.03% Eletron S.A.). The Brazilian government holds twelve Golden Shares.
54. Embraer's capital ownership in December 2013: 10.38% Oppenheimer Fund, 5.34% Thornburg Investment, 5.49% Baillie Gifford, 7.82% Previ (Banco do Brasil pension fund), 5.37% BNDESPAR and 65.60% others. The Brazilian government holds a Golden Share.
55. Brasil Foods ownership structure in December 2013: 12.26% Previ (Banco do Brasil pension fund), 12.10% Petros (Petrobras pension fund), 7.87% Tarpon, 4.87% Blackrock, 2.46% Vale pension fund, 1.08% Sistel, 0.29% BNDES and 59.07% others.

REFERENCES

Abinee. *Panorama econômico e desempenho setorial 2013*. São Paulo: Associação Brasileira da Indústria Elétrica e Eletrônica, 2013.

Amann, Edmund. "Globalisation, industrial efficiency and technological sovereignty: evidence from Brazil." *The Quarterly Review of Economics and Finance*. Vol. 42 (2002): 875–88.

Amann, Edmund, and Frederick Nixson. "Globalisation and the Brazilian steel industry: 1988–1997." *The Journal of Development Studies*. Vol. 35 (1999): 59–88.

Arbix, Glauco, and Andrés Rodriguez-Pose. "Strategies of waste: bidding wars in the Brazilian automobile sector." *Workshop on the Brazilian Automotive Industry: Foreign Direct Investments and the Business–State Relations*. Oxford: St. Anthony's College, University of Oxford, November 2001.

ATKearney. *FDI confidence index 2002*. Alexandria, VA: Global Business Policy Council, ATKearney, 2002.

Automotive News. "Top suppliers: North America, Europe and the world." Detroit, 17 June 2013.

Bernardes, Roberto. "Passive innovation system and local learning: a case study of Embraer in Brazil." *1st Globelics Conference: Innovation Systems and Development Strategies for the Third Millennium*. Rio de Janeiro, 2003.

BNDES. *BNDES 60 anos: perspectivas setoriais*. Edited by Felipe Lage de Sousa. Rio de Janeiro: Banco Nacional de Desenvolvimento Econômico e Social, 2012.

Bonelli, Regis. "Labour productivity in Brazil during the 1990s." *Texto para Discussão 906*. Rio de Janeiro: Instituto de Pesquisa Econômica Aplicada, IPEA, 2002.

Costa, Ionara, and Sérgio Robles Reis de Queiroz. "Foreign direct investment and technological capabilities in Brazilian industry." *Research Policy*. Vol. 31 (2002): 1431–43.

Cysne, Rubens Penha. "Macro- and microeconomic aspects of the reforms." In *Brazil in the 1990s*, by Renato Baumann, 39–88. Basingstoke: Palgrave, 2002.

Dahlman, Carl and Claudio Frischtak. "National systems supporting technical advance in industry: the Brazilian experience." In *National innovation systems: a comparative analysis*, by Richard R. Nelson, 414–50. New York: Oxford University Press, 1993.

Doctor, Mahrukh. "The interplay of states and markets: the role of business–state relations in attracting investments to the automotive industry in Brazil." *Working Paper CBS-40-2003*. Oxford: Centre for Brazilian Studies, University of Oxford, 2003.

DTI. *The top 800 UK and 600 European companies by value added 2004*. London: Department of Trade and Industry, 2004.

Embraer. *Annual Report 2004*. São José dos Campos, 2004.

Evans, Peter. *Dependent development: the alliance of multinational, state and local capital in Brazil*. Princeton: Princeton University Press, 1979.

Exame on line. "Ambev investirá US$100m na República Dominicana." 12 February 2004. http://portalexame.abril.com.br/empresas/conteudo_29877.shtml.

———. "CADE reprova compra da Garoto pela Nestlé." 04 February 2004. http://exame.abril.com.br/negocios/noticias/cade-reprova-compra-da-garoto-pela-nestle-m0064061.

Ferraz, João Carlos, and Nobuaki Hamaguchi. "Introduction: M&A and privatisation in developing countries—changing ownership structure and its impact on economic performance." *The Developing Economies*. Vol. 40 (2002): 383–99.

Financial Times. "BP to invest $560m in biofuels with Brazil ethanol joint venture." London, 25 April 2008.

———. "China: a nation's hopes rest on a Flying Phoenix." London, 14 July 2008.

———. "Deal's collapse raises more questions." London, 14 November 2002.

———. "Gerdau pays $4.2bn for US rival." London, 12 July 2007.

———. "Gerdau: family-owned operations set the pace." London, 13 June 2006.

———. "Globalisation: companies must expand to prosper." London, 14 November 2010.

———. "Growing appetite for ethanol puts strain on Brazil's cane millers." London, 26 January 2006.

———. "Nestlé acquires Brazilian rival." London, 01 March 2001.

———. "Nestlé ordered to sell Brazilian unit." London, 05 February 2004.

———. "Sukhoi turns swords into ploughshares." London, 14 July 2008.

———. "Telemar and Brasil Telecom in R$6bn merger." London, 27 April 2008.

———. "US signs green fuel deal with Brazil but fails to address market access." London, 10 March 2007.

Furtado, João. "Globalização das empresas e desnacionalização." In *Desnacionalização: mitos, riscos e desafios*, by Antônio Corrêa de Lacerda, 13–42. São Paulo: Editora Contexto, 2000.

Ghemawat, Pankaj, Gustavo Herrero, and Luiz Felipe Monteiro. "Embraer: the global leader of regional jets." *Case Study 9–701–006*. Boston: Harvard Business School, 2000.

Goldstein, Andrea. "From national champion to global player: explaining the success of Embraer." *Working Paper CBS-17–2001*. Oxford: Centre for Brazilian Studies, University of Oxford, 2001.

Gonçalves, Reinaldo. *Globalização e desnacionalização*. São Paulo: Editora Terra e Paz, 1999.

Greco, Antônio do Monte, and Carlos Sidnei Coutinho. "Açominas: um exemplo polêmico de privatização." *Proceedings of the 'X Seminário de Economia Mineira'*. Diamantina, 2002.

IEDI. "Emprego e renda—2003: Um ano de desemprego e de queda acentuada do rendimento nos grandes centros urbanos." São Paulo: Instituto de Estudos para o Desenvolvimento Industrial, 2004.

———. "Produtividade do trabalho na indústria: evolução crescente." São Paulo: Instituto de Estudos para o Desenvolvimento Industrial, 2004.

InBev. "Interbrew and AmBev establish InterbrewAmBev: the world's premier beer." *Press Release*. Leuven and São Paulo, 03 March 2004.

Jank, Marcos Sawaya, Maristela Franco Paes Leme, Andre Meloni Nassar, and Paulo Faveret Filho. "Concentration and internationalisation of Brazilian agribusiness exporters." *International Food and Agribusiness Management*. Vol. 2 (2001): 359–74.

KPMG. "Mergers and acquisitions research 2014, 1st quarter: mirror of transactions undertaken in Brazil." São Paulo, 2014.

Lacerda, Antônio Corrêa de. *Globalização e investimento estrangeiro no Brasil*. 2nd edition. São Paulo: Editora Saraiva, 2004.

Mendes de Paula, Germano, João Carlos Ferraz, and Mariana Iootty. "Economic liberalisation and changes in corporate control in Latin America." *The Developing Economies*. Vol. 40 (2002): 467–96.

Mitsubishi Aircraft News. "Mitsubishi regional jet schedule update." *Press Release*. Nagoya, 25 April 2012.

Molano, Walter. *The logic of privatisation: the case of telecommunications in the southern cone of Latin America*. Westport, CT: Greenwood Press, 1997.

Moreira, José Roberto, and José Goldemberg. "The ethanol program." *Energy Policy*. Vol. 27 (1999): 229–45.

Moreira, Maurício Mesquita. "Capital nacional na indústria: reestruturar para sobreviver." In *Desnacionalização: mitos, riscos e desafios*, by Antônio Corrêa de Lacerda, 43–65. São Paulo: Editora Contexto, 2000.

Noam, Eli M. *Telecommunications in Latin America*. Oxford: Oxford University Press, 1998.

Posthuma, Anne Caroline. "Industrial renewal and the inter-firm relations in the supply chain of the Brazilian automotive industry." *Workshop on the Brazilian Automotive Industry: Foreign Direct Investments and Business-State Relations*. Oxford: St. Anthony's College. University of Oxford, November 2001.

Ramos, Lauro, and Marcelo Britto. "O funcionamento do mercado de trabalho metropolitano brasileiro no período 1991–2002: tendências, fatos estilizados e mudanças estruturais." *Texto para discussão 1011*. Rio de Janeiro: Instituto de Pesquisa Econômica Aplicada, IPEA, 2004.

Revista Exame Melhores e Maiores 2009. São Paulo: Editora Abril, July 2009.

Revista Exame Melhores e Maiores 2012. São Paulo: Editora Abril, July 2012.

Revista Exame Melhores e Maiores 2013. São Paulo: Editora Abril, July 2013.

Revista Exame Melhores e Maiores 2014. São Paulo: Editora Abril, June 2014.

Revista Valor: Grandes Grupos. "Os dez anos que mudaram o Brasil." Rio de Janeiro: Valor Econômico, December 2002.

Scaletsky, Eduardo Carnos. "A Petrobras e os trabalhadores da empresa estatal." *Revista Universidade Rural*. Vol. 23 (2001): 137–49.

Szapiro, Marina Honorio de Souza. "New opportunities for developing countries in telecommunications: a comparison between Brazil, India and China." *Proceedings of the 5th Globelics International Conference*. Saratov, 2007.

———. *Technological capacity in the telecommunications industry in Brazil: development and impacts of the structural reform in the 1990s*. Rio de Janeiro: Instituto de Economia, Universidade Federal do Rio de Janeiro, 2000.

Valor Econômico. "Governo assume mais risco para levar trem-bala adiante." Rio de Janeiro, 20 December 2012.

Vernengo, Matías. "External liberalization, stabilization, and the labor market in Brazil." *Latin American Perspectives*. Vol. 31 (2004): 62–75.

WSA. *World steel in figures 2014*. Brussels: World Steel Association, 2014.

Final Conclusions

The market-oriented reforms carried out by Brazil in the 1990s led to a profound change in local business. Within a short period of time, there was an impressive surge in foreign investments, a sudden rise in mergers and acquisitions, an intense reshuffle of the ownership structure of the biggest companies in Brazil, a rearrangement of the most dynamic sectors of the Brazilian economy and a rapid rise in foreign trade. The move towards a greater integration of Brazil into the world economy implied, however, the implementation of a series of measures that were largely at odds with its previous development strategy. It included the withdrawal of the state from key sectors of the economy, the liberalisation of the local capital market, the lift of trade barriers, the abandonment of industrial policies and the relentless pursuit of an ideal risk-free environment for private investment (either local or foreign). The objective was to force the Brazilian economy to move away from its state-led model of development and make it step into a new one that was primarily ruled by the market. For the main supporters of the reform, the Brazilian economy would be able to make a more efficient use of its resources and capabilities only by unleashing its market forces. The end result would be an economy more in tune with its real 'comparative advantages' and therefore better suited to reach sustainable growth.

The tendency of analysts to only extol the benefits of the economic reforms let them ignore a far less optimistic side, namely, the impact that the higher exposure to world competition could have on local companies. This was a particularly dynamic period of the world economy in which the very processes of economic liberalisation, greater freedom of capital flow and technology innovation (information technology) contributed even further to stimulate the propensity of capitalism towards industrial concentration. The years that followed the opening up of the world economy did show profound changes in big business. They were marked by an aggressive race for multi-billion cross-border mergers and acquisitions and by the tightening of links between 'system integrators' and their first- and second-tier suppliers. This led to a 'revolutionary' process in 'global business', which was powerful enough to give a new shape to the landscape of the world's most successful firms. The business environment that came about as a result of this process of global integration at the firm level reached such a level of concentration that the great majority of Brazilian companies were simply not able to compete.

Although the opening up of the Brazilian economy forced the move of the domestic companies into an environment of fierce competition with the global giants, it still counted on the support of the most influential sectors of the local business community. Perhaps the most intriguing aspect of the market-oriented reforms in Brazil was this willingness of the Brazilian entrepreneurial class to abandon its links with the state and to opt for an economic liberalisation process that was bound to expose these same companies to an unparalleled degree of competition, bring about a good deal of uncertainty and, in many cases, ultimately put their own businesses at risk. Even when the opening up of the economy revealed itself harmful to some of the biggest companies in Brazil and caused the fast denationalisation of the domestic industry, the support of the Brazilian entrepreneurial class for the reforms was not shaken. On the contrary, the response from the Brazilian business community to the first warning signs about the poor chances of the local industrial sector to compete in a more open environment was that of staying committed to the neo-liberal orthodoxy.

Although the shift toward a greater integration into the world economy exposed the national industry to a degree of competition that it had never experienced before and threw these same companies into uneven conditions of competition, the failure of local companies to compete in a more open environment was considered by the Brazilian business community to be the result of its own domestic limitations. According to local businesspeople, the main barriers for the Brazilian companies did not lie in the challenges brought about by the opening up of the economy but rather in the interventionist presence of the state. The decision of the business community was to concentrate their efforts on combating what they claimed as 'Brazil Cost'. The costs of doing business in Brazil were mainly related to the country's deficient transport infrastructure, too-rigid labour legislation, restrictive monetary system and counter-productive tax system. Their belief was that once these obstacles relating to the 'Brazil Cost' were solved, Brazilian companies would finally be in conditions to compete with their foreign counterparts. The dominance of the mainstream orthodoxy over alternative forms of strategic integration into the world economy is perhaps the most striking feature of Brazil's economic reforms. Even the fast denationalisation of the largest Brazilian companies in the years that followed the opening up of the economy was not enough for Brazilian business leaders to challenge some of the preaching of the neo-liberal orthodoxy.

Another aspect of Brazil's move towards its greater integration into the world economy was the complete rupture from less orthodox principles. This would not have been a major issue had Brazil and Latin America not been so strongly influenced in previous decades by the construction of a development thinking that was characterised by challenging the mainstream orthodoxy. Although it can be claimed that the recent changes in the global economy depict a scenario too distinct and complex to be addressed by the analytical framework of non-orthodox Structuralist and Dependency scholars, their vast experience in dealing with Latin American issues could have at least been used, when necessary, to help provide a counter-view to the mainstream economic thinking. The acknowledgment of different alternatives, which could have promoted a constructive and vivid debate on the most appropriate way of getting themselves integrated into the world economy, was virtually nonexistent. This behaviour is a stark contrast with the intense debate carried out in other major developing economies like China and India in the 1980s and 1990s. To a large extent, the reforms carried out by Brazil merely echoed the economic liberalisation process that was in full swing in Latin America in the early 1990s. In general, these reforms were characterised by a certain lack of long-term planning and by the almost complete absence of tailor-made measures.

For the Brazilian business community, the country's competitive integration into the world economy was chiefly based on a few key policies: to reach economic stability, to liberate the economy from the intervention of the state and to ensure competition through the reduction of trade barriers. Strangely enough, the sole concern with the neo-liberal orthodoxy left little room for business leaders to focus on what should probably have been the most crucial strategy, to empower local companies to compete with their foreign counterparts.

The integration of Brazil into the world economy largely contrasts with processes of economic transition experienced by other countries. China is perhaps the most notable example. Although both countries come from very distinct economic experiences and analysts are generally tempted to highlight their differences in terms of scale, mode of industrial development and degree of rural-urban migration, a more in-depth analysis reveals that these two countries can in fact be united by the challenges brought about by the opening up of their economies. In their move towards integration into the world economy, both countries had to find ways to adapt to the risks of a world business scenario marked by rampant international competition, sweeping takeovers, increasing industrial concentration and the prospect of having their industries completely restructured as their markets were opened.

What differentiates China's approach of integration into the world economy from the Brazilian one is the former's strict commitment to clear long-term goals. China's decision for an 'incremental' and gradual reform was decisive in allowing its companies to adapt to the growing presence of market forces and thus increase their chances of surviving in the adverse environment of international competition. There was a common understanding among Chinese leaders that if the economy were to be more opened, it should be through a strategic way. On many occasions, the measures taken by China were completely at odds with what was recommended by the 'transition orthodoxy'. Drastic 'one cut of the knife' reforms that dominated the economic agenda of the transition economies in the 1990s were rejected straight away by the Chinese government. China refrained from privatising its largest state enterprises and maintained strict barriers on short-term speculative capital. The country also made blatant use of its bargaining power to negotiate better deals with all the economies that were trying to gain access to its booming domestic market. It made use of incentives and subsides to promote exports and made sure that imports were organised 'according to needs'. It circumvented drastic cuts on trade tariffs and permitted competition to be carried out primarily between domestic companies. And above all, from the early years of its opening-up process, China invested in an ambitious plan of building 'national champions' to compete with global corporations. China seems to have fully understood the importance of supply chains in current global business. The Asian giant has made strong efforts to place its companies in the upper end of the value chain.

In the same way that during the period of state-led development Brazil's industrial growth was overshadowed by the competitive capacity of the newly industrialised East Asian economies, like South Korea, in the current stage of greater integration into the world economy, Brazil seems unable to keep pace with the recent spectacular growth of the manufacturing capacity of other large developing economies, like, for instance, China. Thanks to its agenda of strategic integration into the world economy, China has managed, over the last three decades, to increase its share in world trade by more than eight times. More importantly, China's impressive surge in exports has also been followed by successful efforts toward technological upgrading. Brazil, on the other hand, has seen its share in world trade barely improve over the last few decades and the structure of its exports to become strongly skewed towards basic commodities. On the firm level, since the beginning of the opening up of these two economies, the capacity of Chinese companies to move abroad has also been notably higher than their Brazilian counterparts.

With regard to big business, it is impossible to deny that the opening up of the Brazilian economy led to a quick denationalisation of its largest companies. This trend can be easily observed in the changes in the ownership structure of the top 500 companies in Brazil in the 1990s. The only sector that showed a steady growth in this period was that of private foreign enterprises. This growing dominance of multinational corporations in Brazil in tandem with the opening of capital of some of the country's largest companies and the impressive rise of foreign direct investments suggests the emergence of a radical new business scenario in the Brazilian economy: from one that for several decades was chiefly state-led to one of foreign capital-led industrialisation. It must be mentioned, however, that against this trend, the policy of having the state as an inducer of growth was revived to a limited extent during the administrations of President Lula and President Rousseff.

On the foreign trade front, the integration of Brazil into the world economy was marked by the rapid expansion of its commodities sector and the growing relevance of its role as a world supplier of commodity-based products. The opening up of the Brazilian economy seems to have given new leeway for the strengthening of its already vigorous agribusiness (particularly soybeans, orange juice, sugar, cotton, processed meat and poultry), iron ore and steel sectors and the pulp and paper industry. It was mostly due to basic commodities that Brazil managed to ensure its large trade surpluses in the years following the opening up of the economy. The implications of this shift for a newly opened economy are vast. In the new surge of global trade in the late 1990s and in the early twenty-first century, it has been predominantly in the low-value-added sectors that Brazil seems to have achieved its 'real comparative advantage'. However, even these sectors might not be dominated by local companies in the long term, as a considerable number of them (particularly in agribusiness, mining and bio-fuels) are already witnessing a growing participation of foreign investors.

The expansion of basic commodities in Brazil after the reforms may indicate that the country is at risk of having primary and low-value-added goods gaining weight over technology-intensive industry. This would be a surprising outcome, particularly after a long period of state-led industrialisation in which large investments were made in areas such as aerospace, auto parts and telecom equipment manufacturing. The auto parts and telecom equipment industries are two emblematic examples of this recent change of the Brazilian industrial economy. Although demand in these two sectors has registered record highs in Brazil over the last decade, this growth has not been followed by the emergence of any major domestic company. Despite the fact that Brazil counts now with one of the world's largest mobile communication networks with more than 271 million users, the presence of significant domestic companies in the sector has become almost irrelevant. This same conclusion can also be drawn on the automotive industry, which witnessed, in the years that followed the opening up of the economy, the participation of the domestic companies being gradually pushed to the lower end of the value chain. To make matters even worse, Brazil's recent commodity-fuelled vast surpluses have helped to disguise deep inefficiencies of the Brazilian economy, most notably the country's growing dependence on high-tech imports. This eventual move back to basic commodities largely contrasts with the tendency followed by other developing economies, particularly those of South and South-East Asia, where the shift toward greater integration into the world economy was more strategically focused on technology upgrading.

Although the opening of the economy resulted in much-needed gains in productivity, the reforms seemed insufficient to prop up the innovative capacity of Brazilian industry and place it in a more comfortable position in the newly formed global value chains. In many sectors, Brazilian industry was not able to catch up with the fast expansion of major developing economies and may even have lagged behind. This is in deep contrast to other developing economies that made use of this period of transition to strengthen their industry.

This is a period of profound changes in the world economy, where every move can have long-lasting effects, and it is therefore crucial for Brazil to secure an active role in the new global business scenario. Recent events, however, show a very different picture. Apart from a few exceptions like the high-tech aerospace industry and petrochemicals, it is mainly in the commodity-based sectors that Brazil has experienced its most significant growth and its companies have gained larger international recognition. This is an intriguing outcome for a country like Brazil, whose set of reforms originally had the main aim of modernising the economy.

Index

Printed in the United States
by Baker & Taylor Publisher Services

Printed in the United States
by Baker & Taylor Publisher Services